Artful Thunder

Artful Thunder

VERSIONS OF THE ROMANTIC TRADITION

IN AMERICAN LITERATURE

IN HONOR OF

Howard P. Vincent

Edited by Robert J. DeMott and Sanford E. Marovitz

THE KENT STATE UNIVERSITY PRESS

Library of Congress Cataloging in Publication Data
Main entry under title:
Artful thunder.

   Includes bibliographical references.
   CONTENTS: Testimonies. Murray, H. A. A letter to Howard Vincent.
Gildzen, A. A celebration of Howard Vincent.—The eccentric orbit: some
versions of the romantic. Krause, S. J. Romanticism in Wieland: Brown and
the reconciliation of opposites. Mottram, E. Poe's Pym and the American so-
cial imagination. Wright, N. Roderick Usher, Poe's turn-of-the-century artist.
Stone, E. Hawthorne's house of Pyncheon: a theory of American drama. Hoch,
D. G. Walden. Yoga and creation. [etc.] (p.

   1.   American literature—History and criticism—Addresses, essays, lectures.
2.   Romanticism—United States.   3.   Vincent, Howard Paton, 1940-   —
Bibliography.   I.   DeMott, Robert, ed.   II.   Marovitz, Sanford E., ed.
III.   Vincent, Howard Paton, 1904-
PS169.R6A7   810'.9'14   74-21886
ISBN 0-87338-172-6

Contents

Acknowledgements

The generosity, dedication and graciousness of all the contributors aided immeasurably in the growth of this *Festschrift* from proposal in 1972 to publication. Special thanks are due to Hennig Cohen, Frank Fieler, Bernard Hall, Bruce Harkness, James W. McGrath, Martin Nurmi, Paul Rohmann, Edward Stone, and Mary Vincent for their advice, encouragement and support, and to Merald Wrolstad for contributing the design of the volume and to William E. Ward for calligraphy. We also acknowledge the editorial, bibliographical and clerical help of Michael A. DiBattista, Diane Stevenson and James Barbour, as well as the patient assistance of Michele DeMott and Eleonora D. Marovitz.

We would also like to list the following acknowledgements:

Robert J. DeMott gratefully acknowledges permission from Alfred A. Knopf, Inc. to quote from the copyrighted works of Wallace Stevens.

Vivian Pemberton gratefully acknowledges permission from Brom Weber to quote from Brom Weber, *Hart Crane: A Biographical and Critical Study* (New York: Bodley Press, 1948), and Brom Weber, *The Letters of Hart Crane, 1916-32* (New York: Hermitage House, 1952); from the Columbia University Libraries for permission to quote from "Portrait of Aunty Climax," "Auntie Climax," and Brom Weber, *Hart Crane: A Biographical and Critical Study* (New York: Bodley Press, 1948); and from Liveright Publishing Corp. for permission to quote from *The Collected Poems and Selected Letters and Prose of Hart Crane by Hart Crane*. Copyright © 1933, 1958, 1966 by Liveright Publishing Corp.

Gloria Young gratefully acknowledges permission from Basic Books, Inc., for permission to quote from *Poets on Poetry*, edited by Howard Nemerov, © 1966 by Howard Nemerov, published by Basic Books, Inc.; from Howard Nemerov, for permission to quote from "Holding the Mirror up to Nature," "The Loon's Cry," "To Lu Chi," and "Writing" from *Mirrors and Windows*, "Painting a Mountain Stream," "Runes" "The Sanctuary," and "White Lightning" from *New and Selected Poems*, "De Anima" from *The Next Room of the Dream*, "The Book of Kells" and "The Salt Garden" from *The Salt Garden*, and selections from *The Image and The Law*; from Princeton University Press to quote from C. G. Jung: *Psychological Reflections, A New Anthology of His Writings 1905-1961*, selected and edited by Jolande Jacobi, Bollingen Series XXXI (copyright 1953 by Bollingen Foundation and © 1970 by Princeton University Press); and from Rutgers University Press for permission to quote from *Journal of the Fictive Life, Poetry and Fiction*, and *Reflexions on Poetry and Poetics*.

Robert J. Bertholf gratefully acknowledges permission from Alfred A. Knopf, Inc. to quote from the copyrighted works of Wallace Stevens; and from New Directions Publishing Corporation and Jonathan Cape Limited to quote from "Bending the Bow," © 1963, 1964, 1965, 1966, 1967, 1968 by Robert Duncan, and "The Opening of the Field," © 1960, by Robert Duncan.

RJD
SEM
July 1974

No jingling serenader's art,
Nor tinkle of piano strings,
Can make the wild blood start
In its mystic springs.
The kingly bard
Must smite the chords rudely and hard,
As with hammer or with mace;
That they may render back
Artful thunder, which conveys
Secrets of the solar track,
Sparks of the supersolar blaze.

Emerson, "Merlin"

Introduction

The ability to hold in tension the frequent appositeness of American literature and thought, from Emerson's ringing perorations in *Nature* and "Self Reliance" to Williams' tough admonition in *Paterson*, "no ideas but in things," is a key to the diversity and dimension of Howard Vincent's world. His mind is an active chrestomathy which gathers varied confluences of literature, as well as art and music, into meaningful wholes, projecting them outward in class and in conversation with all the force, eagerness and freshness of perception as if he were discovering them for the first time. During a creative academic career that spans nearly half a century, he has influenced countless students, colleagues, associates and friends, some of whom raise their voices here in tribute.

It has been more than forty years since he earned his Ph.D. and during that time turned from a promising career in eighteenth century letters to a brilliant one in American literature. After receiving

xiii

his B.A. from Oberlin College in 1926, he entered Harvard's graduate program in English, completing his M.A. in 1927. During the next year he taught at the University of West Virginia, but returned to Harvard in 1928, winning a Dexter Traveling Fellowship there in 1930. From 1931 to 1932 he taught elementary school in Cleveland Heights, Ohio, and the following year finished his Ph.D. at Harvard where he wrote a dissertation on George Colman the Younger. After a year at the University of Pennsylvania's School of Social Work he went to Hillsdale College, Hillsdale, Michigan, where he served as Chairman of the English Department from 1935-1942, and from which he received an honorary doctorate in 1958. His next move took him to Chicago, there eventually to serve as Chairman of the English Department at Illinois Institute of Technology from 1946 to 1961. He interrupted his tenure at IIT to lecture as a Fulbright scholar in France at the Universities of Lyon and Bordeaux in 1954-1955, and to serve, from 1955 to 1957, as Director of Libraries in Paris for the United States Information Service, helping as well to found the Centre Cultural Americain. Following another Fulbright post in Belgium in 1961-1962, he moved to Kent State University where, in 1968, he was honored as one of the first two University Professors in Kent's history, a rank he still holds. During Spring 1967, he was once again a Fulbright lecturer, this time in American Studies at the University of Rome, and in 1973-1974, he was a Visiting Professor at the Sorbonne.

Like Melville's Tranque whale, this skeletal outline of Howard's career hardly does justice to the larger forms of his life and works. His unflagging energy, his perpetual openness to the influx of new experiences and ideas, his willingness to extend himself for others, constitute the "radiant gist" of his personality. Howard has taken seriously a quotation he is fond of repeating, Melville's query to Hawthorne, "Lord, when shall we be done growing? As long as we have anything more to do, we have done nothing." At the age of 70, when most men are content to rest from their labors, Howard continues to write, to teach and to travel. Remarkably, in the past half dozen years alone he has organized several Melville conferences, from Kent to London and most recently in Paris (viz., the poster reproduced on page 104), published the brilliant and critically acclaimed *Daumier and His World* (the result of thirty years devoted avocation), edited *Melville and Hawthorne in the Berkshires*, published two pamphlets on Melville, a collection of essays on *Moby-Dick* and one on *Billy Budd*, as well as a full-length study of *White-Jacket*, and he fulfilled a long standing dream to journey to the Marquesas Islands—all of this while working on his *magnum opus*, "The Mirror of American Literature." Even at the moment *Artful Thunder* celebrates his past achievements, he is already living beyond them, creating new ones.

Howard Vincent's legacy is manifold. He teaches constantly, by instruction and by example. The range of his intelligence and interests, the effectiveness of his teaching, the warmth of his personality, amaze and delight those who know him. And the man exists in his books as well: his best scholarship, *The Trying-Out of Moby-Dick*, *The Tailoring of Melville's* White-Jacket, and *Daumier and His World* proves that impeccable, stimulating statements about literature and art can be made with sensitivity and liveliness. But yet, a little lower layer, closer to the center of the man: Howard Vincent demonstrates it is still possible for a human being to age with dignity, grace and beauty.

Artful Thunder honors only one of several intellectual spheres in which Howard is equally exceptional. However, his preferred teaching of American literature, particularly the 19th and 20th century Romantic tradition, provides a natural basis for this book. The collection gathers the original work of some representative men and women—friends, students and colleagues of several generations— and offers itself as one statement in a field of many possibilities: a synecdoche of a fuller, more comprehensive testimony to Howard if Time, Strength, Cash and Patience had been more abundant.

Part One

Testimonies

Henry A. Murray

Dedication

*Of an Intended, But Unfinished, and Hence Absent
Contribution to this Festschrift
Written in the Form of a Letter
That Reveals the Logic of
the Author's Measureless Gratitude to his Noble Patron
and Benefactor in the Arts*

Howard P. Vincent

Hail to thee gallant Howard, staunch friend, despite my sins, for a full quarter of a century, or let's say, for three hundred moons or more, if you favor crazily-wise Babbalanja's mode of reckoning. Even before starting this declaration of my indebtedness I could see that only a tiny fraction of my hoarded heaps of nugget truths about your admirable self and works could possibly be accommodated within the allotted stint of space; and that the first question to be settled would inevitably be: in terms of what rule or criterion could the process of selection be best ordered. Autonomous head scratching—perhaps to magically induce the breaching into consciousness of the needed rule—had scarcely begun when I happened to glance at a scrap of paper on which was printed a short sentence which instantly stopped the scratching. It was one of Emerson's wonderfully succinct apothegms: *"Only so much do I know, as I have lived."* Eureka! Here, exactly on time, was a fortuitously offered gem of usable wisdom that was better than anything my head could have concocted as a simple rule to choose by, especially if the sentence were somewhat irreverently altered to read: *Only so much will I relate* (about you Howard), *as I have personally experienced.*

At one stroke this rule canceled all presumptuous urges that might otherwise have arisen in this outsider to crane his neck over the wall of your hushed discipline and start bellowing praises of your multifarious accomplishments as scholar, author, editor, teacher, and initiator of burgeoning enterprises in the sphere of American letters. No. Emerson's ten-word apothegm saved you from that embarrassment. Instead, you have a host of discriminating insiders, young and old colleagues, who are eminently qualified to expound on the distinctive virtues of your grand tapestry of achievements.

Thus in its first trial of strength my rule-linked conscience proved invulnerable. But now, alas, with less surplus motive power to support it, conscience is on the point of being torn from its attachment by a certain irresistible temptation, a temptation to hazard a conjecture—with complete confidence, I may say, in its unverifiable validity—regarding your active participation in a cultural trend which, by a strict reading of the rule, is out of bounds for me. However, since I too experienced this trend to *some* extent, through my eyes and on my pulses, a little casuistry should be enough to conceal, if not to repair whatever rent in the integument of conscience may have resulted from my willfulness. Anyhow, here is the unrestrainable conjecture: that without your plenitude of heart and intellect, sparkling, bubbling, and overflowing generously and delectably for more than three decades, the Melvilleans of our land would be less plentiful than they patently are today, less zealous, less knowledgeable, and less prolific. In short, my charismatic friend, you have not expended your resources of learning and exuberance in vain: in your own lifetime, you have appreciably raised the power, and notably enhanced the quality of this forever invaluable current of the Zeitgeist.

Having just acted on Oscar Wilde's assurance that the best way to get rid of a temptation is to yield to it, I am ready to be absolved, to turn over a new leaf, and, vowing strict allegiance to Emerson's sage prescription, to confine my remarks to the signal effects you have had on the person I presumably know best, on his humoral affairs (the cyclical intemperance of black and yellow bile) and on his Melvillean endeavors. But to arrive at some appreciation of these things, it seems that you will have to suffer quite a splurge of egotism from me, such as the insertion of the two following sentences in order to provide some autobiographical perspective. One sentence—plagiarizing the language of guess who—states that from my thirty-first year, exactly half a century ago, I date my life as avocational pursuer of the ever-elusive and ungraspable phantom of Melville's ongoing psychic life, the master-key to the understanding of its nature being the "golden haven" which I could be only unreasonably ambitious of attaining. The second sentence merely tells of my continuing this pursuit (as I still am): researching, reading, reflecting, and revering, with paper and pencil within reach, ready for any hypothetical insight that might surface. This for twenty-five often-interrupted years, during which solitude, privacy, and anonymity were prized, accorded first priority, and, by edict of the superego, publications and public utterances were banned. And then suddenly, in the middle of this unhurried intro-verted search for minor and major keys and clues to keys, I was struck by a resistless blast of eloquent persuasion emanating from no less a figure than Professor Howard Vincent of whose enviable repute in Melville circles I had already been partially informed. Sir, it was you, your beguiling medley of masterful articulate maneuvers—your vi-sions of realizable creations, your waxing tides of zeal and optimism, tactical flexibility, nimble logic, considerate yet implacable persistence —it was these which shook me loose, put a burr under my tail, dragged me out of the obscurity to which I was attached, and literally forced me to assemble my numberless jottings of stray thoughts, ap-preciations, dubious aperçus, conceivable interpretations, et cetera, and make a concerted effort of several months duration to digest them into publishable sentences for an Introduction to *Pierre*, Melville's least intelligible book.

From what I have just written a reader might be led to believe that you—the almost invariably successful hunter and capturer of authors for books and of speakers for symposia—had been laboring under the impression that I was some species of big game, and that you would have to bring your entire repertoire of strategies to bear on the task of compelling my assent to your proposal. Not at all. I was inwardly won over in close to record time—never mind how close precisely—, but was playing "hard to get," because your opening gambits so enchanted me that I couldn't bear to end so rare an opportunity to learn at first hand how another man's resistance could be politely and artfully dissolved. And the compliments! the delicious compliments! bestowed with such tactful modulation that my bristling skin defenses against humbug were given no cause to rise to the occasion. In other words, I was made to feel that even the most spicy, perchance the most fragrant of your compliments could be safely swallowed (with salt galore of course), since to no injurious extent were they inflationary. To be sure they were gloriously embellished and exaggerated, but, so far as I could see, always by your visceral buoyancy, never by fraudulent calculation.

Here is just the place for some (expletive deleted) wise guy to announce that my last remarks constitute an all-too-obvious "cover" for the veritable and most parsimonious explanation of the ease with which you swayed me to a full acceptance of your first offering of a job—namely, that you are a born and bred arch-flatterer who knows an arch-narcissist, his hereditary victim, when he sees one. Period. Half true, let's face it, but too banal for comment. I have a bevy of other explanations in which Chance, my favorite determinant, plays a decisive role. For instance, how was it that you were chosen as editor-in-chief of what was intended to be the first American edition of Melville's complete works? This was one of the most fortunate happenings in my life, since there could hardly have been more than one chance in a hundred that any other appointed major domo would have dared to jeopardize his reputation in the world of belles-lettres by choosing as editor of *Pierre* a surgical chemical psychologist, recently released from the Office of Strategic Services. Of all Melville's books, *Pierre* was certainly the one from which a burrowing, subcutaneous psychologist with secret biographical aspirations had most to gain in the way of analytical experience and understanding of some uncommon and profound psychic states, not to speak of certain rare rejoicings of the aesthetic imagination. In fact, for me, hardly a working day passed that I failed to learn something new, exciting, and notably worth remembering. And so, regardless of what factors were involved in your risky original choice, in your powers of persuasion and encouragement, in your allowing me to write an Introduction of a hundred pages instead of ten, and then in offering me plenty of opportunities to cross the boundary between our two disciplines and learn how the other half, your half, talked and thought—I was so invigorated and advantaged by all this that I was no more elusive than a sitting duck when, a few years later, you great persuader and encourager, picked me, for the second time, as target of your weaponry, and finally, about ten years after that, for the third time, in anticipation of the Bartleby symposium in 1965.

Now, if you happen to feel at this moment that I have been over indulging my propensity for blarney, please join me in taking a cool, hard look at pertinent facts and figures: *Fact* 1. I have ventured into print in celebration of Melville's genius only three times since first reading *Moby-Dick* fifty years ago, and each of those ventures is unquestionably attributable to you as prime mover. *Fact* 2. No other professional writer—let's say no other member of the MLA—has ever proposed any scribblings from me; that is, you are the sole man of letters who has dared to bet on the possible existence of arousable potentialities in me. *Conclusion.* You are the *sine qua non* of literary authorship in me: no Vincent, no publishable cortical secretions from Murray. This cause and effect sequence has been as regular as a law of Nature. Since I happen to be quite a bit more pleased than displeased with the outcome of each of our conjoined efforts, and since the noxious notion that these may have done more harm than good to the estate of literature has been artfully oblivionated, I must confess your effect on my avocational career as well as on my humoral equilibrium has been experienced by me for a quarter-century as totally and unambiguously beneficent. Wonder ye then at the magnitude of my indebtedness?

Corollary. What is true for me is true for other varieties of Vincentians.

Alex guidzen

A Celebration of Howard Vincent

It was like having never heard Ives or having never seen one of Joseph Cornell's boxes. I wasn't prepared. I'd just sit each day on the hard-bottomed chair watching this white-haired man turn into a hippocampus, undecided between galloping across the frontier or swimming out among the dolphins.

Ned Rorem says most people's character is revealed through their eyes. With Howard Vincent it was the eyes that were my clue. I was an undergraduate. I read daily assignments but felt lost in class: all the parades came into town at the same time. Instead of illuminating Hawthorne he'd be grappling with a "brackish reach of shoal off Maddaket," and before I was with him he would be considering "the inconsistencies of Scarlatti." My notes were in circles. But I knew there must be a key. And it was in his eyes. I'd watch his eyes and begin to see the complexities of his subconscious like the myriad nooks of Piranesi's prisons. An idea caught in spidery minutiae would begin breaking away to surface. The eyes revealed the flight. Then the careful upturning of his lips into that inevitable smile of recognition. His hands would weave the wonder before it was translated into words. Then there was no stopping it. The idea would become sound cracking the room's silence. He had formed and communicated a connection.

But what he really shared was the formulation of the connection. The meaning of process. His method at first overwhelms. You're certain he's making relationships that you're not. But exposure to the layers of his eclecticism is the same as examining the scales of Agassiz's haemulon. When you discover what the man's been doing and how it's done you are joyous.

9

Once he has introduced you to process Howard doesn't rest because his life is process. This inexhaustible collagist mentally clips and files as a daily procedure. And he brings to his every activity the full resources of his reading, thinking, and energy. "When I hear music, all I was I am," wrote Richard Howard. The line could have been spoken by Howard Vincent.

Part Two

"The Eccentric Orbit":
Some Versions of the Romantic

Romanticism in *Wieland*:
Brown and the Reconciliation of Opposites

I

Serious fiction in America begins with Brockden Brown. That Romanticism in our fiction also begins with him is more difficult to affirm. Even at the level of gothicism, the strictly romantic element in Brown—mystification—was after all rather carefully circumscribed —a common concession to middle-class objections against flights of the imagination. And, if it be agreed, as various literary historians have pointed out, that Brown "naturalized" the mysterious in much the way Anne Radcliffe did by eventually giving what he called "out-of-nature incidents"[1] a plausible, and indeed factual explanation, then what we are left with would seem to be little more than a veneer— if not a hoaxed—romanticism, in its uses, mere technical legerdemain. Was it not his aim in *Wieland* that miraculous "appearances" would be "solved" in a way that corresponded "with the known principles of human nature"? And did he not insist that the more glaring of them could be historically authenticated?[2] Early reviewers took Brown at his word, observing that "novelty of action" in his works differed markedly from the "German wonders" which "do not exist in nature," so that readers might "enjoy the society of flesh and

1. William Dunlap, *The Life of Charles Brockden Brown* . . . (Philadelphia: James P. Parke, 1815), II, p. 100.
2. "Advertisement," *Wieland; or the Transformation* (New York: H. Caritat, 1798). All textual citations will be to this, the first edition of the novel, with page references hereafter given in the body of the paper.

13

blood, in the midst of all these marvellous events, and see nothing done but what a human agent [was] capable of doing."[3]

Nonetheless, when Brown's novels were reissued in the 1820's, and critics tried for the first time to deal with them in historical perspective, they generally had the sense that what Brown's performance added up to was by and large romanticism. Some went so far as to call him "the founder of the romantic school of American literature."[4] Predictably, later critics like Charles Dudley Warner, mindful of the standards of "Realism," regarded Brown's romantic bent in a pejorative light, or patronized it as productive of "sentimental musing," criticizing his scenery and characters as "unreal" and his use of horror as "sometimes dangerously near the ludicrous."[5] Late nineteenth and early twentieth century literary historians saw Brown as merely an acknowledged romantic and precursor of Poe and Hawthorne, a writer who in adopting the gothic romance involved himself with "the first extravagant contribution of fiction to the Romantic movement."[6] More recent criticism has been divided on the matter. Among those denying that Brown was much of a romantic—if any at all— Harry Levin has taken the position that "he was completely committed to the postulates of the Enlightenment" and delighted in "rationalistic explanations" of the supernatural.[7] F. O. Matthiessen veered toward the other extreme in seeing a capacity on Brown's part for elevating the "stock trappings of romanticism" to a rather high order of literary enterprise. "Brown's turbulence," Matthiessen held, "was the product of a passionate imagination that transformed the mechanical horrors of the Gothic novel into something really felt, as

3. Anon., "Critique on the Writings of Charles Brockden Brown," Port Folio, 6 (July, 1811), 33.

4. William B. Cairns, British Criticisms of American Writings, 1815-1833, Univ. of Wisconsin Studies in Lang. and Lit., No. 14 (Madison: Univ. of Wisconsin Press, 1922), p. 200.

5. Washington Irving (Boston: Houghton, Mifflin Co., 1881), pp. 12-14.

6. Hjalmar H. Boyesen, Literary And Social Silhouettes (New York: Harper & Bros., 1894), pp. 59f. Percy H. Boynton, A History of American Literature (Boston: Ginn & Co., 1919), p. 104.

7. The Power of Blackness (New York: Alfred A. Knopf, 1958), p. 21.

he explored a mysterious borderland between fantasy and reality."[8] The contemporary view most frequently encountered is that while Brown questioned the eighteenth century theory of sensationalist epistemology (stemming from Hartley, and behind him, Locke) and challenged the authority of Reason, he only moved "in the direction of a romantic theory of knowledge" but fell short of reaching it because, lacking the advantage of Coleridgean influence, he had no theory of the romantic imagination as creative force.[9]

To some extent, the variation of opinion on Brown and romanticism suggests that critics of differing persuasions have been touching different parts of the elephant—a pair of them in fact. There was, after all, no more just one Brockden Brown than there was, as Lovejoy pointed out some time ago, only one romanticism. "I am conscious of a double mental existence," Brown once remarked.[10] His use of the double (Stephen Calvert and his twin, Edgar Huntly and Clithero Edny) and his portraying the two-sidedness of a given character (Wieland and Ormond) are direct reflections of his own divided allegiances—allegiances often divided on just such issues as those of Rationalist and Romantic which pervaded his transitional era.

Actually, aside from his being attracted to opposing philosophies, a certain manic volatility seems to have been constitutional with Brown. "I have been raised to a sublimer pitch of speculation," he wrote Dunlap, "only to draw melancholy from the survey of the con-

8. *American Renaissance* . . . (New York: Oxford Univ. Press, 1941), p. 201.

9. Donald A. Ringe, "Early American Gothic: Brown, Dana and Allison," *American Transcendental Quarterly*, 19 (Summer, 1973), 4. Robert Hemenway, who has also attempted to more closely define Brown's romanticism, suggests that it lies in his creating "dilemmas which are insoluble through neo-classical principles," and in his implication that "irrationality is the governing force in human affairs." "Fiction in the Age of Jefferson: The Early American Novel as Intellectual Document," *MASJ* 9 (Spring, 1968), 97.

10. He was referring to the fact, he said, that, when writing, his ideas would "flow naturally and irresistibly through the medium of sympathies which steep them in shade, though the feelings they bring are so pleasing as to prevent my perceiving it." John Bernard, *Retrospections of America, 1797-1811*, ed. Bayle Bernard (New York: Harper & Bros., 1887), p. 252.

trast between what I am and what I ought to be."[11] Interestingly, the
very process of conversion that was responsible for these conflicting
states of mind made them an inner source for the major romantic
strain in Brown's fiction. Even in his personal correspondence, the
dualism apparently produced an intense creative effect. Having received a rather emotional letter from Brown, his rationalist doctor-
friend, Elihu Hubbard Smith, was struck by the peculiar blend of
feelings it contained. "Sentiments so opposite," Smith noted, "yet so
intimately combined and interwoven, gave it [the letter] an interest
in our hearts which sensibility could not but cherish, and which reason hesitated whether she should welcome or disclaim." Chiding him
for his "delight in mystery," Smith describes a tendency in Brown
that closely resembles the disposition of the romantic imagination "to
be affected," as Wordsworth had it in his famous "Preface," "by absent things as if they were present":

> Do you, of choice, give to the simplest circumstances the air of
> fiction or have you been so long accustomed to deal in visionary
> scenes, to intertwine the real with the imaginary, and to enwrap
> yourself in the mantle of ambiguous seeming, that your pen in-
> voluntarily borrows the phraseology of fancy, and by the spell
> of magic words still diffuses round you the mist of obscuring
> uncertainty? The man of Truth, Charles! the pupil of Reason
> has no mysteries.[12]

Although he assimilated the essence of romantic sensibility, it
should be understood—before one goes any further with the matter
—that, in terms of subject, there were some kinds of romantic Brown
was not, and some he was. Among other things, he was clearly neither
a Wordsworthian devotee of nature, a Shelleyan celebrant of Promethean affirmation, nor a precursor of Byronic egotism. Rather, the sort
of romantic affinities one customarily finds Brown most at home with
lie in his preoccupation with the melancholiac temperament (with
the "darker passions," as they said in his day), in his psychological

11. Harry Warfel, *Charles Brockden Brown: American Gothic Novelist*
(Gainesville, Fla.: Univ. of Florida Press, 1949), p. 87.
12. Warfel, pp. 56, 58.

symbolism (whereby, as one critic points out, landscape in *Edgar Huntly* doubles as a sort of symbolic geography of the troubled mind[13]), and in his demonstrating the inability of Reason and the Senses to cope with the Irrational and Daemonic. Moreover, the Daemonic had a compelling appeal in itself, in much the way that Clara Wieland seems to have been hypnotically drawn to Carwin, quite against her will. Dunlap might well have been speaking for Brown in noting that Carwin is "a character approaching to the sublime, from the mystery thrown around him."[14]

However, the monstrous is not merely an attribute of obviously devious types like Carwin, Craig, or Welbeck. In its most potent form, it images the turmoil of our inner world, and in doing so becomes an illuminative and heuristic device. Consider Clara Wieland's falling asleep in her little summer house retreat and dreaming that her brother beckons mysteriously to her from beyond a pit, which she is saved from falling into on feeling someone catch her arm and exclaim, "Hold! hold!" with "eagerness and terror." Shaken from her dream she finds herself surrounded by "deepest darkness" and plagued by images "so terrific and forcible" as to make it temporarily impossible for her to distinguish between sleep and wakefulness (73f.). Nor is this the only time her subconscious forces her to look toward the danger that accrues from a source which her conscious mind refuses to entertain as hostile. Finally, it is not reason, but sheer terror, bred of the animal instinct for survival, that arms Clara with the will to reject suicide, in her awesome confrontation with Wieland, and to decide that she would plunge her penknife into his heart, if need be, however "insupportable" it might be to her rational mind to strike down "a brother thus supreme in misery" (271f.). "Terror enables us to perform incredible feats," she notes (271), revealing the critical solvent of her dilemma. The contemplation of terror as a quickener of psychic energies that take us beyond our ordinary powers instances, of course, the closeness of Brown's world to Poe's. It

13. Kenneth Bernard, "Charles Brockden Brown and the Sublime," *Personalist*, 45 (Apr., 1964), 247.
14. Dunlap, *Life*, II, p. 15.

also asserts the existence of an ideological seriousness in Brown that makes talk about his seeming carnival use of the gothic somewhat otiose.

A number of critics have commented on the tensions that Clara Wieland is beset with. She, better than most characters, displays the dualistic consciousness of Brown himself; and, as with the artist, it is the very acuteness of her sensitivity—and her consequent need to account for the contradictions of experience—that stimulates these tensions. At one point she feels herself so utterly torn by the "implacable contention" of the "separate parts" of her psyche (171) that she declares, "the poet's chaos was no unapt emblem of the state of my mind" (172).

This tension of opposites functions in *Wieland* as a major manifestation of Brown's romanticism—as the "artful thunder" that gives his fiction its artistic power. It is so organically woven into the novel's structure that one finds it not alone in the turmoil affecting its major characters (beginning with the father's being destroyed by what should have been his salvation—a craving for "devotional sentiments" [5]), but in their modes of thought and expression as well. Intimately real as the story is to Clara, she is aware, she says, that it would have to be rejected as "incredible" were her testimony without corroboration (2). Even mere introductory material is treated in the language of opposition, setting the mood of what is to follow. Thus, Wieland's disposition is regarded as suggesting a "thrilling melancholy" (23), and with Pleyel—his optimistic counterpart—one finds a nature given to an "almost boisterous" gaiety, which, however, is "capable of yielding to a grave deportment" (26). The two men are described as friends whose "creeds . . . were in many respects opposite"; where one found confirmation of his faith, the other found grounds for doubt: "moral necessity" vs. "intellectual liberty," Calvinism vs. Reason (26). The initial impression of Carwin is likewise a composite of opposites, which will become accentuated as the story progresses: it was "wholly uncertain, whether he were an object to be dreaded or adored, and whether his powers had been exerted to evil or to good" (84). Clara is particularly given to thinking in oxymoron terms. She liked Louisa Conway so much, for example, that she "often shed tears of pleasure at her approach, and pressed her to [her] bosom in an agony of fondness" (29). Some of this vocabulary one must discount, of course, as not so much purposive as a sort of natural carry-over of the stylistic conventions of eighteenth century sensibility. What seems distinctive with Brown, however, is the special interaction of opposite values and the kind of results (often considered beneficial) that it yields. Thus, in accounting for the strained moroseness of Wieland's mood, Clara observes, "some agitation and concussion is requisite to the due exercise of human understanding" (24).

In short, what seems unique about this insistent polarity on Brown's part is that his opposites are in some fashion *reconciled*. And he does this systematically enough that I would venture to propose the result is an operational demonstration of the Coleridgean idea of the reconciliation of opposites—a clear case, if one wishes, of practice preceding theory (as it should, neo-classicism notwithstanding), though there is not, nor need there be, any evidence that Coleridge had Brown in mind (surely, he did not), or that Brown was deeply read in the German sources (Kant, Schelling) from whom Coleridge derived his views. With respect to the passages just cited, it can be seen that Brown's opposites are not only reconciled, but they dialectically need one another. Wieland is said to lay aside some of his gravity at Pleyel's approach and to feel a void at his leaving (27). Negative sentiments have a way of inspiring positive ones. On the first instance of their hearing disembodied voices, Clara grudgingly concedes the miraculousness of the incident and says that while her wonder was excited, it was "unmixed with sorrow or fear," as might have been expected, and, instead, awakened in her "a thrilling, and not unpleasing solemnity" (39). Although her meaning is vague and although she later declares herself "a stranger . . . to that terror which is pleasing" (52) in connection with a subsequent incident (Brown's way of telling us he is not dealing in mere gothic claptrap), she explicitly sublimates her shock by speculating that she has perhaps had some empirical intimation of spiritual presence, and "an awe," she says—underscoring that *she too* is a Wieland—"the sweetest and most solemn that imagination can conceive, pervaded my whole frame" (53). At this point, she was reconciling the apparent conflict between reason and the senses on the basis that emanations from the supernatural could only be divine—and not diabolic.

To be sure, these are not the most important instances of the principle. I have wanted merely to show its pervasiveness and speciality. Also, that one can pick it up almost at random. However, the reconciliation of opposites is very strongly operative in the central theme of the novel; for Wieland's governing obsession is based on a crucial union of radicals; namely, that the absolutely worst of motives with regard to man—familicide—becomes the highest with regard to God. For Brown's purposes, the underlying human psychology of such a union is apparent enough. As Pleyel explains in his condemnation of Carwin: "The process by which the sympathies of nature are extinguished in our hearts, by which evil is made our good, and by which we are made susceptible of no activity but in the infliction, and no joy but in the spectacle of woes, is an obvious process" (161). It is neither necessary nor possible here to pursue this doctrine through major parts of the novel. Hopefully it will suffice to see how it works in the big climactic scene in which Wieland murders his wife. A masterful scene-builder, Brown nowhere exhibits his romantic thunder with more resounding abandon.

II

Strangely enough, John Greenleaf Whittier is the only critic who has given this powerful scene any detailed attention. In an essay entitled "Fanaticism," Whittier pondered the revolting account of a man whose mind became so unhinged from contemplating the Apocalypse and personal coming of Christ that he dispatched his wife and four children with an axe. Turning to Wieland's "execution" of a similar "baleful suggestion," Whittier declared, "In the entire range of English literature there is no more thrilling passage." The masters of the old Greek tragedies "have scarcely exceeded the sublime terror of this scene." Significantly, what makes it so artistically compelling for Whittier is "the coloring of the picture . . . [in] an intermingling of the lights of heaven and hell,—soft shades of tenderest pity and warm tints of unextinguishable love contrasting with the terrible outlines of an insane and cruel purpose, traced with the blood of murder." Moving into the scene proper, Whittier recounts the ironic interplay of conflicting emotions: "The murderer confronted with his gentle and loving victim in her chamber; her anxious solicitude for his health and quiet; her affectionate caress of welcome; his own relentings and natural shrinking from his dreadful purpose; and the terrible strength which he supposes is lent him of Heaven, by which he puts down the promptings and yearnings of his human heart, and is enabled to execute the mandate of an inexorable Being,—are described with an intensity which almost stops the heart of the reader."[15]

Examined structurally, Wieland's reconstruction of the murder in his courtroom confession is a masterpiece not only of the clash of highly charged passions, but of their startling reconciliation—which is what yields the intense aesthetic affect that so impressed Whittier. Prefacing his recitation of the deed, Wieland thanks God for his "bounty" that He did not ask "a less sacrifice than this. . . ." "Now," he therefore avows, "may I, with dauntless and erect eye, claim my reward, since I have given thee the treasure of my soul" (200f.). Having established the note of paradox, he begins his narration by remarking that his mind that evening was at the outset "contemplative and calm." However, on his way to see his sister, about whose safety there had been some concern following her experience with the voices in her closet, his mind is so unaccountably overtaken by a "torrent of fervid conceptions," that he loses sight of his purpose. He finds himself enraptured over the parental and conjugal love he enjoys, and this gives rise to gratitude and a soaring desire to serve the God who has given him such joy. This at first seems a natural enough sequence, but he suddenly becomes so wrought up that he feels he must actively apprise himself of God's will and offer testimony of his love for Him. Thus are the excruciating terms of his terrible bargain foreshadowed and the tragic inevitability disclosed whereby these opposites—human and divine love—will be reconciled, by the submission of one

15. *The Prose Works of John Greenleaf Whittier* (Boston: Houghton, Mifflin Co., 1889), III, pp. 391-93.

to the fulfillment of the other. Only his willing destruction of that which he most prizes on earth will satisfy his high craving to "attest" his constancy of spirit. There follows the vision and injunction, his initial human rejection of the dreaded demand, and a series of mounting ironies in which his hesitancy increases his agitation (in proportion as his "will was strong," his "limbs refused their office"), which in turn elicits increased solicitude *for him*, in his anguish, from the innocent Catharine. This leads to even greater intensities of revulsion on Wieland's part which, as they show the degree of human feeling he must surmount to meet the divine test, finally, for that reason, impell him to get on with it. In the act of strangling her, he thrice relaxed his grip, on the appeal for compassion in her looks, until, castigating himself for prolonging her agony, he does kill her (201-09). Throughout, Brown plays up the evident perversity of his needing to derive spiritual satisfaction from what is humanly most hateful to him. That nothing less than that evil will do for that good is the exact formula for their reconciliation.

However, the artistically most forceful part of the scene occurs not in the prelude or during the act itself, but in the aftermath, where it takes no small skill to sustain the climactic peak—no less to build yet another higher one when the narrative momentum would seem about to turn downward. But build it Brown does, and brilliantly, in a fantastic succession of syntheses formed by the reconciliation of opposites. The first of these Wieland experiences in his moment of sheer triumph. The deed *has* actually been done; and its being "past recal," [sic] he can glory in having "successfully subdued the stubbornness of human passions" (209). He is reconciled to what he has done because he overcame enormous human compunctions and the urgent fear of his possibly failing the rare chance to prove the completeness of his faith. He gets so carried away by the fact that this unbelievable reconciliation has indeed been achieved that he lifts the corpse in his arms, lays it on the bed and gazes upon it with delight—which in the state of reconciliation enjoyed, satisfies both his still unquenched reverence for Catharine and his pride in having accomplished the impossible. On this afflatus, there is released an unparalleled perversity of joy which, in its union of pleasure with the gruesome, discloses yet another—the harshly grotesque—level of opposition reconciled. It takes the tension of that fusion to keep the ugliness of the scene from overwhelming it. "Such was the elation of my thoughts," Wieland cries, "that I even broke into laughter." With this colossal laugh, the flood bursts:[16] "I clapped my hands and exclaimed, 'It is done! My sacred duty is fulfilled! To that I have sacrificed, O my God! thy last and best gift, my wife!' " By its very nature, though, the elation is doomed to fade, which Wieland half realizes the instant after he has felt himself soaring "above frailty." "I imagined I had set myself forever beyond the reach of selfishness; but my imaginations were false" (209f.). The reason Wieland keeps falling out of harmony with his emotions is obvious enough. He has tried to reconcile the genuinely irreconcilable; hence, to have succeeded must seem a delusion—certainly a shock to the human heart.

Not only does his rapture ebb, but it takes merely one look at his wife for his "joyous ebullitions" to vanish. The synthesis falls apart as the one opponent feeling he had to transcend in order to achieve his purpose, itself gains ascendancy, and the euphoria that made their reconciliation possible turns to horror. As if recovering from a nightmare, Wieland says, "I asked myself who it was whom I saw? Methought it could not be Catharine . . . the woman who had lodged for years in my heart . . ." (210). Lapsing into "desperate and outrageous sorrow," Wieland now has the clash of feelings go out of balance in the other direction: "The breath of heaven that sustained me was withdrawn, and I sunk into *mere man*." His reaction is to leap from the very floor and dash his head against the wall, uttering screams of horror. He pants after "torment and pain." "Eternal fire, and the bickerings of hell, compared with what I felt, were music and a bed of roses" (210).

His dejection phase, however, lasts not much longer than the elation had. For he is shortly thanking God that "this degeneracy was transient." He thinks upon the key reconciliation motif—what he did

16. There is a special kind of ghastly release in the gothic laugh. Faulkner once suggested something of what it was like: "*only when you are hungry or frightened do you extract some ultimate essence out of laughing. . . .*" *Absalom, Absalom!* (New York: Random House, 1972), p. 130.

was "a sacrifice to duty"—and is "*calm*," apparently restoring his sense of transcendence. It then occurs to him, though, that while the avenue of human consolation provided by his wife is closed, others—namely, his children—still remain open to him. And this of course suggests that the comfort associated with them must also be dashed on the same terms that his love for his wife had to be obliterated. Thus, "to dispell the mist" that was beginning to obscure his dearly bought reconciliation, he senses the need of "a new mandate." The scene mercifully ends with Wieland's hearing the charge that his children must be "offered"; and one foresees that he will have to remount the heights, at the permanent cost of his humanity (210f.).

To the court he knows he must seem a criminal, but in the "Omnipotent and Holy" tribunal he feels he will be judged as having given "obedience" in "the test of perfect virtue, and the extinction of selfishness and error." Death may come when it will; he is secure, as he puts his reconciliation in its ultimate terms, in knowing that the less men think of him the more he perceives he has fulfilled the condition for his highest aspiration—the assurance of salvation (215).

The enclosing outer irony that this will all collapse with the revelation to Wieland that he has indeed been deluded affords the compensating opposite by which Clara at the end may suggest the need to frame "juster notions" of "divine attributes" and human fallibility, and thus restore some semblance of the moral balance Wieland's mania had destroyed (298). Still, Wieland is not *all* monster. For Clara's final vision of a moral balance is what presumably inspires all great quests for a *more lasting* reconciliation of the worlds of man and God than life allows; and it is precisely this ideal Wieland had sought and which had eluded him, as it does all of us.

Poe's Pym,
and the American Social Imagination

I

Paul Valéry understood that Poe was a superb craftsman of modern literature, referring to him as "that great literary technician, the first to compose the scientific story, a modern cosmogony, the description of pathological phenomena."[1] Baudelaire and Mallarmé recognized Poe's engineering of socio-psychic effects. In America, Hart Crane placed Poe in the New York subway, the focal Hell of his 1930 America. Poe's roots were in the modern condition itself, the state of displacement and disinheritance which is the material of major American and European writers from his decade onwards. Poe's centrality for America is evidenced in the nature of the relationship between his nonnaturalistic forms of fiction and American culture. Furthermore, Poe exemplifies changes in western sensibility focused on the transition from belief in creativity as "an inspired profession" within a religious context to an action "freed from dependence on religious systems."[2] Baudelaire wrote, in the spirit of Poe as Walter Benjamin rightly observes, that the "time is not distant when it will be under-

1. Walter Benjamin, *Charles Baudelaire, A Lyric Poet in the Era of High Capitalism,* trans. Harry Zohn (London: NLB, 1973), p. 43.
2. Harold Rosenberg, *The Tradition of the New* (New York: Horizon Press, 1959), pp. 103 ff. Cf. Allen Tate in "The Angelic Imagination: Poe as God," *The Forlorn Demon* (Chicago: Regnery, 1953), p. 60, who says "Poe is thus a man we must return to: a figure of transition, who retains a traditional insight into a disorder that has since become typical, without being able himself to control it."

stood that a literature which refuses to make its way in brotherly concord with science and philosophy is a murderous and suicidal literature."

Poe's art is related to methods of "scientific experiment" and "re-
discovering the creative energies of the whole community."[3] This freedom entails an initial alienation from the values of capitalist society
and its Christian supports. In compositional practice, it entails a
change from sporadic inspiration to conscious experiment and planning, from illusionist fiction to forms which appear fantastic but in
fact probe reality, and still take place within the area of popular fiction rather than academic or "high" culture, an elitist or genteel literature. Poe's mysteries are elucidatory, not priestly. In a letter of 1831
he criticizes poetry presented as metaphysics based on vague inspira-
tional procedures likened to an ill-defined "Nature," and objects to
the Romantic utilitarian beliefs of Wordsworth and Coleridge that
their products were morally useful in a nonmetaphysical and direct,
eighteenth century manner:

> As regards the greater truths, men oftener err by seeking them
> at the bottom than at the top; the depth lies in the huge abyss
> where wisdom is sought—not in the palpable places where she
> is found. The ancients were not always right in hiding the god-
> dess in a well.[4]

This "Letter to Mr. ———" (later published as "Letter to B———"
in 1836) Poe used as preface to his 1831 *Poems*, and throughout his
subsequent career worked for a theory and practice of invention
which refused metaphysical profundity as a gambit to attract attention. "The Ancient Mariner" and "Kubla Khan" appealed to him
more than Coleridge's autobiographical retracings because their energy is structured in narrative and description without insistent explanation from the poet's beliefs. In the *Marginalia* articles published
between 1844 and 1849, he emphasized the structure of words rather

---

3. Rosenberg, pp. 107-108.

4. *Edgar Allan Poe: Representative Selections*, Margaret Alterton and Hardin
Craig, eds. (New York: American Book Company, 1935), p. 245. Hereafter
identified as *EAP*, and included parenthetically in the text.

than antecedent emotions in the artist, insisting on "deliberateness," "method," "control," "the capacity of inducting or compelling" the condition of vision and the ability to embody, continue and transfer it to memory in order to "survey it with an eye to analysis" (*EAP*, 411). The resulting fiction is to be "a synthesis of inspiration and conscious method." As Harold Rosenberg says, "Science should leap ahead by means of intuition . . . poetry, however, must produce scientifically."[5] Poe understood that his methods were not entirely original. "The Philosophy of Composition" in 1846 begins with a quotation from a note Charles Dickens wrote in 1842 on Poe's "examination . . . of the mechanism of *Barnaby Rudge*":

> By the way, are you aware that Godwin wrote his 'Caleb Williams' [1794] backwards? He first involved his hero in a web of difficulties, forming the second volume, and then, for the first, cast about him for some mode of accounting for what had been done. (*EAP*, 365)

The "web" plot is a spatial narrative involving the reader in an overwhelming sense of movement within a determined area. By the time that Poe published his prize-winning story "MS. Found in a Bottle" in 1833 (in the *Baltimore Sunday Visitor*, which offered the competition), private reading had increased to the point where it was no longer liable to the kind of suspicious scorn embodied in Jane Austen's *Northanger Abbey* (1818). Reading Poe is not a public or family event but a private entrance of the solitary body into a field of stimulus without immediate social interference. The reader enters an enclosed space lit, perhaps, by that gas light which is the technological basis of so much of nineteenth century literature and which emphasizes shadow and flickering movement as much as it enlightens. Poe knows how we respond to latent or actualized claustrophobia and agoraphobia as bases of our confidence or its undermining. How we feel distance and movement into space controls confidence, even in those conditions which Poe offers in *Eureka* (1848)—that universal space is spatial logic, that the structure of his plot extends into that universe in which "the plots of God are perfect" and "the universe is

5. Rosenberg, p. 110.

a plot of God." Poe's fictions, therefore, are means by which a man places himself in relation to universal structure.

But that structure does not include a systematic psychology, through which automatic explanations for "mystery" may be provided with all the aplomb of Walpole rationalizing his materials at the conclusion of *The Castle of Otranto*. Poe is free to compose so that universal plot may overwhelm and it is precisely that invitation to the reader which is termed "morbid horror"[6] by a twentieth century rationalist. In fact, the morbidity lies within the sustaining myth of competitive individualism in capitalist society, most recently rabid in the United States. If Poe has roots in society, it is in a culture which assumes that the individual is isolated and that this condition is best stated as "a problem" to be solved by the individual and not by the society which holds him. In Poe's world the individual has no sense of home or of society as a beneficent whole in which he can have confidence, even in some "appointed place." God may have his plot, but the self has no "corresponding metaphysical conception of the natural universe as an ordered unity which harmonizes with human ideals."[7] On the contrary, in Poe's world "there is no underlying order and each individual must find his own way of dealing with chaos," even if it comes to simply describing one's inevitable fate and throwing the bottled account into the ocean currents. *Eureka*, the Dupin detections, and the escape tales (especially those with special co-operation with the elements) are dramatizations of tension between order and chaos, the myth of the free individual and the fact of social enclosure, in which Poe works for the stability of reason against uncontrollable psychic, elemental, sexual and social forces. Stability usually takes the form of one person's power over another and its consequences, or over natural

6. Wayne C. Booth, *The Rhetoric of Fiction* (Chicago: University of Chicago Press, 1961), p. 203.

7. Henry Bamford Parkes, "Poe, Hawthorne, Melville: An Essay in Sociological Criticism," *Partisan Review*, 16 (February 1949), 159. Two recent critics study spatial dimensions in *Pym*: see David Halliburton, *Edgar Allan Poe: A Phenomenological View* (Princeton: Princeton University Press, 1973), esp. pp. 257-260; and Robert Carringer, "Circumscription of Space and the Form of Poe's *Arthur Gordon Pym*," *PMLA*, 89 (May, 1974), 506-516.

elements and their scientific structure (including human body matter). His field is the embattled individual in a society of competition and Christian guilt. His fascination with omnipotence, cruelty and logic is not private fantasy but a method of coming to terms with the whole field of psychic and social tension. In any totalitarian society, whether capitalist or communist or fascist, readers will be found who recognize Poe's fascinations as their own, willingly or not.[8] To label his work "morbid" is complacent naiveté, or perhaps ignorance of fundamental relationships between self and society in the modern West.

American society in particular has been dominated by the Success Ethic—every man a winner in an acquisitive complex, a psychopath of Emersonian self-reliance, an example of Marx's perceptions in 1844 that man "has himself become the tension-ridden being of private property."[9] Poe had little confidence in democracy, human perfectibility, social reform, theories of progress and "natural goodness," nor did he indulge in early nineteenth century obsessions with countryside at the expense of the city. He preferred city life and despised the mob, was suspicious of anything which threatened the individual man (including female emancipation). He defended slavery as a property right, loathed any form of what he called "every-man-for himself confederacy," and believed that there were "laws of *gradation* visibly impressed upon all things in both the moral and physical universes"; and that "Democracy is a very admirable form of government—for dogs." Poe as Virginian is an unreconstructed Southerner, without the sentimentality of Southern agrarian aristocratism. He was, however, more tolerant and liberal than reactionary and believed persistently in the elevation of society by education for "the heart and intellect fully developed." But like most individualist liberals who fear revolutionary change, he was a bundle of contradictions, at his firmest in this dream of genius:

8. Henry Bamford Parkes, *The American Experience*, 2nd ed., rev. (New York: Alfred Knopf, 1955), pp. 186-187, 196-197.
9. *Economic and Philosophic Manuscripts [of 1844]*, trans. in *Karl Marx: Early Writings*, trans. and ed. T. B. Bottomore (New York: McGraw-Hill, 1963), p. 148.

Genius is confined to no rank—it is to be found in all grades of society. Spread elementary education among the people, extend to them the means of improvement, and superior minds wherever fortune may have placed them, will not long remain in obscurity. Their inherent vigor will break through difficulties, surmount obstacles, and supply the deficiencies occasioned by the want of a collegiate education. (*EAP*, lxxvi)

To Poe, therefore, any change must take place within stasis. The paradigm of revolution in Kuhn's sense is remote from his thinking.[10]

The action of *The Narrative of Arthur Gordon Pym*, written when Poe was twenty-eight, already shows the configuration of his sensibility. The armature is traditionally mythic: the journey out, the young man's figure of adventure outward towards manhood, the voyage from home, the sea crossing towards possible death and rebirth, changed return or absorption into the far land or the earth or the sky. *Pym* embodies an exploration for which no civilized upbringing prepares the hero. Women have no part. Love is a dog's licking and pawing of a man. The closest human relationship is loyalty or disloyalty between shipmates in extreme situations, including cannibalism. Pym is therefore related to Romantic voyages in Coleridge, Byron, and Shelley, and beyond them, to Melville, Baudelaire and Rimbaud. Within a highly artificial legend, physical and psychological facts, taken more or less for granted, are placed at the disposal of a dialectic between catastrophe and recovery, and finally synthesized into an image of absorption which is neither. The geography of Pym's voyage from northeast America to Antarctica is also his interior topography, through terror and deception to resolution. His reversals and escapes move steadily towards chaos and primitivism, since his journey out is also back, to a culture of ciphers and hieroglyphics, to what men are historically.

Pym's own preface contains two significant factors. First, the narrative is stated as connected detail but told from memory as an "appearance" of the truth it really possesses, told under the force of imag-

10. Thomas S. Kuhn, *The Structure of Scientific Revolutions*, 2nd ed. (Chicago: University of Chicago Press, 1970), pp. 10-12, 37, 77, 144.

inative excitement. Secondly, Pym was diffident about being believed until Mr. Poe encouraged him and he wrote his voyage as fiction, a "ruse" which succeeded when parts of it were first published as "fable." In this way he signals his procedure: imaginative truth offered in the form of fable (printed serially in 1837, complete in 1838, reprinted complete in 1841). As literary engineering, Pym is a control of memory through a fictitious voyage to an imaginary, yet necessary, world: "the realm of memory," the world of the unconscious whose story exists with a latent content which appeals to the reader's unconscious levels of reading, as well as to the whole body that reads. The result is therefore a more inclusive experience than simplified naturalism.

In the "Marginalia" (Jan. 1848), Poe once wrote that a book should be written called "My Heart Laid Bare," a revolutionary work, because explicitly true to its title:

> No man dare write it. No man ever will dare write it. No man *could* write it, even if he dared. The paper would shrivel and blaze at every touch of the fiery pen.

Baudelaire planned *Mon Coeur mis à nu* as a book of the modern artist, the Dandy who "should live and sleep in front of a mirror."[11] Poe's paper did not burn but his heart lies in *Pym*, his dandy mirror, its scope larger than mere narcissism. *Pym* is a mirror with a hole in it through which life itself rushes, as in many of Poe's stories, controlled by inhuman forces which the human force of the artist projects. The climax of the tale is an extreme situation for the engulfed self, but even this moment of psycho-geography has an origin outside Poe's psyche. Mercator's map of the Polar Gulf showed a place near the towering black rock of the North Pole itself where the ocean

11. In *Introduction to Poe: A Thematic Reader*, ed. Eric W. Carlson (Glenview, Ill.: Scott-Foresman, 1967), p. 543, Baudelaire himself looked upon *Mon Coeur mis à nu* as a "terrible book" which would have raised bourgeois society against him, the notes for which in fact expose him in the central image of the modern artist, the Dandy who "should live and sleep in front of a mirror." See *My Heart Laid Bare and other prose writings*, ed. Peter Quennell (London: George Weidenfield and Nicolson, 1950), p. 177; and Jean-Paul Sartre, *Baudelaire* (Paris: Gallimard, 1947).

rushed into the inside of the Earth. When Poe was nine, John Cleves Symmes declared to the world from St. Louis, Missouri, that "the earth is hollow and habitable within . . . that it is open at the poles." He called for volunteers to descend and claim a utopia, "a warm and rich land stocked with thrifty vegetables and animals, if not men." He called to Sir Humphry Davy and Baron Von Humboldt for backing, but the public ridiculed him. Two years later in 1820, Adam Seaborn wrote a novel called *Symzonia: A Voyage of Discovery*—a voyage to "the abode of a race perfect in their kind," perfectly white utopians living under the South Pole, living on natural foods and free from "the bloody sweat of slavery,"[12] and the polar opposite of the "darkness of skin and grossness of features" of Africans and, of course, American slaves.

Jeremiah Reynolds defended Symmes and the polar holes; Poe remembered the defense. Perfection as white, the fascination with whiteness, and the alternation of white and black—the pattern of moral and racial color theory in the Christian West—penetrate *Pym* in 1837, as they do *Moby-Dick* and *Uncle Tom's Cabin* in 1851 and 1852 respectively, and *Pudd'nhead Wilson* in 1894. All four works, strung out in the historical space of nineteenth century American culture, concern isolated men discovering the nature of dominance and submission in societies divided along the color line. They are deeply western works and deeply American.

II

Poe's inside story begins with a preliminary voyage from Nantucket where Pym was born, the northeastern American island of whalemen and whale legend. Where Melville's first chapter begins "Call me Ishmael," Pym begins with his own identity (which is to be challenged rather than built) and his class solidity, rooted in the whaling industry:

12. Quoted from Seaborn by Sydney Kaplan, "Introduction" to *The Narrative of Arthur Gordon Pym* (New York: Hill and Wang, 1960), p. xiii. This section of my essay is indebted to Kaplan's entire introduction.

My name is Arthur Gordon Pym. My father was a respectable trader in sea-stores at Nantucket, where I was born. My maternal grandfather was an attorney in good practice.[13]

This was the scene of Poe's own childhood and Pym's grandfather's money came from stocks in Edgarton New Bank. The inference is clear: from defined American prosperity within the class inheritance an American boy once again sets forth into the uncertain. In New Bedford, on the mainland of Massachusetts, Pym owns a sail-boat named after Ariel, an energy trapped and freed by the controls of white magic. Pym's spirit is moved by tales of South Pacific whaling voyages told by the father of his friend Augustus Barnard. Poe anchors his opening firmly in the economic center of America from the 1830s to the 1860s, the whale oil industry: it is from here that Pym makes his figure of outwards.

In the opening chapter the structure of *Pym* is initiated: men deliberately in conflict with the elements, the nonhuman other of the basic proposition of Earth and sky; men in a state of changed consciousness, intoxication, the "ecstasy" of adventure (*SW*, 250); the mate's mutinous disobedience and its parallel in the young men's deception of their parents; the series of reversals of appearance into reality, with Pym and Barnard apparently dead, both saved by what might kill, or nearly killed by what was intended to save. The world of reversals has begun. Refreshing night turns to deadly gale. For men, it is a chaos of relativity, here solved by a rescue and return home. But the next adventure, inspired by the first, is a voyage much farther out. The initial catastrophic voyage spurs Pym to greater excitement, to "the life of a navigator." The need for thrill takes the form of desire to re-experience disaster, suffering, despair and the unpredictable sea—all of which Barnard fears. Pym's sensibility has the imagination of disaster:

My visions were of shipwreck and famine; of death or captivity among barbarian hordes; of a lifetime dragged out in sorrow

13. *Selected Writings of Edgar Allan Poe*, ed. Edward H. Davidson (Boston: Houghton Mifflin, 1956), p. 249. Hereafter identified as *SW* and included parenthetically in the text.

and tears, upon some gray and desolate rock, in an ocean unapproachable and unknown. (*SW*, 257)

These, he knows, are common dreams of "melancholy" men, but he takes them as prophecies of "a destiny which I felt myself in a measure bound to fulfil." The initial pattern of reversal is reinforced psychologically: "our intimate communion had resulted in a partial interchange of character" (*SW*, 258). The change becomes the deliberate preparation for extreme living, away from land, banks, the whaling industry and parental authority. Young Pym voyages to test truths of the parental world of received order and morality, to discover the real within the apparent. His personality is that of the philobat,[14] the person whose pleasure lies in arousing and bearing anxiety, through loss of balance, stability and contact with firm earth. His thrill lies in leaving the region of customary confidence in the social and rooted: the man who increases his thrill by progressively throwing away equipment in an exposed situation, whose confidence is a magical sense of personal potency, actively or latently erotic, who wishes, or in fact is compelled, to live dangerously, and who thrusts into what he will call virgin forest, or climbs a virgin peak.

Pym seizes the chance to sail in the whaler *Grampus* and risk parental disinheritance; he pretends to study, swallows his hypocrisy in "wild and burning expectation" (*SW*, 258), dreams of his "scheme of deception." Barnard forges a letter to enable Pym to leave his parents, and at New Bedford Pym plays the offended sailor to deceive his grandfather in the street. On the *Grampus* (the word means both a blowing, dolphin-like whale and a person who breathes aloud, and carries with it the tones of grandpa or "grampa" in both mockery and the sense of repetition of adventure from generation to generation) Pym is concealed in the hold in an iron-bound coffin-shaped box—a second apparent death buried in the labyrinth of the ship's cargo. The deception theme is here connected with Poe's obsession with premature burial and all forms of fateful enclosure.

Barnard's father is in command of the ship—a further release from

14. Michale Balint, *Thrills and Regressions* (New York: International University Press, 1959), chapter 2 ff.

the parental to be achieved. After three days the putrefying meat in the hold gives Pym breathing difficulties and affects his dreams into forms of disaster. He reads Lewis and Clark's account of their expedition to the mouth of the Columbia River between 1803 and 1806, a classic of American exploration, commissioned by Thomas Jefferson and exemplifying the new nation's westward destiny. Pym's dreams Poe dreams—being smothered to death by demonic figures and embraced by serpents with "fearfully shining eyes" which stare at him "earnestly," alone in limitless deserts or among great leafless grey tree trunks in endless succession:

> Their roots were concealed in wide-spreading morasses, whose dreary water lay intensely black, still, and altogether terrible, beneath. (*SW*, 265)

He is forced awake by a nightmare in which a Sahara lion bears down on him: he comes to, "stifling in a paroxysm of terror," to find it is his Newfoundland dog, Tiger. The dream desire for helplessness is comically resolved, but the reality remains, within and outside the dream. The book's pattern is again exemplified: deliverance from the overpowering, the division of appearance and reality, the experience of power in recovery. Since his watch has run down, his darkened timeless existence in the hold labyrinth generates a significant series of images which are all dreams of dominance and submission; but Pym's waking existence also exemplifies universals of reality and appearance, surface and latent meaning, which are the common interpretative processes of living. He is nearly killed or starved in the labyrinth —archetypally, the body and the world, to be resolved as a spatial puzzle-form of energies. Tiger acts as Pym's intermediary between states. The message tied to him proves to be a deception, the first illegible message in the book. But he is a loving companion in darkness as Pym's energy is slowly expended to "a condition nearly bordering on idiocy" (*SW*, 271). When the earlier glimmer of the message is re-read on its torn up pieces, by phosphorous light (the dog had eaten the candles) rubbed into the writing indentations, all he can read is: "*blood—your life depends upon lying close*" (*SW*, 273). The word "blood" affects him profoundly, a term of "mystery," "suffering" and "terror" rather than positive life, and it is in fact written in Barnard's blood and therefore literally a "life" writing.

The *Grampus* carries Pym outwards, and Poe's detailed, hallucinatorily realistic prose holds the total situation and atmosphere controlled. A mutiny on the *Grampus* proves to be the reason for Pym's "incarceration" in the "trap" of his condition. Another rebellion against authority, this is the second mutiny in the book and the second involving Barnard's father, who is overthrown in violence and bloodshed followed by drunkenness. The only restraining crew member is Dirk Peters who is not white but, through his mother, half Upsarokas Indian from the source of the Mississippi, America's geological main artery. He is four foot eight, ferociously ugly, bald, strong—a hairless dwarf, a recurrent figure of strength and phallic power in mythology. His head is immense, indented on the crown, "like that of the head of most Negroes," and covered by a wig from Spanish dog or American bear, forms of American or Americanized beast. In fact, Peters appears as a kind of indigenous Hercules. His teeth are long and protruding—indications of power and energy—and his face appears to be "convulsed" in silent laughter (*SW*, 281). Nantucket stories report him doubtfully sane. Peters is in fact daemonic—a chthonic hairy-man suggesting men's bestial inheritance, a restraining moral force for life, a life-saver, and completely unlike conventional American white nineteenth century salvation figures—again a part of Poe's pattern of deception.

The *Grampus* crew divide and quarrel until only thirteen men are left, (including Pym), and these are drunk. Throughout this section the wind increases, and the ship careens forward violently under minimal human control. Pym, Peters and Barnard plan to overthrow the mate and take charge—a third statement of rebellion. But by now there are other significant structural elements within the relaxed style of the narrative at this stage. First, Peters tried to attract the mutineers to sail as pirates in the South Seas where "perfect security and freedom from all restraint are enjoyed" in the "deliciousness of the climate," "the abundant means of good living," and "the voluptuous beauty of the women" (*SW*, 287). It is partly a wish to rescind responsibility for competitive democratic society and its depredations, partly a wish to revert to infantile security, partly a desire to conquer the helpless and rule in a state of secure sensuality over a cheap labor force, whether women, Negroes, Polynesians, children or the proletariat. The dream forms a utopia of the senses, an anti-puritan abundance and leisure, within a work-conscious society which holds it as axiomatic that to work is to be good, but secretly knows this to be a nonsensical trap created by priests, kings and other exploiters of labor. In American culture it is also the opposite of the frontiersman-pioneer myth which sustains the need to move westwards in space to complete the traverse of the continent, invade Asia and make for the Moon. Secondly, Pym drains his last water in a fit of "perverseness" which he admits is infantile, and then smashes the bottle. Ironically, the sound saves his life, since it indicates to Barnard that he remains alive. The trivial incident is part of survival within reversal. A man's existence is suspended from chance incidents and contingency. The unpredictable in one scheme of life is predicted in another. Meaning depends on the program in which it is realized. Thirdly, Poe details the packing of cargo in this ship's hold in order to demonstrate both potential danger (loose packing) and how Pym escapes by squeezing through and making his way to a trap-door. Apparent danger through carelessness may be man's salvation, even if the ship itself is rendered unstable.

Poe's methods by now will be clear and obvious. The method is the message. In chapter VII he provides a long section on methods of laying-to a ship in a storm, with accurate accounts of sea and wind, and methods of controlling natural elements by human techniques—men manipulating nature, and therefore an analogue of life itself, the ship as instance of the society of men within nature, the basic proposition or "things as they are." *Pym* is a fable of extreme conditions as men move through the basic human and nonhuman energies. Likewise the basic proposition may instance resistance to control—the moon's control of the tides, its degree of visibility, like the force of winds, are facts beyond human will to cause or control, especially in pre-steamship lore. Wind and air have always been instances of energy for birth, destruction, flight, health, technology. Nature is the sum of our myths of the basic proposition, and *Pym* is enacted in statements and reported speech which constitute a narrative of events. Relationships between characters do not develop; they exist, as the ship's movement exists. *Pym* is not meticulous; it is written by a survivor, and as a relatively early example of Poe's fiction, it over-employs *terror*, *fear*, and *horror* to develop redundantly what has generally been dramatized. Clearly, *Pym* is not the bourgeois social novel as it had developed since the eighteenth century. The ship is a traditional synecdoche for society, but what is Pym's function within it? It conceals him, he is buried in it inactively; when he tries to join it, it is through rebellion, mutiny, revolt and chance. From this point on the ship will be his means of moving out of society towards the unknown, the altogether other. This is to be a fiction of the self alone. A society does not hold him. He makes his own way to discover the world as if it were new, and merge with it.

Pym suggests that the mate can be deceived by a psychological trick, playing on his "superstitious terrors and guilty conscience" (*SW*, 302) since he poisoned the seaman Rogers. Pym dresses in the dead man's clothes—that is, pretends to be dead in order to survive. The mate dies of shock—the appearance kills and is therefore reality. The ship loaded with the dead is now manned by four men, an image of a derelict, disintegrated society after revolt, at the mercy of indifferent sea and wind. Poe uses no pathetic fallacies, moralized nature, or Providence immanent in the elements. A phrase like "the mercy of God" is merely an echo of order, having no plot function. The moral pattern is man's; man's choice causes disaster. Pym is fulfilling his desire; he is no Robinson Crusoe but nearer to the Ancient Mariner in his wilfulness. As the four survivors lash themselves to the mastless hulk, rudderless and swept by the sea, Pym passes into a second state of "partial insensibility." Again his "pleasing images" show the inner condition of the book: everything is in motion, objects in "endless sucession" (*SW*, 313); Pym's interior life is one with the exterior forward motion of the ship in the elements. The images recur in the apparatus of Poe's imagination: ships, large birds, balloons, things driving furiously forward, images of will and compulsion. The motion of the body in space is a basic urge, profoundly unsocial in its mobility, but reflecting competitive society in its driven state. This whole section describes suffering by wind and sea, hunger and exhaustion, a condition of existential privation in which a man is reduced to a body. The detail precludes abstraction of any kind. Poe imitates the conventions of sea-voyage fiction and documentary, with references to good and bad fortune, Providence, prayers, the ship's log, and so on. But emotional atmosphere governs; they endure in a state of almost unimaginable anguish. At its climax in chapter X, the ship of death itself appears, one of the most haunting myths of sea literature.

Extreme joy at seeing another ship turns, first, to extreme horror at the deception, and then to acknowledgement of the reality. The ship's crew, seemingly alive in their places, are dead, and Poe stresses this *appearance* of life and the *smell* of death (*SW*, 319-320). One man smiles perpetually in ironic appearance of welcome, and the irony is developed in a series of events which make the intolerable bearable, culminating in the moment when a gull drops a piece of flesh at the feet of Parker, the fourth man on the *Grampus* wreck. Pym immediately thinks what he dares not express: cannibalism, the event in which man becomes part of an extreme survival pattern. The man becomes the gull, feeding on man, the natural feeding on the dominated, in an ultimate circle of despair. Nature's neutral beasts take their existence where and how they can. In a state of nature—at sea, for instance—beasts and men draw near and compete for survival. The gull is not evil since it cannot be moral. Morality becomes relative when men are driven to bestial limits, and in American nineteenth century experience cannibalism was no fantasy—in fact, the history of Indian-white conflicts, the Donner party, and life at sea in whalers are deeply related in this region of sacrifice.[15] The sacrifice of

15. On either side of Poe's book lie two major events through which its position here is definable. In 1821, Owen Chase published his *Narrative of the Most Extraordinary and Distressing Shipwreck of the Whaleship Essex*. The whaleship was sunk by a sperm whale in the Pacific in 1820; the crew struggled for three months in open boats; six men who died of natural causes were eaten for survival; Owen Coffin, the cabin boy, was shot and eaten after lots had been drawn as to both victim and executioner: "It fell upon Owen Coffin to die, who with great fortitude and resignation submitted to his fate. They

the human by the human is rooted in all societies' power structures, the basic fact of consumer society or any system in which some men are cannibalized for political, religious or economic purposes. The root question, re-inserted into social theory by Charles Darwin's investigations and summaries later in the century, is already present in Poe's novel. Poe simply concludes chapter X:

> it is utterly useless to form conjectures where all is involved, and will, no doubt, remain forever involved, in the most appalling and unfathomable mystery. (*SW*, 322)

Disaster has causes whose convoluted sources constitute mystery—a definition of destiny or Providence, in fact. The book begins to form its center—the urge to mystery rather than rational analysis, to what is unknowable rather than mapped geography.

The narrative now descends again into a period of less intensity, as it gathers for the next climax and employs conventional details of the shipwrecked sailor's existence. Chapter XIII quotes significantly from Pym's diary: after the cannibal feast and a feast on pickled tortoise and tortoise water, and the advent of calmer weather which enables them to find and to dry food from the stores, the three survivors feel "recruited in spirits and strength." He emphasizes the relativity of good and evil in conditions of endurance. Moral standards are based on fluctuation in the pleasure and pain of human life. Ethics derive from the contingencies of existence. Endurance, fortitude and stoicism are the order of the day, despite the threat of imbecility (*SW*, 341).

In chapter XIV they are rescued by the *Jane Guy*, a British ship whose name suggests ambivalent sexuality. But the rescue is not a so-

---

drew lots to see who should shoot him: he placed himself firmly to receive his death, and was immediately shot by Charles Ramsdale, whose hard fortune it was to become his executioner" (ed. Bruce R. McElderry [New York: Corinth, 1963], p. 93). Beyond *Pym* lies the Donner party of 1846, emigrants moving westward too late in the year, harrassed by Indians and their own dissensions, and trapped by severities of the Sierra Nevada mountains, where they were forced to cannibalism. See George R. Stewart, *Ordeal by Hunger*, rev. ed. (Boston: Houghton Mifflin, 1960); and William H. Goetzmann, *Exploration and Empire* (New York: Alfred Knopf, 1966), pp. 267-270.

lution. Jane is the captain's wife *or* mother, and the new ship continues the journey outward and southward. The third and last stage of the voyage Poe calls "a frightful dream"—that is, it has the sensuous intensity and absence of conscious control associated with memory, the unconscious, and the sources of dream life:

> The incidents are remembered, but not the feelings which the incidents elicited at the time of their occurrence. I only know, that when they did occur, I *then* thought human nature could sustain nothing more of agony. (*SW*, 345)

Moving towards this peak, the narrative opens with travelogue details, latitude and longitude factualness, points about the South Sea islands, and the fair weather. When the Antarctic ice is sighted Poe gives some history of southern voyages. The material is presented without overt excitement. But at the end of chapter XIV, Pym urges Captain Guy to press southward farther, against the other men's advice to return. He suspects that the captain's deficiency in "energy" and "spirit of enterprise" will prevent him from solving "the problem" of the Pole, which he believes not to be sterile:

> While . . . I cannot but lament the most unfortunate and bloody events which immediately arose from my advice, I must still be allowed to feel some degree of gratification at having been instrumental, however remotely, in opening to the eye of science one of the most intensely exciting secrets which has ever engrossed its attention. (*SW*, 364)

The proving of Symzonia is a mania which risks life: Guy wishes to go home; Pym has relinquished the concept of home. In the struggle of confidence, Pym's will to catastrophic destiny, his need to solve a problem, his sense of enterprise and science, drive him to ridicule Guy into continuing, so that his figure of outward may be completed. In chapter XVIII, signs of land and growth are picked up, and Poe's inventive imagination takes over from his parody of documented voyage. Those configurations in human sensibility which fuse the memory of the known with the inventions of desire generate, first, the carcass of an animal—a *land* animal:

It was three feet in length, and but six inches in height, with four very short legs, the feet armed with long claws of a brilliant scarlet, and resembling coral in substance. The body was covered with a straight silky hair, perfectly white. The tail was peaked like that of a rat, and about a foot and a half long. The head resembled a cat's with the exception of the ears—these were flapped like the ears of a dog. The *teeth* were of the same brilliant scarlet as the claws. (*SW*, 365)

Strange beasts in mythical fiction exemplify the energic abundance of the planet and the imagination; they represent the flawless surprises against reductive systems afforded by nature and human nature. All other forms of life, but especially those of animals, draw life together in the human apprehension of the Earth; the imagination creates out of nature fantasies which are only slightly more fantastic than nature.[16] That the Antarctic beast of Pym's memory is nameless places it within the dualistic imagination of the West: its red teeth and claws suggest the blood of predatory life; its combination of rat, cat and dog suggest the ambiguity of whiteness and bestiality—dirtiness and viciousness coupled with perfidy and fidelity. When the human beings of the Antarctic appear they are black, apparently simple and ignorant. But simple opposition to beast and human whiteness is soon demolished. The blacks enact a role expected of them by the whites. White and black are the signs of an *imago mundi* built of deception and reversal.

Pym's relationship to Captain Guy is now reversed and he exerts considerable "influence" over him as they proceed south. After anchoring in a black sand bay, they begin to explore the totally novel land. Poe's inventiveness is now completely in charge of the narrative. The water is thick, gummy and shaded "in veins" of various purple tints which remain separate from each other:

16. It is the source, for instance, of James Thurber's "A New Natural History," including his drawings of "A Garble with an Utter in its Claws," "The Hoodwink on a spray of Ragamuffin," and many others followed by "A Gallery of Real Creatures" all of whom appear fantastic in some way, yet have names which place them in imagination as well as zoology: "The Tasmanian Devil," "Bosman's Potto," "The Spider Muck-Shrew." See *The Beast in Me and Other Animals* (New York: Harcourt, Brace, 1948), pp. 151-178.

their cohesion was perfect in regard to their own particles among themselves, and imperfect in regard to neighbouring veins. . . . The phenomena of this water formed the first definite link in that vast chain of apparent miracles with which I was destined to be at length encircled. (*SW*, 370)

For Pym, this water of original power is the central instance of the region of his destiny, desire and will, the basic proposition of fluid energy to which he has given himself from the first recognition of what his life is to be.

The final section of *Pym*, from chapter XX, is a journey into the interior, through a rocky gorge in the form of a huge labyrinth (the second in the book), dark and high-walled. As the small party, which includes Dirk Peters, Pym and a third man, squeeze through a fissure to examine some shrubs bearing nuts, a huge "concussion" collapses the gorge in total darkness. Pym is buried alive (the second premature burial in the book). The hints of betrayal in chapter XX are substantiated; the "accident" is part of a pattern of deception and reversal. The accident of penetrating the fissure saves Pym from "living inhumation" (*SW*, 381), and once again rebirth is possible. Pym and Peters survive and leave the corpse of their companion, Wilson Allen (his name combines Poe himself with the *Doppel-gänger* figure in his story of 1839, "William Wilson"). Once again, too, the third man is killed off. In fact, the apparently friendly blacks had engineered the burial in the labyrinth with considerable ingenuity, an example of that tradition of mazes constructed "with the purpose of luring devils into them so that they might never escape." But for Pym it is also an experience of initiation and the "loss of spirit in the process of creation"[17] which is the Fall preceeding rebirth, terrifying because it is the center of a human nightmare of premature entombment, living death in all its forms, suffocation, the condition of helplessness which reduces a man to a baby state, and the fear of darkness. Resurrection forms from a "glimmer of light"

17. J. E. Cirlot, *A Dictionary of Symbols*, trans. Jack Sage (New York: Philosophical Library, 1962), p. 166. On this point, see also Joseph Moldenhauer, "Imagination and Perversity in *The Narrative of Arthur Gordon Pym*," *Texas Studies in Literature and Language*, 13 (Summer, 1971), 267-280.

(as in traditional conclusions to initiation rituals) and "a patch of blue sky." But the black threat to white consciousness and its assumptions, to the idea of a subordinate class of human beings, remains.

In chapter XXIV Peters again discerns, through courage and skill, a way out of the labyrinth. The two men's shirts are fashioned into a rope with which their escape is made and which links them so closely that Peters virtually becomes Pym's *alter ego*. Descent into the chasm is an occasion for another Poe theme, the pleasure and fear of great height and depth: "I found my imagination growing terribly excited by thoughts of the vast depth yet to be descended" (*SW*, 396). Poe's description of the descent shows his interest in common fears at this early period of western analytical introspection. The very act of desiring not to be conscious produces a vivid anticipation of disaster which corresponds to his needs and dreams early in the book: "I found these fancies creating their own realities. . . . [M]y whole soul was pervaded with *a longing to fall*; a desire, a yearning, a passion utterly uncontrollable" (*SW*, 397). The desire lies in the man latently; he produces his own wish for death, for velocity of movement, for crossing the boundary into unconsciousness. The desire to look down, to embrace vertigo, becomes actual falling and swooning. What he imagines to be a dusky fiend in Hell turns out to be the half-cast Dirk Peters whose ugly body saves him. The traditional fall into Hell is parodied; it is as if the mythical Fall is deprived of religious context and retains its original human and erotic motivation: to yield to the daemonic, to resign to the dark man who exemplifies inner darkness. Pym, the white American, falls into the arms of a man part Indian, part of the apprehensiveness of the white for the dark races. Both personal and cultural myths are fused into this complex single action. Within the book's pattern, apparance again changes to reality, death to life, and fiend to savior. Pym is actually suspended from Peters and is then released from him into rebirth.

In the final short chapter, Pym and Peters, with the aid of Nu-Nu, a black prisoner, escape in a canoe—an image of America: one white, one half-cast and one black in a single boat, together with the examples of ancient pre-human life—three Galapagos tortoises. They leave the black land and head farther south. On the fifth day, the

North wind drops and only the current propels them on. Neither man is agitated but Pym cannot understand Peters' expression and he himself grows numb in a reverse polar winter of warmth:

> I felt a *numbness* of body and mind—a dreaminess of sensation
> —but this was all. (*SW*, 404)

Within this incipient closing of consciousness, on March 6th, in the Spring journey to the South, the pervasive vapour draws nearer and whiter as the water grows hot to the touch. After violent agitation of both liquid and vapour "a fine white powder" like ash falls on them. The black prisoner, Nu-Nu, lies in a state of abandoned half-conscious terror, and for the first time it is noticed he has black teeth. Poe's polar blacks are the image of the white's necessary dream of perfect blackness. On March 8, a white animal, like the tabu animal encountered earlier, floats by as if heralding the finale. Pym tries to capture it but he is overcome by "a sudden listlessness." The heat increases. Peters says little or nothing. The black Nu-Nu barely breathes. On March 9 the white powder continues and the vapour increases, embodied as

> a limitless cataract, rolling silently into the sea from some immense and far-distant rampart in the heaven. The gigantic curtain ranged along the whole extent of the southern horizon. It emitted no sound. (*SW*, 405)

Several days later the canoe enters the total blank of whiteness and silent movement. Pym's daily log stops and we have two last entries —that the only sound is the tabu cry, "*Tekelili!*," now made out of nature itself, by the reappeared and retreating birds. Then Nu-Nu dies, and Pym writes:

> And now we rushed into the embraces of the cataract, where a chasm threw itself open to receive us. But there arose in our pathway a shrouded human figure, very far larger in its proportions than any dweller among men. And the hue of the skin of the figure was of the perfect whiteness of the snow. (*SW*, 405)

The embracing figure is sexless and shrouded, and concludes the voyage. But Pym and Peters survive, where the black man dies, in the vision of total whiteness, the blacks' tabu, and the opposite of the black hellish land. There is no horror, only a certain awe ending the current of desire, an apotheosis of warmth, milkiness, whiteness—the elements of absorption into white security, of a young man's dream of fulfillment through defeating the black and entering the kingdom of the white. The event is not evaluated but left as imaginative narrative, a conclusion to the book's structural dialectic, a synthesis about which no comment is offered. The fable which began with rebellion ends with an entrance into the center of white superiority, an apotheosis from which Pym will survive to tell the tale. The narrative on its own states the dialectic of reality and appearance, and resolves it in an embracing image. Then Poe's second *persona* takes over from his first, Pym, and adds a "Note" which gives Pym's sudden death and the loss, therefore, of any further writings in the accident which, ironically, killed him (back in the world of accident his white experience did not protect him). Peters cannot be found, although he is said to be alive and well and living in Illinois. The nature of any possible interpretation is carefully stated by Edward H. Davidson:

> The farther Pym goes, the more perception is external or is represented outwardly in action or horror or death. An act of perception is a fulfillment in physical sensation; nothing is known until it is felt or endured; the muscle and the brain are very close. Hunger and thirst are demonstrations of rational intelligence; killing is a measure of the mind's knowledge of survival; love and hate are realized only in the caresses of a dog or in the trickery or fidelity of a shipmate. All thought seems to occur outside the mind, as though the human mind were at every turn the victim of thought and action long anterior to itself. Thought is first known "somewhere," then it is manifested in some physical demonstration, and finally it is known as an idea and concept.[18]

18. *Poe: A Critical Study* (Cambridge: Harvard University Press, 1957), pp. 173-174; and "The Tale as Allegory," *Interpretations of American Literature*, ed. Charles Feidelson and Paul Brodtkorb (New York: Oxford University Press, 1959), pp. 63-83. For a survey of some recent scholarship on *Pym*, see J. V. Ridgely, "Tragical-Mythical-Satirical-Hoaxical: Problems of Genre in *Pym*," *American Transcendental Quarterly*, ♯24, Part I (Fall, 1974), 4-9.

At the very end, the "Note" speculates on the native black language, blandly and unhelpfully except for an italicized quotation at its conclusion, an aphorism which in fact concludes *The Narrative of Arthur Gordon Pym*:

> *I have graven it within the hills, and my vengeance upon the dust within the rock.* (*SW*, 407)

This can be read to instruct that the language, the script, the chasm shapes and the complete narrative of Pym's desire exemplify the permanence of human experience both historical and psychological. Poe is concerned with facts of human destiny:

> They who dream by day are cognizant of many things which escape those who dream only by night. In their grey visions they obtain glimpses of eternity, and thrill, in awaking, to find that they have been upon the verge of the great secret. In snatches, they learn something of the wisdom which is of good, and more of the mere knowledge which is of evil. They penetrate, however rudderless or compassless, into the vast ocean of the "light ineffable" and again, like the adventurers of the Nubian geographer, "*agressi sunt mare tenebrarum, quid in eo esset exploraturi*" (*EAP*, 160)

The Nubian geographer, here at the beginning of "Eleonora," is Claudius Ptolemy in the second century; the quotation means "they entered the sea of darkness in order that they might explore what was therein"; and the sea of darkness is the Atlantic Ocean (*EAP*, 517). Poe's voyage of exploration takes place in America in 1837. The final italicization draws on the Old Testament image of the Ancient of Days in the Book of Daniel, Jehovah, "whose garment was as white as snow, and the hair of his head like pure wool," and on the New Testament image, in the Revelation of John, of the white Divinity whose voice is as "the sound of many waters" and whose raiment, in Matthew, is "white as the light." Poe also recalls Revelations 2:17:

> To him that overcometh will I give to eat of the hidden manna, and will give him a white stone, and in the stone a new name written, which no man knoweth saving he that receiveth it.[19]

19. Quoted by Kaplan, pp. xxii-xxiii.

Pym's Spring revelation of a man's psychic change is an entry into the renewal of confidence in the divine myth of whiteness interpreted as a permissive alibi for the eternal combat of white against black at all levels of that dualism. The voyage of exploration is a journey of confirmation. The detailed know-how of the documentation—a peculiarly American pleasure which links, for example, Cooper, Twain and Hemingway—is placed at the disposal of the color myth.

III

In *Pym*, Poe dramatizes the tradition of an original division between black and white, darkness and light. The chasm writing is God's word, and it is timeless. Black and white are eternal; the subordination of black to white is forever; it is God's decree. Poe's education, reading and subsequent cultural imprinting produced *The Narrative of Arthur Gordon Pym*. Those feelings of family love and antagonism which he shares, of course, with all men, are formed within his training. The work of literature emerges at the intersection of culture, nurture and the unchanging body. Poe's cry of "Reynolds" on his death bed in 1849 was indeed part of "the literary fragments that rose to the surface of his breaking mind,"[20] out of the resources of his only novel. Pym's experience may have taken its origin in what Baudelaire termed "l'exception dans l'ordre moral" (he was considering Poe), but the total structure of the novel is embedded in the genesis of slavery, and the information which gives believers in the divine sanction of slavery their confidence. This pattern of reversal and deception leads toward survival within a destiny which turns out to be the apotheosis of white permissions to be supreme. Pym penetrates the region of dread and fall until complexity becomes simplicity; whiteness is the extreme reduction of variety, the logical absolute which resolves the antithetical structure of the novel for the hero, but leaves him superior to the enemy—blackness, blacks, the devil. He becomes his choice, the destiny of his human potential worked

20. Alexander Cowie, *The Rise of the American Novel* (New York: American Book Company, 1948), p. 306.

out within the directions of American white Christianity. The plot exposes the fact that there comes a moment when a man may not change his character; for Pym it comes at a young age in New England. The ritual of sacrifice and rebellion leads to a world where, to use the terminology of Jean-Paul Sartre, relations with other people gradually become minimal and finally negative. The hero lives not for other people (*être-pour-autrui*) but for self (*être-pour-soi*). But such a life is entirely sanctioned by the doctrine of individualism in the West. *Pym* is a *Gestalt* of Poe's sensibility; as Allen Tate observes:

> An imagination of any power at all will often project its deepest assumptions about life in symbols that duplicate, without the artist's knowledge, certain meanings, the origins of which are sometimes as old as the race.[21]

Pym is in one clear sense a form of that part of himself which once wrote: "my whole nature revolts at the idea that there is anything in the universe superior to myself." Salvation for the white hero is damnation for the sons of Ham. In Harry Levin's terms: "The 'constant tendency to the south' . . . takes on special inflection, when we are mindful of the Southern self-consciousness of the author. His letters and articles reveal him as an unyielding upholder of slavery, and as no great admirer of the Negro"—nor of white men who favoured Abolition: "In the troubled depths of Poe's unconscious, there must have been not only the fantasy of a lost heritage, but a resentment or a social phobia."[22] Levin reminds us of Poe's story "The System of Dr. Tarr and Professor Feather" in which the pampered lunatics of a French asylum revolt against their keepers and tar and feather them, a punishment frequently afflicted on Negroes and abolitionists in the South, and obviously symbolic of black and white phobias. But

21. "Our Cousin, Mr. Poe," in *The Forlorn Demon*, p. 88. Grace Farrell Lee, "The Quest of Arthur Gordon Pym," *Southern Literary Journal*, 4 (Spring, 1972), 33, says that the importance of the mythic structure of the sea journey "may be unconscious, but whether Poe was aware of the significance of his episodes or not matters little. The structure exists, and it arose from his imagination."

22. Harry Levin, *The Power of Blackness* (New York: Alfred Knopf, 1958), pp. 120-121.

Poe's story continues: the guardians revolt themselves, like an army of "chimpanzees, orangoutangs, or big black baboons," and beat the lunatics into submission. The story exemplifies profound apprehensiveness about black-white tension, a theme to which Poe constantly returned, not least in his poem "The Raven," the very original of the dark and the deathly.

Poe's novel is a paradigm of both social relations and personal need. All the information moves towards the Self absorbed into the Other in order to achieve another life beyond revolt, a dream of being totally absolved from outlawry. Poe's "The Colloquy of Monos and Una" (1841) moves out from a consideration of the meaning of "born again," and attacks the infection of democracy or "universal equality":

> in the face of analogy and of God—in despite of the loud warning voice of the laws of *gradation* so visibly pervading all things in Earth and Heaven—wild attempts at an omni-prevalent Democracy were made. (*EAP*, 429)

Nature is thereby deformed, taste perverted, the inheritance from China, Assyria, Egypt and Nubia confirmed in disaster. "The Art-scarred surface of the Earth" has to be purified from "rectangular obscenities," enter "the smiling waters of Paradise," and be purged. Monos and Una enter a kind of death from which they recover consciousness in an ideal state of oneness and alertness in a new Earth. They enter a sixth sense state of "duration" free from the horrors of change, decay and time. Perhaps it is this ecstasy that the philobat reaches for. Richard Byrd, in his flight over the South Pole, was at one point reminded of Poe's whitenesses.[23] Whitman seems to have recalled Poe in his dream of Pym at the helm of Ariel, Shelley's boat named after Shakespeare's free spirit.[24] Jules Verne's "completion" of Pym, *Le Sphinx des Glaces* (1895), misinterprets Poe's novel and tidies it up with a French rationalist nineteenth century urge for explanation. Henry James recognized the power of *Pym*, and so did

23. Cowie, p. 305.
24. Kaplan, p. ix.

T. S. Eliot (in a passage excised from the *Waste Land* manuscript). C. A. Dake's *A Strange Discovery* (1897) makes Pym's white embracing figure simply a huge statue on a Utopian island of wise men and beautiful women, with one of whom Pym falls in love (the Tsalalian teeth are explained as artificial). The girl is killed and Pym returns to America, leaving the Baconian *New Atlantis* and its Antarctic House of Salomon for ever.

But most extraordinary of all is the tale in *Blood on the Sea* (1962) by Donald McCormick, which investigates a famous case of cannibalism which confronted the later Victorians. When Captain Dudley of the *Mignonette* was wrecked, he found himself adrift in a rowing boat with two men and a cabin boy. To survive, they killed the sick boy and ate him. Returning to England, Dudley was condemned to death, but the sentence was reduced to six months in prison. Early in his fateful voyage, Dudley had been reading *Arthur Gordon Pym* and the cabin boy's name was that of the cannibalized seaman in Poe's story—Parker. Before setting out in his ship, Captain Dudley had rescued a flower-girl from drowning, and when he went into exile in Australia after his release from prison, this girl turned up representing herself as the cabin boy come to haunt him. In Australia, people on the Sydney waterfront used to shout at him: "Who ate the boy?". When he left for a peaceful idyllic life on a Pacific island with the flower girl, the incidents leading to the boy's sacrifice were re-enacted. Dudley returned to Australia and became the first victim of plague there.

His case is clearly what Poe called *"perfect consistency,"* a logical continuity within the single integument of the universe. The phrase appears in *Eureka*, a work which demonstrates Poe's firm understanding that cosmological description—whether Genesis, *Paradise Lost* or twentieth century science fiction—is always fiction, and that religion itself is a kind of science fiction:

> *the Universe* . . . in the surpremeness of its symmetry, is but the most sublime of poems. Now symmetry and consistency are convertible terms:—thus Poetry and Truth are one. A thing is consistent in the ratio of its truth—true in the ratio of its consistency.

A perfect consistency, I repeat, can be nothing but an absolute truth.[25]

His main guide for men is, therefore, "symmetrical instinct" as distinguished from "the superficial symmetry of forms and motions." The organizational basis of poetry/truth is "the really essential symmetry of the principles which determine and control form and motion." In the essential morphology of natural energy nothing is formless. The goal of human experience—the South—is to experience and to feel the energic connections between natural self and natural environment, human body and the body of the world. That this may be either a mania for hierarchy or a madness for the unchanging absolute is the core of Poe's vision. How near to the center of the American Dream that vision remains, has become increasingly obvious. The most recent descendant of Poe's science fiction structure of racism is William S. Burroughs 'Exterminator,' with the major difference that Burroughs not only understands the nature of power but also the extent of its threat. In one section of his novel, "The Coming of the Purple Better One," his logic produces the ideal candidate for President in an electronically manipulated ape, mouthing the racist platitudes of America against "Nigger loving Communistic agitating Sheenies," hippies and Yippies as versions of the single animal Enemy. Earlier in this section of his book, Burroughs reminds us, as did Malcolm X in his *Autobiography*, of one implication of Poe's aboriginal black threat: "All the signs that mean anything indicate that the blacks were the original inhabitants of this planet. So who has a better right to it?"[26]

Poe and Pym persist in the American social imagination because of their subversion of the great dream of union and stability,[27] a power

25. In *Edgar Allan Poe: Selected Prose, Poetry, and Eureka*, ed. W. H. Auden (San Francisco: Rinehart, 1950), p. 580.

26. *Exterminator!* (New York: Viking Press, 1973), pp. 105, 99.

27. Walter Bezanson, "The Troubled Sleep of Arthur Gordon Pym," *Essays in Literary History*, ed. Rudolf Kirk and C. F. Main (New Brunswick: Rutgers University Press, 1960), p. 172, notes that with Poe "we must settle for the visual and latent force of the oneiric projection, the disturbing painting nailed to the mind's wall."

recognized in a major political novel of the 1970s in America in which Poe once again appears almost as a living character:

> Historians of early America fail to mention the archetype traitor, the master subversive Poe, who wore a hole into the parchment and let the darkness pour through. . . . A small powerful odor arose from the Constitution; there was a wisp of smoke which exploded and quickly turned mustard yellow in color. When Poe blew this away through the resulting aperture in the parchment the darkness of the depths rose, and rises still from that small hole all these years incessantly pouring its dark hellish gases like soot, like smog, like the poisonous effulgence of combustion engines over Thrift and Virtue and Reason and Natural Law and the Rights of Man. . . . It's Poe who ruined us, that scream from the smiling face of America.[28]

28. E. L. Doctorow, *The Book of Daniel* (New York: Random House, 1971), p. 177.

Nathalia Wright

Roderick Usher:
Poe's Turn-of-the-Century Artist

The influence of Edgar Allan Poe on the French Symbolist movement has been acknowledged from the beginning by the major Symbolists themselves—by the poets Baudelaire, Rimbaud, Mallarmé, and
Valéry in three successive generations, and by many others belonging
or related to that movement. That Poe influenced several later painters and composers is also known, though less often discussed. The
chief paintings and drawings inspired by his works are Gauguin's
Nevermore, Odilon Redon's album of lithographs *To Edgar Poe*,
James Ensor's album of lithographs with the same title, his *Domain
of Arnheim* and *Vengeance of Hop Frog*, Manet's lithographs to
illustrate Mallarmé's translation of "The Raven," and Ryder's *Temple of the Mind* (based on "The Haunted Palace"). In addition, Klee
is known to have read Poe. The chief composer influenced by Poe
was Debussy. Sibelius and Prokofiev expressed admiration for his
works, and Schoenberg acknowledged reading many of them. Ravel's
The Gibbet is based on "The Raven."[1]

1. The chief studies of Poe's literary influence in France are C. P. Cambiare,
The Influence of Edgar Allan Poe in France (New York: G. E. Stechert & Co.,
1927); Léon Lemonier, *Edgar Poe et les Premiers Symbolistes Français* (Paris,
1923), *Edgar Poe et la Critique Française de 1845 à 1875* (Paris: Presses Uni-
versitaires de France, 1928), *Les Traducteurs d'Edgar Poe en France* (Paris:
Presses Universitaires de France, 1928), *Edgar Poe et les Poètes Français*
(Paris: Éditions de la Nouvelle revue critique, 1932); P. F. Quinn, *The French
Face of Edgar Poe* (Carbondale: Southern Illinois University Press, 1957);
Jean Alexander, ed., *Affidavits of Genius: Edgar Allan Poe and the French
Critics, 1847-1924* (Port Washington, N.Y.: Kennikat Press, 1971).

Another example of a significant relationship between Poe and certain later artistic movements has not thus far been examined—that represented by Roderick Usher in "The Fall of the House of Usher." Usher is one of Poe's typically withdrawn, dreaming characters, who insofar as they create their own worlds may be considered in a broad sense artists or poets.[2] Only four of these characters, however, produce specific works. The Venetian in "The Visionary" (1835; later entitled "The Assignation") is apparently the author of the poem first printed separately with the title "To One in Paradise" (1834), which describes his dream life with his loved one and forecasts his death. In "Ligeia" (1838) the title character composes the poem later published separately with the title "The Conqueror Worm," forecasting Ligeia's death and making the "drama" or "play" of life appear intolerable. The artist in "The Oval Painting" (1842) paints the likeness of his wife, in the process transferring her life to his canvas and so killing her. Neither the Venetian nor Ligeia is primarily a poet, however, and the painter in "The Oval Portrait" is not a very significant figure.

Only one major character in all Poe's work is cast primarily and

For painters who were inspired by Poe or knew his works, see *Baudelaire on Poe*, tr. Lois and Francis E. Hyslop, Jr. (State College, Pa.: Bald Eagle Press, 1952), p. 32; *The Graphic Works of Odilon Redon* (New York: Dover, 1969), nos. 12-18; Libby Tannenbaum, *James Ensor* (New York: Museum of Modern Art, 1951), pp. 65, 84, 85, 87.

For composers who knew Poe's works and those who wrote musical settings for them, see Mary G. Evans, *Music and Edgar Poe* (Baltimore: The Johns Hopkins Press, 1939), p. 9, *et passim*. For Poe's influence on Debussy, see Edward Lockspeiser, *Debussy et Edgar Poe* (Monaco: Editions du Roches, 1962) and *Debussy: His Life and Mind* (New York: Macmillan, 1962), I, 211-214, II, 139-152, *et passim*. Early in his career Debussy was engaged on a symphony based on "The Fall of the House of Usher," and during the last two decades of his life he worked on operas based on that story and "The Devil in the Belfry," but he completed none of them.

2. Richard Wilbur considers them all poets in his construction of "the myth of the poet's life," drawing on the entire Poe canon, including the tales of ratiocination and the pseudo-philosophical *Eureka* and "The Colloquy of Monos and Una." See *Poe*, ed. Richard Wilbur (New York: Dell Publishing Co., 1959), pp. 7-39.

significantly in the role of a producing artist: Roderick Usher. For this reason alone he merits analysis in this role, an analysis he has not thus far received. Most interpretations of the story present it as simply an exploration of the subconscious: a dream of the narrator, the illustration of an idea, horror generated for its own sake, the psychological consequences of fear, the development of a vampire theme, and above all the dissolution of a mind.[3]

When Usher is viewed as an artist, he not only appears more complex and more credible than he does in these interpretations, but he also prefigures certain poets, painters, and composers who actually emerged in the late nineteenth and early twentieth centuries, largely in Europe but in the United States as well. Usher is a Symbolist poet, an Abstract painter with a tendency to Surrealism, and a composer with characteristics similar to those of the Impressionists. As a practitioner of three different arts, he is further comparable with later artists who attempted to fuse two or more artistic forms. As an artist who has detached himself from the physical world as well as from society and who lives in a world of his own imagining or dreaming, he is also an anticipation of later figures in fiction and poetry—and in life—who did the same.

As a poet, Usher writes the poem first published separately with the title "The Haunted Palace,"[4] which is in all essentials a Symbolist work. It exemplifies the principle held by both Poe and the Symbolists that the effects of poetry should approximate in indefiniteness those of music, it combines the perceptions of different senses, and it confuses the imaginary and the real.[5]

3. Jay B. Hubbell, "Edgar Allan Poe," in *Eight American Authors*, rev. ed., ed. James Woodress (New York: W. W. Norton & Co., 1971), pp. 30, 31. The only view of Usher corresponding to that presented here which has been found is that expressed by Lockspeiser in *Debussy: His Life and Mind*: "Yet we may truly see his [Debussy's] work as the child of Roderick Usher himself, the prototype of the new artist embracing poetry, painting, and music" (I, 213).

4. The poem first appeared in the *Baltimore Museum*, April, 1839. The story and the poem together first appeared in *Burton's Gentleman's Magazine*, Sept., 1839.

5. This summary analysis of the common characteristics of Poe and the Sym-

The poem is closely connected with music, being words for one of Usher's compositions on the guitar. It also centers on two sound and movement patterns: the first, of "spirits moving musically/To a lute's well-tunèd law" and of a "troop of Echoes" which "came flowing, flowing, flowing/And sparkling evermore"; the second, of "Vast forms that move fantastically/To a discordant melody."[6] There is less confusion of different sense perceptions than in Poe's other poems, but the very nature of the music-accompanied dance makes the visual and auditory perceptions virtually one.

The main symbol in both the poem and the story is a house, which is identified in a conventional way with its inhabitants, but in a private and arbitrary way with rational and subsequently with irrational or destructive thought. Thus a "correspondence" (in Baudelaire's terminology) is set up between observed and imagined phenomena. A better example of such a correspondence, however, is Usher's theory that a vital relationship exists between physical and nonphysical realms. He is sensible of

> an influence which some peculiarities in the mere form and substance of his family mansion, had, by dint of long sufferance . . . obtained over his spirit—an effect which the *physique* of the gray walls and turrets, and of the dim tarn into which they all looked down, had, at length, brought about upon the *morale* of his existence. (281)

He believes in "the sentience of all vegetable things," which he finds manifest in the "collocation" and "arrangement" of the stones of his house,

> as well as in that of the many *fungi* which overspread them, and of the decayed trees which stood around—above all, in the long undisturbed endurance of this arrangement, and in its reduplication in the still waters of the tarn. Its evidence—the evidence

bolists is taken from Edmund Wilson, *Axel's Castle* (1931; rptd. New York: Charles Scribner's Sons, 1947), pp. 13, 19.

6. *Complete Works of Edgar Allan Poe*, ed. James A. Harrison (New York: Fred De Fau & Co., 1902), III, 285. All quotations from the story are from this edition; page numbers are hereafter incorporated in the text.

of the sentience—was to be seen, he said . . . in the gradual yet certain condensation of an atmosphere of their own about the waters and the walls. The result was discoverable, he added, in that silent, yet importunate and terrible influence which for centuries had moulded the destinies of his family, and which made *him* what I now saw him—what he was. (286-287)

As for the subject of the poem—the passage of the monarch or king from sanity to insanity, it indirectly reflects the dislocated sensibility widely expressed by the Symbolist poets, notably Verlaine and Rimbaud. It may also be said to be a variation on the theme of *ennui* popular with them all, especially Baudelaire, Mallarmé, and Verlaine.

Usher as a painter is also a forerunner of later artists. His paintings both delight and mystify the narrator. As Usher's "elaborate fancy brooded" over them, writes the narrator, they "grew touch by touch, into vaguenesses at which I shuddered the more thrillingly, because I shuddered knowing not why." He would, he added,

in vain endeavour to educe more than a small portion which should lie within the compass of merely written words. By the utter simplicity, by the nakedness of his designs, he arrested and overawed attention. If ever mortal painted an idea, that mortal was Roderick Usher. For me at least—in the circumstances then surrounding me—there arose out of the pure abstractions which the hypochrondriac contrived to throw upon his canvas, an intensity of intolerable awe, no shadow of which felt I ever yet in the contemplation of the certainly glowing yet too concrete reveries of Fuseli.[7] (283)

One of the paintings is described in detail:

One of the phantasmagoric conceptions of my friend, partaking not so rigidly of the spirit of abstraction, may be shadowed forth, although feebly, in words. A small picture presented the interior of an immensely long and rectangular vault or tunnel, with low

7. Henry Fuseli (1741-1825) was an Anglo-Swiss painter and draughtsman. His most famous painting, to which it seems likely Poe was referring, was *The Nightmare*, depicting a fiendish mare sitting on the body of a maiden, who is stretched upon her bed in an apparently dying condition.

walls, smooth, white and without interruption or device. Certain accessory points of the design served well to convey the idea that this excavation lay at an exceeding depth below the surface of the earth. No outlet was observed in any portion of its vast extent, and no torch, or other artificial source of light was discernible; yet a flood of intense rays rolled throughout, and bathed the whole in a ghastly and inappropriate splendour. (283)

Thus on one hand Usher appears to be a painter belonging to the Abstract Art[8] movement some three-quarters of a century before its time. This movement is regarded as having been originated by Kandinsky, who abandoned objective for nonobjective painting in 1910. He was followed very shortly by Mondrian. Earlier the Cubists and the Fauves produced paintings which were either abstract or radically distorted representations. Later the number and variety of abstract painters proliferated—especially in the United States, including such different stylists as Hofmann, De Kooning, and Pollock. (The Dutch Mondrian and De Kooning and the German Hofmann all eventually settled in the United States.) Insofar as there seem to have been two main trends among the Abstractionists—one dominantly geometric and usually low-colored, the other dominantly free-form and highly chromatic—Usher is to be associated with the former on the evidence of the single painting by him which is described. His depiction of a white, linear, subterranean area invites comparison with the work of the Cubists (notably Picasso and Braque) and the geometric designs of Mondrian (which often make great use of white), rather than the freer, brighter canvases of the Fauves, Kandinsky, Hofmann, and later painters of abstractions.

On the other hand, when it is considered that the particular painting by Usher which the narrator describes represents the place of

8. It is interesting to note, in view of Poe's early use of the word, that "abstract" as applied to actual painting is first recorded as occurring in 1915 in an article in *The Forum* (New York), describing Walther's *Symphonic Poem in Blue* and a painting by Dove. See *A Supplement to the Oxford English Dictionary, Volume I. A-G.* Ed. R. W. Burchfield, (Oxford: Clarendon Press, 1972). The *Forum* article is misquoted, however, Dove's name being given as Dore.

Madeline's entombment before she dies, Usher appears to be an early Surrealist, whose composition reflects the subject on which his subconscious has become fixed. The Surrealist movement, officially founded in Paris in 1924 by the poet-painter André Breton, emphasized the importance of dreams and the associations made by the subconscious. It is chiefly represented by the fantastic and often catastrophic content of the works of Dali, Miró, Klee, Ernst, Tanguy, and Blume. Among its forerunners were Redon and de Chirico as well as some of the early Expressionists. The name of the movement was coined by the Symbolist poet Guillaume Apollinaire. Indeed, in 1925 the Surrealists claimed as their literary spokesmen the whole group of Symbolist poets. Usher's painting, in its emptiness and its architectonic design, as well as its foreboding air, seems most comparable to the vacant public squares and passageways of de Chirico. It may also be regarded as a pictorial version of the three "tomb" poems of Mallarmé—those about the tombs of Poe, Baudelaire, and Verlaine.

Usher as a composer of music is less distinctly characterized than he is as a poet and a painter. His compositions are nevertheless notable. "I listened, as if in a dream," writes the narrator, "to the wild improvisations of his speaking guitar. . . . His long improvised dirges will ring forever in my ears. Among other things, I hold painfully in mind a certain singular perversion and amplification of the wild air of the last waltz of Von Weber" (282-283).[9] Usher's music is more closely related to his withdrawn situation than is his practice of any other art. A "morbid condition of the auditory nerve," explains the narrator,

> rendered all music intolerable to the sufferer, with the exception of certain effects of stringed instruments. It was, perhaps, the narrow limits to which he thus confined himself upon the guitar, which gave birth, in great measure, to the fantastic character of his performances. But the fervid *facility* of his *impromptus* could

9. Karl Maria von Weber (1786-1826) was the earliest and perhaps the most important representative of German romantic opera. Presumably Poe refers to Weber's *Aufforderung zum Tanz* (1819). It became best known in the orchestrated version of Berlioz, who incorporated it in his adaptation of Weber's opera *Die Freischutz* (1841).

not be so accounted for. They must have been, and were, in the notes, as well as in the words of his wild fantasies (for he not unfrequently accompanied himself with rhymed verbal improvisations), the result of that intense mental collectedness and concentration to which I have previously alluded as observable only in particular moments of the highest artificial excitement. (283-284)

In its limitation, its improvised nature, its unreal effect, and its connection with verbalization, Usher's music seems to forecast that of the Impressionists. Chief among them—the originator and the only composer to remain identified with the style known as Impressionism—was Debussy. Other composers who exhibited that style to some extent include Roussel, Ravel, and Dukas in France, Delius in England, Palmgren in Finland, and Charles Griffes in the United States. Most of Debussy's compositions—and the Impressionistic compositions of the others—are short, including songs (Debussy composed many of the verses for his songs) and works for strings, all are distinguished for their departure from classical form and their disguised tonality, and many are based on literary works. If a particular composition by Debussy were to be singled out for comparison with Usher's music it might best be *La Cathédrale engloutie*, which was possibly inspired by some twenty pictures by Monet of the west front of the cathedral at Rouen. Like Usher's music in general, this work by Debussy has a funereal and an unreal air, and like Usher's musical poem it evokes a central image of an architectural structure. Insofar as the palace in the poem corresponds to Usher's house, standing beside a tarn, it also evokes, like Debussy's work, the image of water.

Usher's practice of the three arts of poetry, painting and music is at least as significant as his achievement in any one of them. It is a forecast of the tendency of artists throughout the last decades of the nineteenth and the early decades of the twentieth century to combine two or more art forms—particularly to combine them in another way than Wagner did in his music-dramas. It is interesting in this connection that one of Usher's compositions is said to be a variation on a work of Weber, whose operas point toward Wagner's achievement.

Most of the Symbolists aimed to fuse poetry and music, as many of the Impressionist composers produced music related to words. Debussy may be said to have carried the Symbolist movement into music. Indeed, of all these artists, Debussy seems to have had the broadest artistic conciousness if not creative power, encompassing the forms of music, poetry, painting, and dance. He was well acquainted with the major Impressionistic painters, from whom the Impressionistic style in music got its name, and he sometimes talked of his music in terms of painting. His fame was established by his *L'Aprés-midi d'un faune*, based on the poem with that title by Mallarmé and subsequently played as the score for the ballet also so-titled. Debussy's masterpiece is the opera *Pelléas and Mélisande*, based on Maeterlinck's play with that title (itself derived from Poe, in particular from "The Fall of the House of Usher").

The most striking example of the fusion of art forms during this period—following but differing from that achieved by Wagner—was the ballet. As presented by the impresario Diaghilev in the second and third decades of the twentieth century, it brought together music, painting (in stage settings), dance, and usually narrative. One of the earliest and most famous of those ballets was *L'Aprés-midi d'un faune*, based on Mallarmé's poem, with Debussy's music, and with choreography as well as dancing by the most brillant and original member of Diaghilev's company, Vasilav Nijinsky.[10] Redon was invited to provide the decor and when he declined, it was done by Bakst. Other Impressionist composers who wrote ballet scores include Dukas and Ravel.

At this point, the dance in Usher's poem should be looked at more closely. Beginning with measured movements, it ends in chaotic ones, as "A hideous throng rush out forever,/And laugh—but smile no more" (286). With Diaghilev, the classical Russian ballet, with its rigidly predetermined movements, began to come to an end, as more verbal content and freer positions were adopted. Fokine's radical theory of choreography and Nijinsky's uninhibited dancing in *Scheherazade* prepared the way, but more than any other single performance *L'Aprés-midi d'un faune* may be said to mark the transition. Nijinsky not only abandoned the classical movements in favor of a succes-

10. The fullest account of Nijinsky is Richard Buckle, *Nijinsky* (New York: Simon and Schuster, 1971).

sion of tableaux; he also carried out in positions and gestures the erotic content of Mallarmé's poem. Later choreographers and dancers, especially in the United States, have tended to be completely free and to defer to a nonmusical theme or plot. Among them Martha Graham is most prominent.

When Usher's several artistic talents are taken together, it appears that he is above all a potential creator of ballets.[11] His individual compositions have a close relationship to each other, appearing finally as parts of a unified imagined whole which is more impressive than any of the parts themselves. It is a poetic-musical-dramatic work of art, having dirge-like music, a libretto and dance about madness, and a dual setting of the exerior and the interior—including painted burial vaults—of a decaying house. Actually, later generations produced no single talent in such a variety of art forms.

In his withdrawal from the world and society into a kind of dream life, Usher also prefigures speakers or characters in Symbolist poetry and in such related prose as Huysmans' *À Rebours*, Villiers de L'Isle-Adam's *Axel*, Pater's *Marius the Epicurean*, Maeterlinck's *Pelléas and Mélisande*, and Proust's *À la Recherche du Temps Perdu*. The only room in the Usher house which is described, Usher's "studio" (279), has windows which were

> long, narrow, and pointed, and at so vast a distance from the black oaken floor as to be altogether inaccessible from within. Feeble gleams of encrimsoned light made their way through the trellised panes, and served to render sufficiently distinct the more prominent objects around; the eye, however, struggled in vain to reach the remoter angles of the chamber, or the recesses of the vaulted and fretted ceiling. Dark draperies hung upon the walls. (277-278)

The reason for Usher's situation is, however, an unusual one. He suffers from an obscure, congenital malady. The letter he writes the narrator, imploring him to come for a visit, "gave evidence of ner-

---

11. It is interesting in this connection that the score of one of Diaghilev's most successful ballets, *La Spectre de la Rose*, danced by Nijinsky, was the waltz by Weber apparently cited by Poe in "The Fall of the House of Usher."

vous agitation" and "spoke of acute bodily illness—of a mental dis-order which oppressed him." As is later explained,

> his very ancient family had been noted, time out of mind, for a peculiar sensibility of temperament, displaying itself, through long ages, in many works of exalted art, . . . a passionate devotion to the intricacies, perhaps even more than to the orthodox and easily recognisable beauties of musical science. (275)

After the narrator arrived, Usher

> entered, at some length, into what he conceived to be the nature of his malady. It was, he said, a constitutional and a family evil, and one for which he despaired to find a remedy—a mere nervous affection, he immediately added, which would undoubtedly soon pass off. It displayed itself in a host of unnatural sensations. . . . He suffered much from a morbid acuteness of the senses; the most insipid food was alone endurable; he could wear only garments of certain texture; the odours of all flowers were oppressive; his eyes were tortured by even a faint light; and there were but peculiar sounds, and these from stringed instruments, which did not inspire him with horror. (280)

In consequence, he had not left his house for many years.

Many turn-of-the-century artists (as well as those of other periods) withdrew from society for varying lengths of time and suffered in varying degrees from neurasthenia or hypochondria. The most conspicuous example and the one whom Usher most closely resembles is Proust. Usher's malady, as has not hitherto been pointed out, is apparently a severe allergy affecting all his senses. Proust suffered most of his life from attacks of asthma, beginning when he was nine and increasing in intensity during his later years, caused chiefly from certain odors, among them flowers and leaves. He was also hypersensitive to light and to cold and, when engaged in writing, to ordinary loud sounds. Consequently he early formed the habit of sleeping during the day and writing at night. For years he was virtually incarcerated in his bedroom, which served also as a dining, writing, and reception room. It was kept at a nearly stifling temperature, and when he went out he wore unusually heavy overclothing. For nearly a decade—during which time he wrote most of his novels—the bedroom was cork-lined, and after he gave that one up he customarily plugged his ears with cotton. As palliatives, he used narcotics (including opium) and fumigations. It is suggested that Usher resorts to liquor and opium. His voice is described by the narrator as having

> that abrupt, weighty, unhurried, and hollow-sounding enunciation—that leaden, self-balanced and perfectly modulated gutteral utterance, which may be observed in the lost drunkard, or the irreclaimable eater of opium, during the periods of his most intense excitement. (279)

Unlike Usher, however, Proust had major social ambitions and kept up a variety of social connections throughout his life.[12]

Three other points of comparison between Usher and Proust are worth noting. Like Usher, Proust was profoundly responsive to music. He not only described musical motifs and performances in his novel; he brought musicians into his bedroom to play for him, and on one occasion, over a period of several evenings, he listened to performances of the opera *Pelléas and Mélisande* over his telephone while lying in bed. Both Usher and Proust were, moreover, intimately and ambiguously connected with a female relative—Usher with his sister and Proust with his mother—in a relationship which combined love and an apparent desire for the death of the woman. In their final hours both men were confronted and apparently helped to their deaths by these female figures: Usher by the return of Madeline from her tomb to fall fatally upon him, Proust by an hallucination of a dark woman whom he described as fearful and apparently addressed as "mother." Finally the illnesses of both Usher and Proust are connected in a vital yet mysterious way with their production of artistic compositions.

12. See George D. Painter, *Proust* (Boston, Toronto: Little, Brown and Company, 1965), 2 vols., *passim*. For an illuminating discussion of the relationship between physical and nonphysical realms, pertinent to the sensibility of both Usher and Proust, see Gaston Bachelard, *The Poetics of Space*, tr. Maria Jolas (New York: Orion Press, 1964).

In the end, those critics who believe that Roderick Usher dies a madman may be correct. Most of them fail, however, to recognize the significance of his artistic talents and the diversity of the pressures upon him. The two most conspicuous instances of madness in the world of art in the last hundred years are Vincent Van Gogh, whose loose form and high color prepared the way for a variety of new art movements, including Abstract Art; and Nijinsky, whose dancing was first to depart radically from the classical tradition. As an artist, Roderick Usher has distinguished company among poets, painters, musicians and choreographers for at least a century after his time.

Edward Stone

Hawthorne's House of Pyncheon:
A Theory of American Drama

The political earthquake that overthrew the French monarchy kindled democratic blazes in Europe that burned throughout the nineteenth century, eventually settling down at its close into a steady hearth-fire of socialistic theory. The flames of Europe's political holocaust even lit up the distant shores of the new American republic, burning brightest in the century's mid-most year, 1851. At that time the new nation's eminent fiction writer, Nathaniel Hawthorne, and his young neighbor, Herman Melville, produced results of great importance for American literary history. While that "ruthless" democrat Melville was invoking through *Moby-Dick* the great egalitarian God of Andrew Jackson in attempting an epic about a Nantucket sea captain, the other "democrat" (as his host in "The Hall of Fantasy" calls him) was revealing his susceptibility to the prevailing "fever" of his times by writing the first American Democratic Tragedy, *The House of the Seven Gables*. In it he staged a quiet little artistic as well as political revolution of his own.

When the French Revolution abolished class distinction and substituted "Citizen" for "My Lord" and "Peasant," it took the first step toward abolishing the distinction between kings and commoners in the dramatic art. Its protagonists during the next century parade the evidence of change. "Our adventures nowadays are no less astonishing, diverting, and incredible than those of the past," Fernand Desnoyers wrote in 1855. "There are even plenty of bourgeois whose existence will arouse as much curiosity some centuries hence as that

69

of Mercury and good old Jupiter."[1] Off with the heads, not only of real contemporary French but of legendary Greek kings. "In three days the year 1819 would be over," Balzac wrote in *Eugénie Grandet* (1834). "In three days a terrible drama would begin, a bourgeois tragedy without poison, dagger or bloodshed; but, for the actors in it, it would be crueler than all the tragedies enacted in the famous family of the Atridae."

Certainly American political attitudes in the 1840's and 1850's partook of the democratic spirit at work in Europe. Emerson had seen in the Shaker community in 1842 "an experiment of socialism which so falls in with the temper of the times," and had sensed (in "Politics," around the same time) that "Democracy is better for us [in America] because the religious sentiment of the present time accords better with it." The literary critic, E. P. Whipple, was finding the sympathy for the poor and humble which characterized Dickens' work to be "in a great degree characteristic of the age": "The sentiment of humanity, indeed, . . . has become infused into almost all literature and speech . . . . [One] cannot . . . breathe the atmosphere of his time without . . . perceiving occasionally a liberal opinion stealing into his understanding."[2] Emerson, who spoke in "The American Scholar" of the "literature of the poor . . . the philosophy of the street" as a "great stride"—what wonder that he was excited when *Leaves of Grass* arrived, with its trumpet call to freedom? The nonchalant frontispiece pose of the new commoner who was its author revealed no Good Grey Poet, harvester of the golden fruit of Longfellow's "Sea Weed," but the banner-bearer of a political movement, a man aware of the power of the fellow-countrymen whose virtues he was proclaiming in his Preface: they had the air, he sensed, "of persons who never knew how it felt to stand in the presence of superiors." All these were versions of the "exaggerated youthful faith in the glory of their institutions" around the middle of the century.[3]

1. George J. Becker, ed., *Documents of Modern Literary Realism* (Princeton: Princeton University Press, 1963), pp. 82-83.

2. *North American Review*, 69 (October, 1849), 395.

3. Merle Curti, "Young America," *The American Historical Review*, 33 (October, 1926), 55.

That Hawthorne should eventually ally his art to the cause of liberal politics would seem predictable, not only from the facts of his life (as witness his membership in the Brook Farm commune) but from the characteristic pronouncements of his pen. Arthur Miller, trying to account for the decline of tragedy in our own times, suspects that "we are often held to be below tragedy"; we believe that "the tragic mode is archaic, fit only for . . . kings." Yet, he insists, "the common man is as apt a subject for tragedy in its highest sense as kings were." Actually, the "thrust for freedom" and the "revolutionary questioning of the stable environment" inherent in tragedy are as possible to the common man as to exalted man.[4] Hawthorne never thought otherwise.

Andrew Jackson's impact on Melville stamped itself on *Moby-Dick*; Hawthorne himself had walked to the outskirts of Salem to see Jackson in 1833; touring Europe in 1858, he would wish that this native of a South Carolina village had been painted by no less than Raphael; and seeing Abraham Lincoln close up in the White House in 1862, he recognized behind that grim-looking, shaggy exterior a true dignity. But if Arthur Miller is right, a democracy's common man should be considered as capable of deep stirrings as its great men. And early in his career Hawthorne had frequently said as much, particularly in the *Mosses From an Old Manse*. With the traditional eloquence of "the hereditary legislator" he wished to match the "wild power" of some backwoodsman's language ("The Procession of Life," 1843). "Peer and plowman" he would muster "shoulder to shoulder." In "The Old Apple Dealer" (1845), he found a fascinating paradox. Was it less than witchcraft that whereas many a "noble" form had vanished, the "faded and featureless" figure of an old man selling apples and gingerbread at a railroad station should have lodged in his memory? Not dignity nor venerability—what with his abject hopelessness and despondency, it was pity that the old man inspired. "Yet, could I read but a tithe of what is written" in the old man's mind and heart, "it would be a volume of deeper and more comprehensive import than all that the wisest mortals have given to

4. "Tragedy and the Common Man," *New York Times*, February 27, 1949, Sec. II, pp. 1, 3.

the world; for the soundless depths of the human soul and of eternity have an opening through your breast." This is not only a definition of man as stated by Christ and restated by the Declaration of Independence and the transcendentalists: it may also serve as an introduction to the heroine of the final act of Hawthorne's American Oresteia, Hepzibah Pyncheon. Richard Sewall's finding about *The Scarlet Letter* and *Moby-Dick*, that "Both novels show clearly that their authors were sensitive to the problem of making the tragic vision real to nineteenth-century democratic America,"[5] can be applied as well to *The House of the Seven Gables*.

If it was Ibsen who demonstrated that "A vital drama had to be in vital relation to the actual problems of the modern world,"[6] then we may think of the Hawthorne whose curtain rises on an old woman opening up a store to support herself and an ex-convict brother as Ibsen's forerunner. What Muller says about "The first great bourgeois tragedy," *Ghosts*, we can say about *The House*: an obvious source of its power is "the tragic sense of inevitable doom" with which we can equate Greek fatalism or Hebraic transmission of sins of the fathers.[7] (If reconciliation averts further fatal consequences in *The House*, so does it in the Oresteia, not to speak of other Greek tragedies.) Whereas Chekhov's art is not high tragedy, nor in conformance with Aristotle's terms, still, because of its "fuller 'recognition' of tragic possibility," it is a "more complete picture of life . . . than . . . in any ancient tragedy except Shakespeare's."[8]

The American Democratic Tragedy, then, would be a conflict conceived along the lines of both the Greek tragedy that was and the European domestic play to come, retaining some of the old machinery but taking its characters from the new class, fitting it out in modern dress. It would, as we shall see, reverse Aristotle's values: in it, plot would be secondary to character. The clue to its "distinctive essence"

5. Richard Sewall, *The Vision of Tragedy* (New Haven: Yale University Press, 1959), p. 3.
6. Herbert J. Muller, *The Spirit of Tragedy* (New York: Alfred Knopf, 1956), p. 274.
7. Muller, pp. 264-265.
8. Muller, pp. 290-291.

would be "not its ancient form but its unique content, its new spirit."[9] Although Muller is talking here about Greek tragedy, his description fits American Democratic Tragedy, both being the product of an important emerging society.

That the authors of *The House* and *Moby-Dick* should project their tragic vision in the form of the novel rather than the play seems, in retrospect, an artistic sequel to a political change. If, by 1870, an American critic could assert that "prose fiction now occupies the place held by the drama during the Elizabethan age,"[10] this "rapid growth of the novel into the 'most characteristic literature of modern times' was due to the development of political democracy. With [it] the individual became more important and could more and more shape his own future. As a result, he became interested in his own character."[11] Or to democracy's concomitant, complexity: "The tragic spirit has turned to the novel for expression," Herbert Muller believes, "since it is a form better suited than drama to a complex age, permitting both more amplitude and more inwardness."[12] It was this last quality that distinguished Hawthorne's first heroine of the American Democratic Tragedy, Hepzibah Pyncheon, from her forbears of the Greek stage.

That his novel should be modeled on the Greek is understandable. Only a few months after *The House* appeared, Hawthorne published a children's book based on various Greek myths. Richard Sewall (who feels that Hawthorne borrowed from Sophocles' Antigone for his characterization of Hester Prynne) writes that "he more than once indicated" his "sense of kinship with Greek and Elizabethan tragedy."[13] This could refer to the reflections of Miles Coverdale at the close of "The Wood-Path" chapter in *The Blithedale Romance*

9. Muller, p. 36.

10. Thomas W. Higginson, "Americanism in Literature," *The Atlantic Monthly*, 25 (January, 1870), 59.

11. W. C. Roscoe in the *National Review* in 1856; rptd. in Richard Stang, *The Theory of the Novel in England 1850-1870* (New York: Columbia University Press, 1959), p. 51.

12. Muller, p. 250.

13. Sewall, p. 3.

(1852). He thinks of himself as that "calm observer" who recalls "the Chorus in a classic play, . . . aloof . . . and bestow[ing] the whole measure of its hope or fear . . . on the fortunes of others, between whom and itself this sympathy is the only bond."[14] Or, in *The House* itself, Holgrave's view of his own function is partly to think of himself as a Chorus: neither "to help or hinder [Hepzibah or Clifford]; but to look on, to analyze, to explain matters to myself, and to comprehend the drama which, for almost two hundred years, has been dragging its slow length" over the stage that is the House of Pyncheon.[15] So that when Phoebe immediately comments on his aloofness, scolding him for talking "as if this old house were a theatre" and for looking at the Pyncheon misfortunes over the ages "as a tragedy" such as she has seen acted, he is forced to "recognize a degree of truth" in her remarks. Does he not, a moment later, confess to her that he "cannot help fancying that Destiny is arranging its fifth [and catastrophic] act" for the House? (pp. 217, 218). Earlier Holgrave, trying to help Hepzibah by praising her, had referred to the original Pyncheon-Maule feud, and Hawthorne as well as Hepzibah would appear to have been "not displeased at this allusion to the sombre dignity of an inherited curse" (p. 46). Finally, early in *The House*, where Hawthorne refers to the edifice itself both as having a "human countenance," and being "like a great human heart, with a life of its own" (pp. 5, 27), he practically echoes the opening lines of *Agamemnon*, the first part of Aeschylus' trilogy, wherein the Watchman

14. Nathaniel Hawthorne, *The Blithedale Romance* (Columbus: Ohio State University Press, 1964), p. 97.

15. Nathaniel Hawthorne, *The House of the Seven Gables* (Columbus: Ohio State University Press, 1965), p. 216. Further references will be parenthetically included in my essay.

Austin Warren notes that in *The House* "The community forms, in terms of literary tradition, a Greek chorus, to the happenings in his protagonists' inner lives. . . . [T]he chorus partly comments . . . on what goes forward at the center of the stage, partly utters traditional maxims and apothegms which are too general. In Hawthorne's choruses the same is true." ("*The Scarlet Letter*: A Literary Exercise in Moral Theology," *The Southern Review*, NS 1 [Jan. 1965], 44). See also James W. Mathews, "The House of Atreus and *The House of the Seven Gables*," *ESQ*, 63 (1971), 31-36.

says that "the house itself, could it take voice, might speak aloud and plain" (Richmond Lattimore translation).

The very structure of Hawthorne's drama so closely parallels Aeschylus' that we are justified in wondering whether even his title is an echo of this particular Greek tragedy: his House of Pyncheon *is* a modern House of Atreus. Each house is cursed because of a crime committed by a progenitor; retribution for this brings about retaliation; and the curse is finally lifted in a later generation, the entire action being presented in three stages. In *Agamemnon*, Atreus' unspeakable conduct provokes Thyestes' curse ("Thus crash in ruin all the seed of Pleisthenes"), which bears fruit in Agamemnon's murder by Aegisthus, son of Thyestes; in *The Libation Bearers*, Aegisthus is in turn murdered by Agamemnon's son, Orestes; and in *The Eumenides*, vengeance on Orestes by the Furies is finally averted by a reconciliation of the Furies and Athena by Apollo that lifts the original curse. The curtain of Hawthorne's first act rises on a seventeenth-century stage, with a Pyncheon bringing about the murder for witchcraft of a Maule, who curses him; in the second act, taking place in the eighteenth century, the grandson of the murdered Maule gains revenge on the grandson of his ancestor's murderer by so enchanting the grandson's daughter that she dies; in the third and final act, set in the nineteenth century, the two houses are reconciled by the marriage of a representative of each.

It is no wonder, then, that the Aeschylean quality of Hawthorne's novel was called to the public's attention shortly after his death. Elizabeth Peabody, his wife's sister, wrote of *The House* as

> a tragedy that takes rank by the side of the Trilogy of the Agamemnon, Choephoroi, and Eumenides, without the aid of the architecture, sculpture, verse, dancing, and music which Aeschylus summoned to his aid to set forth the operation of the Fury of the house of Atrides that swept to destruction four generations of men. It takes two hundred years for the crime which the first Pyncheon perpetrated against the first Maule to work itself off. . . . [T]he curse of the first Maule upon the first Pyncheon is at last replaced by a marriage blessing and bond, laying to sleep the Fury of Retribution. . . .

The only true difference she found in this outcome: Hawthorne's "is undoubtedly due to the Christian light which the noble heathen lacked; it is love . . . that undoes the horrible spell."[16]

In the next generation of literary criticism, Paul Elmer More brought to light a more pervasive and more important difference. In *The House* and other stories involving an ancestral curse, he had been "struck by something of similarity and contrast at once between our New England novelist and Aeschylus, the tragic poet of Athens." Despite the vast gulf between the two civilizations, he confessed, "I know not where, unless in these late romances, any companion can be found in modern literature to the Orestean conception of satiety begetting insolence, and insolence calling down upon a family the inherited curse of Atè. It may be reckoned the highest praise of Hawthorne that his work can suggest any such comparison with the masterpiece of Aeschylus." More then probes the truly radical departure of Hawthorne's version of tragedy. Although the two writers dealt with the same concepts of fate and inherited evil, their methods were "perfectly distinct": "The Athenian too represents Orestes, the last inheritor of the curse, as cut off from the fellowship of mankind; but to recall the Orestean tale, with all its tragic action of murder and matricide and frenzy, is to see in a clearer light the originality of Hawthorne's conception of moral retribution in the disease of inner solitude."[17]

In 1941 F. O. Mattheissen agreed with More ("Such an accumulation of oppressive evil upon the roof of one family hardly falls short of the terrible imagination of Aeschylus") and with his definition of the difference between the two conceptions of tragic action. If (unlike O'Neill in *Mourning Becomes Electra* and Eliot in *The Family Reunion*) "Hawthorne gave no indication that he was thinking of the example of Greek tragedy," at least he thought of the final action of *The House* as the end of a drama. In fact, by introducing the two philosophical laborers who appear early and late in the novel, "Haw-

16. Elizabeth Peabody, "The Genius of Hawthorne," *The Atlantic Monthly*, 22 (September, 1868), 359-360.

17. Paul Elmer More, "The Solitude of Nathaniel Hawthorne," *Shelburne Essays, First Series* (New York: G. P. Putnam's Sons, 1904), pp. 39, 40.

thorne went so far with this analogy as to provide his scene with a Chorus."[18]

But what truly attests to Hawthorne's tragic vision, Mattheissen points out, is not the introduction of technical devices but his characterization of Hepzibah—"his ability to endow such a pathetic character . . . with a measure of heroic dignity. . . . He was aware of the problem of choosing for one of his protagonists" a ridiculous looking, slightly demented old woman fallen on hard times.

> Yet Hawthorne held that if a writer looked "through all the heroic fortunes of mankind," he would find this same mixture of the mean and ludicrous in "the purest pathos which life anywhere supplies to him." This was particularly the case for anyone who wanted to represent human nature as it was in a democracy, a truth that Melville was to proclaim later in this very year, in his eloquent statement of the "august dignity" to be found in his *dramatis personae*, the miscellaneous crew of a whaler. Hawthorne's lead to a similar discovery lay in his final remark in the chapter wherein Hepzibah opened her shop: "What is called poetic insight is the gift of discerning, in this sphere of strangely mingled elements, the beauty and majesty which are compelled to assume a garb so sordid."[19]

It is Mattheissen, then, who finally has identified the timeliness of the spirit that Hawthorne breathed into this woman, who has linked history and art in *The House*. In a democracy, the simple "issues of conscience" can acquire a "dramatic reality."[20] Character *can* overshadow plot, in refutation of Aristotle's insistence in the *Poetics* that "without an action there could not be a tragedy, but without character there could."

This new concept of the tragic potentiality of the average American pervades *The House*. Hepzibah first appears not as a figure in a novel but as an actress on a stage: "Forth she steps . . . a tall figure,

---

18. F. O. Mattheissen, *American Renaissance* (New York: Oxford University Press, 1941), pp. 338-339.
19. Mattheissen, pp. 338-341.
20. Mattheissen, p. 341.

clad in black silk, with a long and shrunken waist, feeling her way towards the stairs like a near-sighted person, as in truth she is" (p. 32). This description embodies the opposing components of the character of democratic tragedy as Hawthorne will shortly define it so memorably. A few pages later he returns to contemplate his heroine in the shop, finding "[i]n the aspect of this dark-arrayed, pale-faced, lady-like, old figure, . . . a deeply tragic character that contrasted irreconcilably with the ludicrous pettiness of her employment" (p. 37)—a repetition of the earlier fusion of conflicting elements. The fact that "in this republican country" the family-proud, socially mighty such as the Pyncheons are always on the verge of ruin, Hawthorne views as nothing short of a "tragedy . . . enacted" as repeatedly as a "popular drama on a holiday" and more moving, even than when in Europe the same fate befalls the hereditary nobility. Finally, at the end of this first scene-chapter, he fills in these brush strokes with the colors that will produce the first heroine in the Democratic American Tragedy. As dramatic artist trying to portray human nature realistically, what can he make of its hopeless mixture of "the mean and ludicrous . . . with the purest pathos" that real life also provides? "What tragic dignity, for example, can be wrought into a scene like this!" No young Antigone has he to offer, but an old, ludicrous woman faced with no more "great life-trial" than earning a living! (pp. 38, 40-41).

Truly, an explanation, an apologia was due his readers. Their values were Shakespearean, and they were accustomed to look, Melville was saying, for another Elizabethan heroine in another drama from old English history. Whereupon down to the footlights the native dramatist advances, his document firmly in hand. Like Melville's invocation at the close of Chapter 36 in *Moby-Dick*, which it may have inspired, it is as moving a manifesto as Whitman's preface a few years later or any of the revolutionary kind circulating through the old countries. Here Hawthorne is pleading that "if we look through all the heroic fortunes of mankind, we shall find this same entanglement of something mean and trivial with whatever is noblest. . . . Life is made up of marble and mud." In place of Aristotle's amalgam of the protagonist highly renowned and prosperous, the distant illustrious personage marred by some error or frailty, the native playright was proposing one of Essex County stone mixed with mud. But this mixture, so far from daunting the tragic artist, should challenge him: "What is called poetic insight is the gift of discerning, in this sphere of strangely mingled elements, the beauty and the majesty which are compelled to assume a garb so sordid" (p. 41). For the equal of this definition, we would have to go back to Pope's concept of man as "the glory, jest, and riddle of the world," or to Hamlet, for whom man is "the beauty of the world, the paragon of animals! And . . . the quintessence of dust."

Now, the *heroic*, the *noble*, the *majestic* that Hawthorne has spoken of inheres in the dignity of the democratic protagonist, whose "issues of conscience" can, Mattheissen thought, acquire a "dramatic reality."[21] That is why, when, not a Queen Clytemnestra, but Hepzibah Pyncheon, spinster, "pale, wild, desperate in gesture and expression, scowling portentously, and looking . . . qualified to do fierce battle" (p. 42), opens her shop in the next scene, the era of the new drama, the American Democratic Tragedy, has begun.[22]

For this was the revolution as it carried over into dramatic art. When Howells defined Henry James's fiction as avoiding the "moving accident" and "all manner of dire catastrophies" and studying "human nature much more in its wonted aspects" and finding "its ethical and dramatic examples in the operation of lighter but not really less vital motives," it was fitting that he spoke of its being derived from Hawthorne (and George Eliot).[23]

When the *Westminster Review* critic of 1866 described George Eliot's novels as "not novels in the ordinary sense of the term—they are really dramas: as the word is understood when applied to 'Hamlet,' or the 'Agamemnon,'"[24] he is merely amplifying the implications of Holgrave, who in "The First Customer" chapter of *The House* asks: "Do you really think, Miss Hepzibah, that any lady of your fam-

21. Mattheissen, p. 341.
22. Hawthorne's mockery faintly but perceptibly tinges Hepzibah's heroism, of course.
23. William Dean Howells, "Henry James, Jr.," *The Century Magazine*, NS 3 (November, 1882), 28.
24. Stang, p. 47.

ily has ever done a more heroic thing, since this house was built, than you are performing in it to-day?" (p. 45).

In Aeschylus' trilogy, Kitto points out, there was "no revelation of motives." (Aristotle had insisted that "incidents and plot are the end of tragedy.") All we know is *that* Agamemnon killed Iphigenia, not *why*. Clytemnestra justifies herself, but "there is no picture of conflicting passions in her heart," for this aspect of the action is "an irrelevant part of the presentation of the tragic heroes." Similarly, the theme of Sophocles' *Electra* "is not the tragic workings of a mind; it is that men of violence do things which outrage Justice, bring retribution, and provoke further deeds of violence. . . . what passes in [the actors'] minds is a minor interest."[25] The same is true of the first two parts of Hawthorne's modern version. These too, we note, describe action of the Pyncheon princes of the land, and long ago. Almost ritualistically the original Pyncheon had been cursed, and he had paid for his greed with his own life. Two generations later the curse had doomed another Pyncheon, this time a young woman. (Albeit here we can see Hawthorne taking a liberty with the Greek original by complicating the motivation of the feuding houses: Alice actually admires the plebeian artisan Matthew; and he, in turn, intends only to humble, not to kill, her.) But the third part of Hawthorne's Oresteia is also the first version of the American Democratic Tragedy. In it the present replaces the past and psychology replaces ritual, and it is precisely the picture of conflicting passions in Hepzibah's heart that defines her dramatic stature. For just as Henry James would insist that the "drama" of *Roderick Hudson* is the drama of Rowland Mallet's "consciousness," so the drama of *The House* is of Hepzibah's momentous struggles, first with the unknown (the public) and its imagined terrors, then with the known (her cousin) and his all too familiar sinisterness.

That is why "The First Customer" truly can yield James' "surprises" for the modern psychologist. Harshness, the elderly spinster can en-

25. H. D. F. Kitto, *Greek Tragedy: A Literary Study* (New York: Doubleday & Company, n. d.), pp. 74-75.

dure, but Holgrave's sympathy evokes both giggles and sobbing. And her conclusions about the "lower classes" are the drama of ambivalence. Hawthorne had found love and hate to be cognates at the end of *The Scarlet Letter*, and now he makes Hepzibah feel not only resentment toward her rude and curious customers from her social inferiors, but also "a sentiment of virulence . . . towards the idle aristocracy to which it had so recently been her pride to belong." Intensity is the word for this "inward . . . history" of Hepzibah's first half-day's heroic deportment in her shop.

What Holgrave identifies as modern heroism, also characterizes the other great dramatic scene, "Clifford's Chamber," following the chapter of Hepzibah's confrontation with Jaffrey Pyncheon late in the novel. She rushes about the darkened house, her mind shuttling between idle trifling and heavy thoughts, as is true of minds in distress. Her grief and pride have so isolated her, she senses, that there are no friends to shield her and Clifford from Jaffrey: any who came, in fact, in response to her appeal would side with Jaffrey. Her faltering faith stamps on her the wretched conviction that God does not care, the vastness of Providence in itself canceling out individual considerations. She herself is the enactment of the "sacred misery, sanctifying the human shape in which it embodies itself" (p. 247) that she thinks of Clifford as being, unnerved as she is "by the scene of passion and terror, through which she had just struggled" (p. 240). In her "native composition" there was "something high, generous, and noble," something "endowed with heroism"; there is a "heroic fidelity" about her—in "Clifford and Phoebe" Hawthorne showers attributes like these on Hepzibah.

It may be true, as the American critics Whipple and Curtis believed, that what resulted from Hawthorne's diligent portraiture was not art but anatomy; that, as the British *Spectator* observed, "he had real difficulty in rising to any tragic crisis," and in his works there is "little of that imaginative *sympathy* with pain which is at the heart of all true tragedy."[26] It is also possible to argue, as Professor Vance does,

26. Stang, pp. 59-60.

that the end product of Hawthorne's efforts in *The House* was more truly tragicomedy than tragedy.[27] But it seems incontestably clear that for the first time in American literature a heroine had appeared in the costume of her own times and from the ranks of the common man to be beset with the struggles heretofore allotted only to the princely ranks in situations of the remote past. Whether hero or tragic hero, it would be idle to dispute, the definitions of tragedy differing as widely as they do (or as Greek tragedies themselves do). Most important are the dimensions of the role in which Hepzibah Pyncheon was cast.

The supporting cast, too, are of a fitting stature. Phoebe's figure "would hardly have suited one's idea of a countess," yet her grace would entitle her to such standing if the society in which she existed made such distinctions. The "new Plebeianism" which she represents has a nobility of its own. (Is not Hepzibah herself "stately"? Has she not a "princess-like condescension"?) As for Holgrave, the potentialities of the New Plebeianism shine from him even more strikingly. In "The Daguerrotypist" Hawthorne says that the ultimate success of the Holgraves of his day "may be incomparably higher than any that a novelist would imagine for his hero," thereby hinting that it may approach the fabulous, the prodigious, the heroic. From this amalgam of the base and the noble, true dignity can also emerge, to be cast in the role until now reserved for the high-born.

Yet a far more impressive demonstration of Hawthorne's leveling principle at work is his treatment of one of *The House*'s minor characters. In him it is possible to take an exact bearing on the progress of the democratic spirit at its work in that age of revolution. W. H. Auden has noted a differentiation in Greek tragedy between the two components of its cast: there was a line between the hero, who was exceptional, and chorus, who were average, that neither could cross. In the tragedy of Christian society, on the other hand, "there is not only an infinite variety of possible characters . . . but overshadowing them all is the possibility of each becoming both ex-

27. William L. Vance, "Tragedy and 'The Tragic Power of Laughter': *The Scarlet Letter* and *The House of the Seven Gables*," *The Nathaniel Hawthorne Journal 1971*, ed. C. E. Frazer Clark, Jr. (Washington, D. C.: NCR/Microcard Editions, 1972).

ceptional and good"[28]—that is, a hero. Kitto cites an example of this classic separation in the *Agamemnon*. When its Watchman opens the play by complaining of the discomfort of his assignment, this is not merely dramatic "decoration" but is functional, for "his ordinary figure gives the scale of those who are to follow; he represents the plain Argive citizen whose sufferings are more than once contrasted with the misdeeds of their rulers."[29] Henry James unwittingly furnishes a basis for comparison in Hawthorne's Uncle Venner, who also appears early on stage. In him Hawthorne introduced "an example of humorous resignation and of a life reduced to the simplest and homeliest elements, as opposed to the fantastic pretensions of the antiquated heroine of the story." This, James looks upon as perhaps "the most striking example of the democratic sentiment" in the entire range of Hawthorne's fiction.[30] Indeed it is also the most striking example of the bridging of the wide gulf between Agamemnon and Watchman in the first part of Aeschylus' trilogy that the democratic dogma had effected. Not only does Hawthorne redesign the classic heroine with parts of mud as well as marble: his chorus (or chorus-level) character Uncle Venner turns out to be constructed of marble as well as mud. As to the earlier old apple dealer, to this handyman is ascribed the possibility of becoming both exceptional and good by virtue of the divine spirit that went into his creation. The peasant who in Queen Elizabeth's day was merely galling the kibe of the courtier, in Andrew Jackson's day is invited to move in with him.

Just as he had never pleaded his case before he created Hepzibah, so Hawthorne rested it with her. In *The Scarlet Letter* he had filtered his vision of the fated characters through the haze of time, working up to the rich dramatic materials of his own age only in the prefatory sketch and humbly admitting inaptitude in not trying to subject them to novelistic treatment. The next year, whereas the theater of *The*

---

28. W. H. Auden, "The Christian Tragic Hero: Contrasting Captain Ahab's Doom and its Classic Greek Prototype," rptd. in *Tragedy: Modern Essays in Criticism*, ed. Laurence Michel and Richard B. Sewall (Englewood Cliffs, New Jersey: Prentice-Hall, 1963), p. 236.

29. Kitto, p. 72.

30. Henry James, *Hawthorne* (London: Macmillan and Co., 1879), pp. 48-49.

Blithedale Romance is only "a little removed from the highway of ordinary travel," still he would not expose its characters to "too close a comparison with the actual events of real lives." While his cast continued native and contemporary, his narrator shuttled between chorus and actor, able only to make guesses at the inner struggles of the heroine.

Hawthorne's final heroine, Miriam of *The Marble Faun* (1860), is a German; his stage, as far removed from Essex County as can be— Rome. And like the Hawthorne of *The Scarlet Letter*, his friend Longfellow would in *The New-England Tragedies* (1868) grope back in the distant American past for the few available materials (the persecution of the Quakers, the witchcraft delusion) of native heroism. Still, the bridge Hawthorne had built in *The House* between ancient theory and modern democracy would attract other travelers. James and Howells would fashion their heroes out of the parvenu merchant princes of their own day, Holgrave reappearing in Christopher Newman and our near-sighted, dingy spinster yielding the stage to the fat-necked, hairy-pawed Silas Lapham: their issues of conscience would acquire a dramatic reality more relevant to readers of the novels in a democracy than those of Antigone or Orestes. By 1925 the protagonist of the new native drama would climb from the ranks of the Salvation Army on the street corner up to the stage of *An American Tragedy*.

David G. Hoch

Walden: Yoga and Creation

Although Thoreau's interest in Indian scriptures has been suggested in a number of places, I do not think the pervasiveness of that influence has been adequately explored and documented.[1] In this essay I would like both to explore the Indian influence on the first two chapters of *Walden* and to suggest how Thoreau relates yoga to the act of artistic creation.

In a letter to H. G. O. Blake (November 20, 1849), Thoreau quotes a passage from *The Harivansa* pointing out that those who practice yoga are "Free as birds in the air" and that they are "disengaged from every kind of chains."[2] Living free is the aim of "Economy" in particular and of *Walden* as a whole. Since freedom is the

---

1. Arthur Christy's *The Orient in American Transcendentalism* (New York: Columbia University Press, 1932) is the pioneer study of the influence of Indian thought on Thoreau. Rather than drawing specific parallels, Christy sees the influences as they affect Thoreau's life style. Both William B. Stein's "Thoreau's *Walden* and the *Bhagavad Gita*," *Topic*, No. 3 (1963), 38-55, and Frank MacShane's *Walden* and Yoga," *New England Quarterly*, 37 (September, 1964), 322-42, point out interesting and cogent parallels between *Walden* and *The Bhagavad Gita*; however, neither uses the translation that Thoreau read. Stein's "The Yoga of *Walden*," *Literature East and West*, 13 (1969), 1-26, uses nineteenth century texts to draw some striking parallels between Thoreau's writing and Indian sources, as does his "The Hindu Matrix of *Walden*: The King's Son," *Comparative Literature*, 22 (Fall, 1970), 303-318, for "Where I Lived and What I Lived For." None of these articles on Thoreau and Indian sources make use of his unpublished notes as I have done in this essay.

2. *The Correspondence of Henry David Thoreau*, ed. Walter Harding and Carl Bode (New York: New York University Press, 1958), p. 251.

aim of yoga, *Walden* is about freedom in this sense. Following this first citation of *The Harivansa*, Thoreau says, "Depend upon it that rude and careless as I am, I would fain practise the *yoga* faithfully."[3] Thoreau's point is clear: he uses yoga to achieve the freedom he desires. He then quotes another passage from *The Harivansa* concerning yoga contemplation, which specifies that the yogi "contributes in his degree to creation" and that "he acts, as animating original matter." Yoga contemplation leads to a homology with the creator and a recapitulation of the cosmogony. Thoreau tells Blake, "To some extent, and at rare intervals, even I am a yogin";[4] his contemplation allows him to participate in the act of creation like the yogi. Hence Thoreau's interpretation of yoga leads him to practice his own art, his writing.

Thoreau directs his readers to interpret *Walden* on many levels. His quotation in "Conclusion" from a work on Hindustani literature establishes this point clearly: " 'They pretend,' as I hear, 'that the verses of Kabir have four different senses; illusion, spirit, intellect, and the exoteric doctrine of the Vedas;' but in this part of the world it is considered a ground for complaint if a man's writings admit of more than one interpretation."[5] Many readers of Thoreau would admit the first three types of interpretation: illusion, spirit, and intellect; few have examined the fourth: the commonplace doctrine of the Vedas, that is, the internal sacrifice or yoga. That *Walden* contains abundant evidence of the legitimacy of this sort of interpretation can be seen in the relationship between the freedom of the yogi which Thoreau points out to Blake and the theme of "Economy."

I

An examination of the structure of "Economy" reveals that it comprises Thoreau's "free papers" (II, 78). The chapter begins and ends

3. *Ibid.*

4. *Ibid.*

5. Henry David Thoreau, *The Writings of Henry David Thoreau* (Boston: Houghton Mifflin, 1906), II, 358. All future references to this edition will be made parenthetically in the text.

with a discussion of freedom. The introduction is a discussion of how man can free himself from slavery to material goods; the conclusion is a quotation from the *Gulistan* enjoining men to be free. The body of the chapter is an elaboration of the theme of how men can free themselves from the "fetters" of economic necessity, echoing the metaphor used in Thoreau's quotation from *The Harivansa* (II, 18). These chains of course include the necessity of procuring a house, clothing, and food.

Addressing his readers in the third paragraph, Thoreau remarks that they appear "to be doing *penance* in a thousand remarkable ways" (II, 4, italics mine). Even the "conscious penance" of the Hindu ceremony of the five fires is not barbarous in comparison with Thoreau's neighbors. At least the Hindu voluntarily sets out to practice mortification. Thoreau's neighbors do it involuntarily. Because of their attachment to things, they begin digging their own graves as soon as they start life. Thoreau observes that a man's "poor *immortal soul*" is "crushed and smothered" by his possessions (II, 5, italics mine).

Thoreau symbolizes the central idea of "Economy" with the metaphor of "Negro Slavery." Compared to a man's being a "slave driver" of himself, the Southern practice seems mild. When a man is the slave and prisoner of his own opinion of himself, "he cannot be free in any sense." Thoreau then asks a question which brings his theme into sharp focus: "Self-emancipation even in the West Indian provinces of the fancy and imagination,—what Wilberforce is there to bring that about?" (II, 8). The introduction to "Economy" focuses on the problem of man's being enslaved to himself.

Religious terms like *penance, immortal soul, divinity, immortal,* and *divine* abound in the introduction to *Walden* and are joined with the slavery metaphor (II, 4-8, *passim*). These do not evoke a Christian framework of allusion however, for Thoreau refers to Christianity ironically. In "Economy," he points out how Christianity thwarts freedom. After saying that the soul should be free and that society imprisons the individual, Thoreau quotes without comment two passages from the Old Testament (II, 32-35). In the first the Lord God pronounces exile on the people of Israel. In the second He declares that He binds all souls to Himself: "Behold all souls are mine" (II,

35). A later reference to Christianity shows the Jesuits to be concerned with physical suffering whereas the Indians, who are being burned at the stake, are superior to it.

Allusions to the Shorter Catechism reinforce this irony. Immediately after Thoreau points out that "The mass of men lead lives of quiet desperation," he says; "When we consider what, to use the words of the catechism, is the chief end of man, and what are the true necessaries and means of life, it appears as if men had deliberately chosen the common mode of living" (II, 8, 9). He parodies the answer to the first catechism—the chief end of man is to glorify God and enjoy him forever—in the following: "Our hymn-books resound with a melodious cursing of God and enduring Him forever" (II, 87). The same is echoed in "Where I Lived and What I Lived For": "For most men, it appears to me, are in a strange uncertainty about it [life], whether it is of the devil or of God, and have *somewhat hastily* concluded that it is the chief end of man here to 'glorify God and enjoy him forever' " (II, 101). Not only are these allusions ironic but they also point up Thoreau's contention that the chief end of man is to free himself.

This is also the philosophy underlying the Indian works quoted in *Walden. The Vishnu Purana*, quoted in "Economy" (II, 11), declares that liberation is the chief end of man. Consider the following passage which Thoreau recorded in his "Note Book": "They [men] . . . are the instruments (Of accomplishing the object of creation, the liberation of soul)."[6] Liberation of soul is also the theme of the *Sankhya Karika*, quoted in "Where I Lived": " 'I have read in a Hindoo book, that 'there was a king's son, who, being expelled in infancy from his native city, was brought up by a forester, and, growing up to maturity

6. *The Vishnu Purana*, trans. H. H. Wilson (Calcutta: Punthi Pustak, 1961), p. 32. This is a reprint of the London, 1840, edition of this work. The quotation also appears in the Thoreau Commonplace Book, p. 187, in the Berg Collection, New York Public Library. I will refer to it hereafter as "Note Book." For permission to examine and to quote from this material, I would like to express my appreciation to:

Henry W. and Albert A. Berg Collection
The New York Public Library
Astor, Lenox and Tilden Foundation.

in that state, imagined himself to belong to the barbarous race with which he lived. One of his father's ministers having discovered him, revealed to him what he was, and the misconception of his character was removed, and he knew himself to be a prince. So soul,' continues the Hindoo philosopher, 'from the circumstances in which it is placed, mistakes its own character, until the truth is revealed to it by some holy teacher, and then it knows itself to be *Brahme*' " (II, 106-107). Notice how the soul's *mistake* here corresponds to Thoreau's reason in "Economy" for the enslavement of most men—"mere ignorance and mistake" (II, 6). Ignorance is also attributed to men who do not practice yoga, as in this passage that Thoreau noted from *The Vishnu Purana*: "Those who have not practiced devotion [yoga], conceive erroneously of the nature of the world. The ignorant . . . are lost in the ocean of spiritual ignorance."[7]

In the Sankhya-Yoga, the Self remains attached to physical matter only as long as it remains ignorant of its true nature. In reality it always is free; however, an awakening of intelligence to this fact is required before the Self can become disengaged from matter or nature. Nature exists only to liberate the soul from this bondage. When all souls are freed, nature will, in theory, cease. That is not to say that nature is unreal. It is real. However, spirit is of a higher order of reality because it remains eternally the same. Nor is Sankhya-Yoga an escape from life. The man who is liberated in this life transcends ordinary levels of consciousness. Since he is no longer subject to the law of Karma, he is completely free of all restraints. He is able to live life fully in this world until his death.

That most men have mistaken the purpose of creation Thoreau indicates in his discussion of architecture with his appropriation of a Hindu metaphor. Though men may construct grand churches, the buildings become coffins: "It would signify somewhat, if, in any earnest sense, *he* [a man] slanted them [a few sticks over himself] and daubed it; but the spirit having departed out of the tenant, it is of a piece with constructing his own coffin,—the architecture of the grave,

7. *Vishnu Purana*, pp. 28, 29; "Note Book," p. 188. See also my "Thoreau's Source for the Story of the King's Son," *Thoreau Journal Quarterly*, 2 (April, 1970), 10-12.

and 'carpenter' is but another name for 'coffin-maker' " (II, 53). Thoreau then equates the house with the body, approximating a similar use in a Hindu text that he read: "As a house forsaken by its occupant becomes dark, so the body, when forsaken by the deity, is filled with darkness; therefore should the divine guest be always retained."[8] Not only is yoga the practice of awakening the spirit, it is the means of retaining the divine tenant of the body. With his use of house-as-coffin, Thoreau evokes his earlier description of coffin-like boxes found by the railroad. A man could use one of those "six feet long by three wide" boxes for a home "and so have freedom in his love, and in *his soul be free*" (II, 32, italics mine). In other words a man who rightly grasps the purpose of creation—the aim of the yoga—can live in a coffin and be free, while an ignorant man transforms a house into a coffin.

Thoreau's use of economic metaphors establishes the same point. He says his "purpose in going to Walden Pond was . . . to transact some private business" (II, 21).[9] Then he introduces a pun "If your trade is with the Celestial Empire, . . ."—pointing out that he means the divine rather than China. Further he says he needs a counting house "in some Salem Harbor" (II, 22). Readers of Hawthorne's sketch "The Custom-House" will remember that Salem was famous for its trade with India. Further, in "Conclusion," Thoreau describes his private sea as "the direct way to India" (II, 354). Thoreau's trade appears to be his practice of yoga. His association of trade, freedom and the soul support this supposition. Few men "own their farms *free* and clear." They are "imprisoned" by their property and possessions, "and only death will set them *free*." Moreover even the few men who are not "pecuniary failures" are "bankrupt" in a worse sense. They do not "succeed in saving their souls" (II, 36, 37, *passim*, italics mine). A man may be a slave most of his life "earning money in order to enjoy

8. William Ward, *A View of the History, Literature, and Mythology of the Hindoos* (London: Kingsbury, Parberry, and Allen, 1822), II, 101. Note that here as elsewhere I retain the spelling and punctuation of the source.

9. Business is employed as a metaphor in *The Bhagvat-Geeta*, trans. Charles Wilkins (London: C. Nourse, 1785), p. 63. For the practice of yoga and his metaphorical use of *business*, Thoreau may have turned to the source cited here.

a *questionable liberty* during the least valuable part of it" (II, 59, italics mine). Contrast Thoreau's evaluation of his own economic venture: "considering the *importance of a man's soul and of to-day,* . . . I believe that [I did] better than any farmer in Concord did that year" (II, 61, italics mine). I have italicized the parts of the quotation which point up the central concern in Thoreau's trade—the soul. Thoreau has traded his beans for rice (II, 179) and comments in "Economy," "It was fit that I should live on rice, mainly, who loved so well the philosophy of India" (II, 67). Thoreau's economy is in the Indian spiritual tradition. It accomplishes the aim of nature by freeing him.

Similarly the conclusion to "Economy" quotes the *Gulistan*, urging man to be free: "be an azad, or free man, like the cypress" (II, 88). Since the Sufi philosophy underlying the *Gulistan* resembles yoga in its emphasis on freeing the soul, the passage is in accord with the earlier portions of the chapter. The cypress is used in the example because it bears no fruit; therefore, it is not obligated to give of itself to men. Unlike a fruit-bearing tree, it remains constant and unchanging. This provides an appropriate conclusion to Thoreau's discussion of charity or "Doing-good." Here he alludes to the yoga of Krishna in the *Bhagavad Gita*. It proposes a system of contemplation wherein the practitioner remains free of whatever material benefit may have accrued from his work; like the cypress in Thoreau's quotation from the *Gulistan*, he remains unchanged and unchanging. Thoreau says, "Probably I should not consciously and deliberately forsake my particular calling to do the good which society demands of me, *to save the universe from annihilation; and I believe that a like but infinitely greater steadfastness elsewhere is all that now preserves it*" (II, 81, italics mine). The specific parallel between this passage and the *Bhagavad Gita* can be seen in a section from the latter that Thoreau recorded in his "Walden Journal." Here Krishna tells Arjuna that each time the world is annihilated he must create it again and preserve it by his practice of yoga; nevertheless, he does not enjoy his creation. "A like but infinitely greater steadfastness" refers to Krishna's yoga, and since he is the incarnation of the preserving god Vishnu, he now "preserves [the world]." Krishna's comment compares favorably with Thoreau's: "Those works confine me not, because I am like one who sitteth aloof uninterested in those works."[10] Thoreau remains as uninterested as Krishna in the works society asks of him. This aloofness parallels Thoreau's attitudes towards his unpublished writings; his reward for these, he says, are in the pains of his labor (II, 19). In other words he is aloof from the results of his works like Krishna. Thoreau admits that the good he does is "aside from [his] main path, and for the most part wholly unintended" (II, 81).

In amplifying this idea he employs the metaphor of the sun as it is used by the Hindus. Rather than doing good, Thoreau says a man should *be* good as the sun *is* bright. The sun does not stop "kindl[ing] his fires" when he is of the brightness of the moon; instead, he "steadily increas[es] his genial heat and beneficence till he is of such brightness that no mortal can look him in the face" (II, 81-82). Just as Thoreau likens the countenance of the sun to that of a man, the Hindus compare the face of the yogi to the sun,[11] the blinding brightness of which is also emblematic of the true Being. As Thoreau noted in the *Isopanishad* [*sic*]: "thou hast, O Sun, concealed by thy illuminating body the way to the true Being, who rules in thee."[12] The sun in Thoreau's example has "the world going about him getting good" (II, 82).

The slave-holder and the Irish laborer also exemplify the distinction between doing-good and being-good. It is not simply the Irishman's clothes that must be changed; he must be transformed internally. The real defect is not his outward poverty—his clothing—but "his taste" (II, 83). By giving him clothing, the philanthropist will not effect a change in the man himself. Just as philanthropy cannot change the Irish worker, so doing-good does not change the slave-holder as long as he fails to alter his life. His doing-good does not change his being. Thus Thoreau criticizes the recognized Christian virtue because it is "a partial and transitory act" (II, 85). A comment

10. *The Bhagvat-Geeta*, p. 79; cf. pp. 52-54; and *Writings*, II, 44.
11. *The Bhagvat-Geeta*, p. 74.
12. Rajah Rammohun Roy, *Translation of Several Principal Books, Passages, and Texts of the Veds* (London: Parbury, Allen and Company, 1832), p. 104; "Note Book," p. 228.

in the *Journal* for 1850 reveals how a man can "become one of the worthies of the world" as Thoreau advocates in this section of "Economy" (II, 87). "With the Hindoos virtue is an intellectual exercise, not a social and practical one. It is a knowing, not a doing."[13] What Thoreau's neighbors call good is a *doing*; his is a *knowing*. This leads to the freedom that the yogi seeks.

Perhaps the most telling allusion to yoga in "Economy" is Thoreau's retort to "a certain class of unbelievers." "I am accustomed to answer such, that I can live on board nails. If they cannot understand that, they cannot understand much that I have to say" (II, 72). Living on "board nails" is an allusion to the practice of yoga as Thoreau learned of it in the *Harivansa*.[14] A yogi is said to have "subsisted" on filings of iron for twelve years. Thoreau's comment about understanding illustrates the pervasive influence that the Indian writings had on him. This is akin to his comment on the Scriptures in "Reading," where he asks, "who in this town can tell me even their titles?" (II, 118).

II

The liberation theme is continued in "Where I Lived and What I Lived For." Thoreau advises his readers in the introduction to the chapter to "live free and uncommitted" (II, 93) and then elaborates on the metaphor from the Hindu texts that instruct the reader in the path to freedom.

In "The Hindu Matrix of *Walden*," William B. Stein shows how the metaphor of awakening underlies the structure of "Where I Lived" especially as it appears in the story of the king's son and the quotation from the *Sama Veda*—"All intelligences awake with the morning."[15] In addition to the rubrics given in these quotations, Thoreau directs the reader to his point in a number of other ways.

The epigraph to *Walden*, taken from "Where I Lived," is a good

13. Bradford Torrey and Francis H. Allen, eds. *The Journal of Henry David Thoreau* (Boston: Houghton Mifflin, 1906), II, 4.

14. *Harivansa*, trans. M. A. Langlois (Paris: Oriental Translation Fund, 1834), II, 483.

15. *Comparative Literature*, pp. 303-318; *Writings*, II, 99.

example of how Thoreau wanted his readers to understand the awakening metaphor. He specifies that Chanticleer, to whom he compares his own wakening cry, is the "Indian pheasant" in "Sounds." An examination of the genetic text of *Walden* reveals that Thoreau's muted allusion in the final draft was quite specific in an early manuscript of "Sounds." Here the bird's Indian origin is sharply emphasized along with "its quenchless inner light" which it has taken from the banks of the Indus and the Ganges to its "imprisonment" in the West.[16] Thus Thoreau's awakening shout has its sources in Indian philosophy.

Thoreau's description of the awakened man is also a rubric. "To be awake is to be alive. I have never yet met a man who was quite awake. How could I have looked him in the face?" (II, 100). This is, of course, a description of the yogi who has awakened his true self. Compare Thoreau's translation of a description of a liberated man in the *Harivansa*: He has a "luminous appearance" "like a sun."[17] Obviously the awakened man, whose face is as bright as the sun, would have a blinding effect on anyone who tried to look at him. In conjunction with the shining face Thoreau makes a statement about awareness in sleep paralleling the joining of the two subjects in the Hindu scriptures. He says, "We must learn to reawaken and keep ourselves awake, not by mechanical aids, but by an infinite expectation of the dawn, *which does not forsake us in our soundest sleep*" (II, 100, italics mine). The similarity of Thoreau's statement to one from "The Sankhya Saru" is striking: "He is liberated in this life . . . whose face shines. . . . He is free even in this life, *who is awake* [to his spiritual nature] *though asleep* [in reference to sensible objects]."[18] The liberated yogi maintains a lucid consciousness even in sleep. With these two allusions Thoreau further underscores the meaning of "awakening" as it is used in *Walden*.

In his next sentence paralleling a passage in the *Bhagavad Gita*,

16. Ronald Earl Clapper, "The Development of *Walden*: A Genetic Text," Dissertation, University of California, Los Angeles, p. 369.
17. *The Transmigration of the Seven Brahmans*, ed. Arthur Christy (New York: W. E. Rudge, 1931), p. 8.
18. Ward, II, 169, italics mine.

Thoreau again alludes to the practice of yoga. He refers here to "the unquestionable ability of man to elevate his life by a conscious endeavor" (II, 100), echoing the language and meaning of a passage he had noted from the *Gita*: "He [the yogi] should raise himself by himself."[19] Elevating or raising the awareness by "a conscious endeavor" can be accomplished by the practice of yoga. Thus "the contemplation" that Thoreau speaks of later in the paragraph refers to the Hindu discipline which evokes the recognition of self identity illustrated in the story of the king's son. It is the path to the awakening of the true Self.

III

Thoreau's introduction of metaphors about his house, i.e., his "seat" of existence—also relates to his practice of contemplation. First he locates himself through the word *seat*. Like the yogi his location is ubiquitous because his dwelling place is in the soul or an integration with the Supreme Being.[20] In one passage Thoreau noted from the *Gita*, Krishna says he is one who "sitteth" while he creates through his practice of contemplation,[21] and in another passage Krishna tells Arjuna: "He [the yogi] planteth his *own seat* firmly on a spot that is undefiled, . . . and *sitteth* upon the sacred grass."[22] Similarly Thoreau describes where he lives: "Wherever I sat, there I might live. . . . What is a house but a *sedes*, a seat?—better if a country seat" (II, 90).[23] Thus in locating his *seat* at Walden Pond, Thoreau establishes his position for the practice of contemplation.

Thoreau's description of the site of his hut also relates to the practice of yoga. He writes that the water "give[s] buoyancy to and float[s] the earth" and that "all the earth . . . appeared like a thin crust . . . floated" on the waters of the pond (II, 97). His depiction

19. *The Bhagvat-Geeta*, p. 62; "Walden Journal," a Thoreau MS in the Berg Collection of the New York Public Library.
20. *The Bhagvat-Geeta*, p. 64; "Walden Journal," p. 44.
21. *The Bhagvat-Geeta*, p. 99; "Walden Journal," p. 44.
22. *The Bhagvat-Geeta*, p. 63, italics mine; "Walden Journal," p. 43.
23. See Stein, "The Hindu Matrix of *Walden*," p. 306.

resembles the description of the earth at the time of creation as described in the *Vishnu Purana*: "[the Supreme Being] upholding the
earth, raised it quickly, and placed it on the summit of the ocean, where
it floats like a mighty vessel, and from its expansive surface does not
sink beneath the waters."[24] The similarity between this description of
the Hindu cosmogony and Thoreau's description of the waters of the
ponds relates his practicing contemplation to the yogi's participation
in the cosmogony, as Thoreau's translation of *The Harivansa* shows.[25]
Further corroboration of this relationship is found in Thoreau's description of his change in "time and place": "I discovered that my
house actually had its site in such a withdrawn, but forever new and
unprofaned, part of the universe" (II, 97-98). In locating himself
here, Thoreau places his seat of existence at the point of the cosmogony to which the awakening of the yogi transports him.

A third place where Thoreau situates himself is near the rarely seen
birds. In describing "where [he] sat," he quotes a passage from *The
Harivansa* about the necessity of having an abode with birds. He says
he has provided himself with birds not by imprisoning them but by
caging himself near them. The caging may be interpreted as his practice of the discipline of yoga. And his soul is compared to a bird as
it is in the *Moonduk-Oopunishud* [*sic*]: "Two birds (*meaning God
and the Soul*), cohabitant and co-essential, reside unitedly in one tree,
which is the body.*"[26] Since Thoreau recorded this in his "Note
Book," the rare bird clearly represents the Divine Self which he realizes in his contemplation, just as the king's son awakens to his true
identity.

IV

Much of the final section of "Where I Lived" is taken up with a discussion of the contrast between appearance and reality. In terms of
yoga this is the discrimination between sensual illusion and transcen-

24. *The Vishnu Purana*, p. 29.
25. *Journal*, II, 190-191.
26. Roy, p. 36; "Note Book," p. 229.

dental reality. Knowledge of the highest reality leads to a union with the creator insuring liberation. Referring to the example used above, Thoreau says those interested in the news or gossip of the day are deluded into thinking that they know a reality. They are the ones Thoreau speaks of when he says, "Shams and delusions are esteemed for soundest truths, while reality is fabulous" (II, 106). In terms of yoga the one real existence is the Self or God. Thoreau says that he seeks things which have "permanent and absolute existence" (II, 106). He looks for "God himself . . . in the present moment" (II, 107).

The image he uses to describe the discrimination of real knowledge is the penetration of the superficial or illusion. He says, "[O]ur vision does not penetrate the surface of things" (II, 107). We need to settle down through the "mud and slush" of "delusion" to find reality (II, 108). Significantly, a passage that Thoreau noted from the *Moonduk-Oopunishud* [*sic*] employs the same metaphor: "Seizing the bow found in the Oopunishuds, the strongest of weapons, man shall draw the arrow (*of the soul*), sharpened by the constant application of the mind to God. Do thou, (O pupil), *being in the same practice*, withdrawing all *the senses from worldly objects*, through the mind directed towards the Supreme Being, hit the mark which is the eternal God."[27] Just as the arrow—the soul—penetrates and hits the mark—reality—so a man contemplating reality cuts through the delusion of the superficial. Or as Thoreau puts it at the end of the chapter, "The intellect is a cleaver [recall the "sharpened" soul above]; it discerns and rifts its way into the secret of things." (II, 109). An interesting correlative to this is found in the "Sankhya Saru": "The person who knows this [that the tree of the world is illusion], with the excellent axe of real wisdom cuts down the tree, . . . and obtains immortality."[28]

Thoreau adopts a similar metaphor to describe the way to a knowledge of reality. If you contemplate reality, he writes, "you will see the sun glimmer on both its surfaces, as if it were a cimeter, and feel its sweet edge dividing you through the heart and marrow" (II, 109).

27. Roy, p. 34; "Note Book," p. 221.
28. Ward, II, 144.

The *Kut'h-Opanishud* [*sic*] describes the process of awakening in similar terms: "for the way to the knowledge of God is considered by wise men difficult as the passage over the sharp edge of a razor."[29] The way to reality in both cases involves the splitting of the individual personality by the edge of divine wisdom.

V

Perhaps the most striking image that Thoreau introduces in "Where I Lived" is his description of the pond. An accurate physical description of Walden, it is also a metaphor for the soul of the speaker. Further the image of the clear, calm lake describes the mind of the liberated man in the Hindu texts. Thoreau's reading shows that he was well acquainted with this metaphor while he was writing *Walden.*

His description of the tranquil pond—"it impressed me like a tarn high up on the side of a mountain, its bottom far above the surface of other lakes, and, . . . its smooth reflecting surface was revealed" (II, 95-96)—compares closely with a depiction of the emanicipated yogi that Thoreau copied from the "Sankhya Saru": "The yogee . . . [who] is always looking inwards, who is happy, profound, benign, . . . enjoys happiness undisturbed *as a lake in a mountain.*"[30] The parallel between these descriptions reveals a source for the lake as a metaphor for the soul; it further shows that Thoreau uses the metaphors of the Indian texts to depict his practice of yoga at Walden.

When water is used as a metaphor for the soul of a common man, it is clouded by the dust of works. The yogi seeks to still the agitation and clear his soul. This is accomplished by the removal of ignorance and the acquisition of knowledge. The soul then becomes "limpid," "clear," and "crystaline." Thoreau uses water to represent the soul in the same fashion. For instance, he attempts to show John Field the path to freedom or "the only true America" (II, 228). However, he fails to convince the man of his error. When he takes leave of Field,

29. Roy, p. 71.
30. Ward, II, 169-170, italics mine; Thoreau records this passage in a Berg notebook entitled "Extracts, mostly upon Natural History," p. 17.

he asks for a drink in order "to get a sight of the well bottom"—the equivalent of Thoreau's Pond (II, 229). What he finds are "shallows and quicksands" and water filled with impurities. And this, Thoreau observes, "sustains life here" (II, 229). Impure and shallow water is emblematic of Field's soul. The woodchopper, who like the King's son, resembles "a prince in disguise" (II, 164), also resists Thoreau's efforts to awaken the spiritual man in him. Thoreau observes of such men that they "are as bottomless even as Walden Pond was thought to be, though they may be dark and muddy" (II, 166). Unlike Walden, which is "nowhere muddy," the woodchopper's soul is darkened by the impurity of ignorance (II, 198).

The pure water of Walden represents Thoreau's awakened soul. Thoreau uses terms like "pellucid," "remarkabl[y] transparen[t]," "pure," and "serenity and purity" to describe the pond (II, 195-222, *passim*). Compare his terminology with a description of the liberated mind that he copied into his "Note Book" from the *Vishnu Purana*: "The pellucid waters of the season were suitably embellished by white water-lilies, as are the minds of the pure by the apprehension of truth."[31] Not only is Walden "pellucid," it is serene and "smooth as glass" (II, 207). The *Vishnu Purana* also describes the soul in terms of waters that are "still and calm" exhibiting "no undulations, like the perfect sage, who has . . . acquired undisturbed tranquility of spirit."[32] In chapter nine, "The Ponds," also, Thoreau employs "pure" and "transparent" to refer to Walden. Likewise the *Vishnu Purana* says, "the waters were as clear and pure as the minds of the wise."[33] The descriptions of Walden, then, correspond to the descriptions of the liberated yogi in the Hindu scriptures that Thoreau read.

Moreover, in "The Ponds" Thoreau identifies himself with the water of the Pond in the poem, "I cannot come nearer to God and Heaven/Than I live to Walden even" (II, 215). The first lines of this poem identify the divine nature of the Pond; the last six lines show the homology of Thoreau with it:

31. *The Vishnu Purana*, p. 417; "Note Book," p. 211.
32. *The Vishnu Purana*, p. 417.
33. *Ibid.*

> I am its stony shore,
> And the breeze that passes o'er;
> In the hollow of my hand
> Are its water and its sand,
> And its deepest resort
> Lies high in my thought. (II, 215).

Thoreau elaborates the epiphany that occurs in "The Ponds" (chapter IX, the midpoint in the eighteen chapters of the book) in the next two chapters "Baker Farm" and "Higher Laws." In the first he images his state of consciousness with "the halo of light around [his] shadow" and explains the freedom he has achieved to John Field (II, 224-230). In the second he expounds further on the transcendental state of mind that he has achieved: "Man flows at once to God when the channel of purity is open" (II, 243).

VI

Thoreau's own interpretation of yoga can be seen most clearly as he associates it with art in "Higher Laws" and "Conclusion." In the penultimate paragraph of "Higher Laws" he proclaims, "Every man is the builder of a temple, called his body, to the god he worships, after a style purely his own, nor can he get off by hammering marble instead. We are all sculptors and painters, and our material is our own flesh and blood and bones" (II, 245). The first draft of this, which is in "Paragraphs Mostly Original," relates Thoreau's concept of art to Hindu discipline. Composed before the end of 1842, it occurs in the midst of a discussion of the Hindus: "With them [the Hindus] life was an art—He is the true artist whose life is his material—every stroke of the chisel must enter his own flesh and blood—and not grate dully on marble."[34] In addition to pointing to the Hindu source of Thoreau's ideas about art and life, this early draft of a portion of "Higher Laws" shows the relationship between the two that Tho-

34. Kenneth Walter Cameron, *Transcendental Climate* (Hartford: Transcendental Books, 1963), III, 963, par. 84. This work contains a transcription and a facsimile of "Paragraphs Mostly Original," a Thoreau MS. in the Pierpont Morgan Library.

reau makes. Like the Hindus he sees the necessity of transforming his life, but more importantly he interprets the Hindu practice with artistic metaphors that reveal what he had in mind when he said, "I would fain practise the *yoga* faithfully." Since the context of the statement has to do with the yogi's contributing to creation and "animating original matter," Thoreau interpreted yoga as a contemplation that led to artistic creation.

This sort of contemplation is shown in the portrait of John Farmer, which concludes "Higher Laws." As Farmer sits down "to recreate his intellectual man," he hears the notes of a flute (the instrument played by Krishna) and they harmonize with his mood: "They gently did away with the street, and the village, and the state in which he lived" (II, 245-246). This transcendence of time and place corresponds to the experience of the yogi. But John Farmer's transcendence is incomplete; because he is not an artist, he fails to transcend his identity.

The role of artistic creation and the relation to the recreation of the self is brought out in "Spring." The "Spring" chapter images the creation of the world: "the coming in of spring is like the creation of Cosmos out of Chaos" (II, 346). Thoreau also describes it as the creation of a cosmic artist: "I am affected as if in a peculiar sense I stood in the laboratory of the Artist who made the world and me" (II, 337-338). Here as elsewhere in "Spring" Thoreau observes the cosmogony and the activity of the Divine Artist.

In "Conclusion" he depicts the transcendence of an artist who homologizes himself with the Divine Artist through his contemplation and artistic creation in the story of the artist of Kouroo. Because the artist is not caught up in "works" as his contemporaries are, he concentrates all of his energy and devotion on his art. Others grow old and die, but he maintains perennial youth. Instead of being overcome by time, he lives beyond its reach. He lives in the timeless moment— the cosmogony. His labors produce another world: "When the finishing stroke was put to his work, it suddenly expanded before the eyes of the astonished artist into the fairest of all the creations of Brahma. He had made a new system in making a staff, a world with full and fair proportions" (II, 360). His identity is thus completely assimilated with the creator. This is the experience of the yogi and, for Thoreau, of the artist.

Thoreau's account of the cosmogony in "Spring" parallels the experience of the artist of Kouroo. It is to achieve this freedom and transcendence that he develops the persona of *Walden*. Thus he frees himself to become the yogi that he speaks of in his letter to Blake and does indeed "practise the *yoga* faithfully."

Part Three

"Affidavits":
The Melvillean Center

MELVILLE AU XXeme SIECLE
6 au 9 mai 1974

Centre culturel américain - 3 rue du dragon 75006 Paris - tel.222.22-70

ZUKA

ZUKA

CONFERENCES..............FILMS................EXPOSITION

PRESENTES par le professeur Roger Asselineau (Paris IV), le professeur Howard P. Vincent (Kent State University), le professeur Viola Sachs (Paris VIII) et le Centre culturel américain.

Donald Yannella

"Seeing the Elephant" in *Mardi*

It is more than thirty years since Luther Mansfield identified certain Melville contributions to *Yankee Doodle*, the satire weekly, in the summer of 1847,[1] but their continuing effect on him as well as that of *Yankee Doodle* and journals like it has been for the most part ignored. Generally, critics have simply noted Melville's interest in this sort of magazine, specifically *Yankee Doodle*, in the period between the publication of *Omoo* in the spring of 1847 and the start of *Mardi* the following fall.[2] Merrell Davis provides an important and happy exception to this critical oversight. His exploration of Melville's reading and literary sources reveals echoes in *Mardi* of the "Authentic Anecdotes" and also of concerns voiced in *Yankee Doodle* before and during Melville's connection with this publication.[3]

My purpose in this essay is to demonstrate Melville's use in *Mardi* of materials from *Yankee Doodle* and its successor *The Elephant*, another satire weekly which had a life of only five issues during January and February, 1848, when Melville was in the second phase of the composition of the novel. It is my view that Melville subtly referred to a contemporary popular expression, a joke about the elephant, which contains striking parallels to the action of *Mardi*. Our awareness of the currency and meaning of the joke affords a glimpse

1. Luther S. Mansfield, "Melville's Comic Articles on Zachary Taylor," *American Literature*, 9 (January 1938), 411-418.

2. For example, see Perry Miller, *The Raven and the Whale* (New York: Harcourt, Brace, 1956), pp. 212-214, and Edward H. Rosenberry, *Melville and the Comic Spirit* (Cambridge, Mass.: Harvard Univ. Press, 1955), p. 188 *n* 1.

3. *Melville's Mardi*, (1952; rpt. Hamden, Conn.: Archon, 1967), pp. 38-39, 54-55, 65-66, 88-89, 157-159.

into Melville's connection with the popular literature of his day and also offers another bit of evidence about the development and rate of progress of the second phase of *Mardi*.

Early in *Mardi* there is curious and provocative use of the image of an elephant. In Chapter 66, as Taji and his party are about to embark on their voyage around the archipelago, Melville describes metaphorically the canoes they are to ride in: "their great black prows curling aloft, and thrown back like trunks of elephants: a dark, snaky length behind, like the sea-serpent's train." After offering some detail about the lead vessel, he writes: "The likeness of the foremost canoe to an elephant, was helped by a sort of canopied Howdah in its stern, of heavy, russet-dyed tappa, tasselled at the corners with long bunches of coconut fibres, stained red."[4] And following some further description of various parts of the canoe, Taji announces: "First went the royal Elephant, carrying Media, myself, Jarl, and Samoa; Mohi the Teller of Legends, Babbalanja, and Yoomy, and six vivacious paddlers."[5] Despite numerous subsequent references to the canoes in the novel, this is the only place in which he uses the elephant metaphor in his descriptions, with the exception of a brief reference to "the regal white elephants of Siam" two chapters later, in an entirely different, unrelated context.[6] Furthermore, in describing native Polynesian vessels in his first two romances, *Typee* and *Omoo*, he had not employed the elephant metaphor.

While it may be argued that the figure was physically appropriate, convenient and fleeting, it appears rather that both its aptness and its transience derive from the topicality of his reference. Melville probably was drawing on the popular expression "To See the Elephant," and when the expression is rightly understood, the implications of Melville's elephant metaphor become significant. The popularity of the elephant expression during the late 1840s is probably best substantiated by the inclusion of the phrase "To See the Elephant" in

4. Herman Melville, *Mardi and a Voyage Thither*, ed. Harrison Hayford, Hershel Parker and G. Thomas Tanselle (Evanston, Ill.: Northwestern Univ. Press, 1970), p. 199.
5. *Ibid.*, p. 200.
6. *Ibid.*, p. 206.

John Russell Bartlett's *Dictionary of Americanisms*, published in 1848. The entry reads:

TO SEE THE ELEPHANT, is a South-western phrase, and means, generally, to undergo any disappointment of high-raised expectations. It is in fact nearly or quite synonomous with the ancient "go out for wool and come back shorn." For instance, men who have volunteered for the Mexican War, expecting to reap lots of glory and enjoyment, but instead have found only sickness, fatigue, privations, and suffering, are currently said to have *"seen the elephant."* I do not remember having ever fallen in with a good origin for the term in this employment of it.[7]

The phrase "To See the Elephant" and the metaphor communicated in the popular culture precisely the sort of eventually disappointing and frustrating quest which lies at the heart of *Mardi*. It appears reasonable to infer that at the outset of this excursion through the archipelago the critical and satirical purposes of the new book were clearly in Melville's mind and, more important, so was the ultimate failure of the quest. I might even suggest that Melville's employing the elephant metaphor rather than one of the conventional phrases, "To See the Elephant" or "Seeing the Elephant," was both subtle and meaningful. The "disappointment of high-raised expectations" for the party, particularly Taji, is not only inevitable but preordained. They do not have to seek the beast; they will *ride* it on their voyage of frustration.

During the summer of 1847, and especially early in 1848, when Melville was composing the portion of *Mardi* including Chapter 66, the elephant joke enjoyed one of its periods of highest currency. The phrase "To See the Elephant" appeared as early as 1835 and as recently as 1964, in an episode on the Richard Boone television show.[8] Ordinarily, the seeker or quester after the knowledge is an innocent,

7. John Russell Bartlett, *Dictionary of Americanisms, Usually Regarded as Peculiar to the United States* (New York: Bartlett and Welford, 1848), p. 290.

8. Mac E. Barrick, "Elephant and Owl," *American Notes and Queries*, 5 (April 1967), 120.

a bumpkin. Some of the heroes of the popular fiction of Melville's time who "see the elephant" are journalist Denis Corcoran's hoosier, who "has all the attributes that peculiarly belong to the back woods-men of the west," comes to New Orleans and undergoes the conventional initiation of the greenhorn in the urban environment.[9] Jim Griswell, another of Corcoran's stereotyped backwoodsmen, is arrested for drunkenness in New Orleans but is not punished "as he confessed he had seen the elephant."[10] The association of the elephant and alcohol was to be most fully exploited in the mid-1850s in *The History and Records of the Elephant Club* by Knight Russ Ockside, M.D., and Q. K. Philander Doesticks, P. B.—pseudonyms for Edward Fitch Underhill and Mortimer Neal Thomson, respectively.[11] This raucous collection recounts the various truths confronted by members of the club during their drinking sprees, for example, when they visit New York Police Courts and theaters. The descriptions of the urban scenes they confront are most frequently rendered with comic, absurd overtones. Confidence games were occasionally the greenhorn's experience, as was the case in Ned Buntline's *The Mysteries and Miseries of New York*, early in 1848. Big Lize, the generous and maternal prostitute, has an accomplice reach through a move-able panel to remove money from her customers' trousers left hanging on a chair.[12] One might also have seen the elephant in military combat, for instance, in the Mexican War, or in California in search

9. *Pickings from the Portfolio of the Reporter of the New Orleans "Picayune"* (Philadelphia: G. B. Peterson, 1846), pp. 46-49. This police report, entitled "A Sketch 'Ower True' Having a Hoosier for Its Hero," was reprinted under the title "A Genuine Hoosier" in *The Cyclopaedia of Wit and Humor*, ed. William E. Burton (New York: Appleton, 1858), I, 233-234. Melville's "The Lightning-Rod Man" was reprinted in the same collection, I, 432-434. A greenhorn is in the process of seeing the elephant in Boston in George P. Burnham, "He Wanted to See the Animal" (1846), *The Cyclopaedia of Wit and Humor*, I, 272-273.

10. Corcoran, "Seeing the Elephant," *Pickings from the "Picayune,"* pp. 142-143.

11. New York: Livermore and Rudd, 1857.

12. (New York: Berford, 1848), I, 13; III, 47-48.

of gold.[13] The point is that whether the search were in the city, on the battlefield, in the gold-fields or any other locale, it invariably recounted the disappointing quest for knowledge and enlightenment, the initiation of the innocent into hard experience.[14]

The most probable immediate source for Melville's awareness of the expression early in 1848 was the satire weekly *The Elephant*, the premise for which had been supplied by a series of articles in *Yankee Doodle* during Cornelius Mathews's editorship when Melville's articles on Zachary Taylor were published.

Melville's interest in the sort of journalism represented by *Yankee Doodle* and *The Elephant* was significant. On October 6, 1847, several days after the last issue of *Yankee Doodle* had appeared on October 2, Evert Duyckinck wrote to his brother George, who was traveling in Europe, that "After three months well applied labor Mathews gets nothing from *Yankee Doodle*, nor Melville, nor Bangs."[15] And on October 23, Duyckinck noted in his Diary: "With Mathews and Melville, in the evening discussed a possible weekly newspaper which should combine the various projects of the kind which *we* [my italics] had entertained for the last few years."[16] Melville's enthusi-

13. Constance Rourke, *Troupers of the Gold Coast* (New York: Harcourt, Brace, 1928), p. 29; and *A Dictionary of Slang, Jargon, and Cant*, ed. Albert Barriere and Charles G. Leland, (1889; rpt. Detroit: Gale, 1967), I, 343-344.

14. For additional references to the elephant, see the citation in Archer Taylor and Bartlett Whiting, *A Dictionary of American Proverbs and Proverbial Phrases: 1820-1880* (Cambridge: Belknap, 1958), p. 119; and *Dictionary of American English*, ed. Sir William A. Craigie and James R. Hulbert (Chicago: Univ. of Chicago Press, 1960), II, 874-875. For their aid in tracing the history and significance of the "elephant" phrase, I wish to thank Professors Hans Bergmann (SUNY, Albany), Walter Blair (University of Chicago), Pascal Covici, Jr. (Southern Methodist University), J. Albert Robbins (Indiana University) and Henry Nash Smith (University of California, Berkeley).

15. Jay Leyda, *The Melville Log* (New York: Harcourt, Brace, 1951), I, 261.

16. Evert Duyckinck, Diary: May 29 to Nov. 8, 1847, Duyckinck Collection, Manuscript Division, NYPL. The "we" which I have italicized has been repeatedly transcribed incorrectly as *he*. Comparison between the *w* in *we* and the *w*'s in *weekly* and *which* and the *h* in *had* in the entry makes it incontestable that Duyckinck was writing *we* and referring to at least two of the three men,

asm for the *Yankee Doodle* venture indeed demonstrates "the range of [his] interests, his keen awareness of the life of his time, and his knowledge of the current humorous conventions," as Professor Mansfield has concluded from his consideration of the "Authentic Anecdotes."[17]

Of equal significance is the abundant evidence that Melville continued to be involved in the literary, intellectual and social life of New York after he moved to the City early in September, 1847. His residence was only about four blocks from Duyckinck's.[18] And during the first three months of 1848, when he was engaged in transforming *Mardi* from travelogue to romance, he was in close contact with Duyckinck, borrowing books from his library and seeing him socially.[19] However reluctant Melville was to have an active social life while attempting to make progress on his new book, he continued in touch with the contemporary scene.[20] Therefore, it seems doubtful that he would have missed Mathews's venture, *The Elephant*, whose short life in January and February 1848 spanned the middle of the period marking the second phase of the development and composition of *Mardi*. This is particularly true in light of his contacts with

---

including himself, rather than to Mathews alone. For samples of the perpetuation of this incorrect transcription and the resulting reference to Mathews, see Willard Thorp, "Introduction," *Herman Melville: Representative Selections, with Introduction, Bibliography, and Notes* (New York: American Book Co., 1938), p. xliii *n* 53; Leyda, I, 263; Davis, p. 55 *n* 7; and Miller, p. 218. It might also be noted that Mathews, who had such high hopes for the new venture, wrote George Duyckinck, who was abroad, in late August and asked him to contact a C. H. Peabody in London and solicit him to act as "agent for *Yankee Doodle* London" (ALS, Cornelius Mathews to George Duyckinck, 31 Aug. 1847, Duyckinck Collection, Manuscripts Division, NYPL). But a few months later George wrote what was the magazine's epitaph: "Y.D. being past surgery it is of course useless for me to call on Mr. Peabody, Norfolk St.— about it" (ALS, George Duyckinck to Evert Duyckinck, 2 Nov. 1847, Duyckinck Collection, Manuscripts Division, NYPL).

17. Mansfield, 418.
18. Davis, pp. 40, 55.
19. *Ibid.*, pp. 62-64, 71.
20. *Ibid.*, pp. 67, 70-71.

Duyckinck. And *The Elephant* was not unaware of Melville's work in progress. In the fourth number, issued on February 12, there appeared the following notice:

> *Cannibalism.*—The following brief extract from a new work, entitled "Travels in the Cannibal Islands, by the author of *Omoo*," is highly illustrative of the manners and customs of the people of those benighted regions. "Dining one day with the King he urged me to try a cut of a cold clergyman, which lay on a side-table; this I declined, much to the King's surprise, with as good grace as I could, professing a great partiality for a dish of fricas-seed mermaid then on the table before me."[21]

In all likelihood, this satirical barb was directed at those who were continuing to attack *Typee* and *Omoo* late in 1847 and early in 1848, for the treatment Melville had accorded the missionaries.[22] Once again, members of Duyckinck's circle rallied round one of their own.

To understand the implications of Melville's elephant metaphor, it is necessary to review the history of the elephant joke among the literati including Duyckinck, Mathews and Melville. The foil for *The Elephant* was *The John-Donkey*, a weekly edited by Thomas Dunn English and George G. Foster; Foster had been the founder and editor of *Yankee Doodle* until Mathews took it in July, 1847.[23] *The John-Donkey* appeared several weeks before *The Elephant*, on January 1, and had a much longer life, folding on July 15, 1848.[24] The rivalry between the two journals forms a small chapter in the history of the battles of the New York literati. Mathews and, as might be expected, *The Elephant* were frequently the objects of satire in

21. *The Elephant*, 12 Feb. 1848, p. 30.

22. Davis, p. 73.

23. Frank Luther Mott, *A History of American Magazines: 1741-1850* (Cambridge: Belknap Press of Harvard Univ. Press, 1957), p. 780. I might add that I have found no reason to suggest a political dimension to this battle between the elephant and donkey. While the donkey was used by Jacksonians in the 1830s, the elephant's association with the Republican Party probably did not begin until about 1860 (Jay Monaghan, "Origin of Political Symbols," *Journal of the Illinois State Historical Society*, 37 [September 1944], 205-212).

24. *Ibid.*, p. 780 *n* 1.

the pages of *The John-Donkey* during the first quarter of 1848.[25] The
attacks by the staff of *The Elephant* on *The John-Donkey* were even
more frequent and intense than those they suffered at the hands of
Foster and English.[26] But *The Elephant* was not simply a foil for *The
John-Donkey*. As Mathews wrote in the leader for the first number,
the new magazine was an extension of one of the more successful
series in *Yankee Doodle* when he was editor during the previous summer. The leader began:

> The public eye, for the last year or so, has been on the look out
> to get a glimpse of that queer animal—known in natural history
> as the ELEPHANT—which has been going abroad night and
> day, in town and out of town, and all over the Continent.[27]

25. Mathews's name was repeatedly misspelled Matthews from the very first
issue (*The John-Donkey*, 1 Jan. 1848, p. 3), and his works were constantly
subjected to derision (for example, "Coroner's Office-Distressing Case," 8
Jan. 1848, p. 24; "New Uses of Chloroform," 12 Feb. 1848, p. 102; "Cross
Readings," 19 Feb. 1848, p. 123; "Treatise on Poetry," 19 Feb. 1848, p. 125;
"Better Still," 11 Mar. 1848, p. 166). *The Elephant* in particular was attacked
throughout its brief life. On the same day that Mathews's new weekly appeared, Foster and English claimed in a half-page ad that *The Elephant* had
been created as a "foil" for *The John-Donkey* by its proprietors (George Dexter of New York had a hand in publishing both weeklies): "It is to be edited
by the great *Puffer Hopkins*, the immortal friend of Duyckink [sic] and all
other sorts of kinks . . ." (*The John-Donkey*, 22 Jan. 1848, p. 64; "Struck a
Vein, at Last!" 29 Jan. 1848, p. 80; "Our Funny Man," 5 Feb. 1848, p. 85).
26. For example, in the second number, issued on January 29, *The John-Donkey*'s "utter destitution of the elements of success, such as are possessed in an
eminent degree by *Punch* and the *Elephant*," was noted. "The *Donkey* has
neither humor nor satire; its fun is spasmodical . . . and the reader is perpetually compelled to laugh at its contributors rather than *with* what they contribute. The *Elephant* is the only entirely comic paper in the country whose humor
is broad and comprehensive, like the eternal ocean itself; and when the *Donkey*
concludes to stand up to the rack of real wit, instead of dealing in pointless
scraps of personality and caricature, there may be a chance for him, and then
but a small one!" ("Struggling Against Fate," *The Elephant*, 29 Jan. 1848,
p. 15).
27. "The Elephant Maketh His Bow: He Unpacketh His Trunk, and He
Asketh in a Loud Voice Saying Who Hath Seen me," *The Elephant*, 22 Jan.
1848, p. [1].

The last few paragraphs of the leader reveal something of the purpose of the journal and the nature and satirical thrust of the elephant joke:

> With a view, therefore, to the better understanding of his character, and to save persons the cost of tedious journeyings to see him, the ELEPHANT has located himself in a back office near to our sanctum. It is his intention to issue thence once a week, for the pleasure and edification of all. During his rambles, you may be sure he has packed his trunk full of curiosities. He has picked up pebbles, too, by the roadside, which he may cast with a sling, against the strong and the witless, or use to pepper vice out of her paint and jewels! The ELEPHANT thinks that when we can make a joke of our follies we are half cured of them. He is determined never to lose a good one because he did not make it; and he prefers even second hand wit, to original dullness.
>
> The ELEPHANT is not so dreadful as he is accredited to be. Full of gambols—clumsy from his great bulk—shall you see him once a week. He is perfectly docile except when enraged by the foolish; and nothing he loveth so much as the dropping of pennies into his trunk! From his great strength, we look for wonders! The ELEPHANT will protect the weak from the strong, and wherever the oppressor is, there will you find his trunk raised to smite; you should not wonder to see him rocking dolls in his huge paws, as quietly as a Miss, and laughing with all his might at the barking of toy dogs, or the gambols of paste board monkeys. He is no politician—but the world's friend. He is of no clique, but of the whole; wherever a tear is to be assuaged, expect that the ELEPHANT will be there with his rude sympathy —wherever abuse, either in rags, or "brocade" exists—look out for his mighty trunk. Honest, good humored and sagacious, turn him not from your door!—you may have worse enemies *there* than the unsophisticated ELEPHANT.[28]

In light of the satire which is so much a part of the latter portion of *Mardi*, particularly in the descriptions of Vivenza and Dominora,[29]

28. *Ibid.*, p. 2.
29. For commentary, see Davis, pp. 84-85, 88-90, 150-159.

the source of the elephant metaphor Melville employed to describe the canoes is significant. The reader with imagination might even perceive certain aspects of the various subjects and styles of *Mardi* as being described appropriately in this leader.

Earlier in the same leader, Mathews made definite reference to the *Yankee Doodle* series which supplied his premise. Cutting at those who sought the elephant in Mexico,[30] he concludes:

> It is a pity they should go so far, and endure so much! But peace be to them! they may see the ELEPHANT at home, now, unless the Government should do them justice!
>
> And then, with wallet lined from sale of kid, and sheep, and fatling cometh cityward the unsuspecting Bumpkin. He, too, would see the ELEPHANT. Pardonable curiosity in one so green! The Bumpkin is a peaceable man! He has little stomach for martial exercise, and goeth not to Mexico to seek him.[31]

The leader goes on to describe the Bumpkin's being conned into buying a watch at an auction ("Thus the Bumpkin seeth the ELEPHANT all at once"), and a citizen who, shunning the auctioneer, seeks the animal at Wall Street among the bulls and bears.

The bumpkin and quest referred to appeared in what was evidently one of the more popular series in *Yankee Doodle* under Mathews, "Various Attempts 'To See the Elephant,' Made in the City of New-York, In the Spring and Summer of 1847, By Joshua Greening, of Esopus." The series enjoyed eleven consecutive weekly installments from July 17 through September 25. An installment appeared in each of the issues which carried a chapter of Melville's satire on Zachary Taylor. In the "Preface" for the hard bound trade-copy, probably written by Mathews in October 1847, it was judged "full of happy turns and cunning strokes of humor. Mr. Greening, the Gull, will be a permanent figure in the comic literature of the country."[32]

This humorous quest-narrative is composed of nine chapters, which

30. For discussion of attacks on the Mexican War in *Yankee Doodle*, see Mansfield, 413.
31. "The Elephant Maketh his Bow," p. 2.
32. "Preface," *Yankee Doodle*, [2], p. iii.

are purported to be faithful transcriptions from a journal kept by Greening, and two letters from him to the editor of *Yankee Doodle*, one which is an introduction to the entire narrative and one which serves as filler between installment-chapters V and VI. Joshua points out in the introduction, dated early July 1847, that his wish is "to give your numerous patrons some reminiscences of my unfortunate efforts, during a few months past, at *seeing the Elephant* in this great and almighty village of Gotham."[33] In the course of his unsuccessful quest this stereotypal bumpkin from the up-state New York village of Esopus has a series of experiences which were stock in urban literature, particularly that focusing on New York City. After a tearful parting from family and beloved, the twenty-three year old seeker has a bout with homesickness while aboard the Hudson River steamer *Roger Williams* and then commences his descent into the urban inferno. He encounters prostitutes, is bilked by a variety of confidence men, including a cab-driver, a dishonest innkeeper, two dishonest judges, and the fast-talking Jewish clothing merchants of Chatham Street. In the last four chapters, the innocent unwittingly enlists in the Army, but fails the physical and so does not have to fight in Mexico; is duped into buying a worthless "Freedom of the City," all-purpose pass; and, finally, stumbles into a hellish tavern, packed with rogues and whores, in the infamous Five-Points section. He is rescued from this last scrape by the police who know of his penchant for being hustled by the sharpers of Manhattan.[34]

---

33. *Yankee Doodle*, 17 July 1847, p. 148.

34. In a letter to his brother George, Evert Duyckinck identified one Bangs as the initiator of "Various Attempts 'To See the Elephant'" (ALS, Evert Duyckinck to George Duyckinck, 14-15 July 1847, Duyckinck Collection, Manuscripts Division, NYPL). Mansfield identifies this contributor as Lemuel Bangs (412); however, it may have been Thomas Butler Bangs who did illustrating for *Yankee Doodle* and according to Mott, collaborated on the New York *Reveille* (*A History of American Magazines: 1850-1865* (Cambridge: Belknap Press of the Harvard Univ. Press, 1938), p. 180). There is some internal evidence to suggest that Mathews may have developed the series which Bangs started. For example, in Chapter 5 of Mathews's novel *Moneypenny, or, the Heart of the World* (New York: Dewitt & Davenport, 1849), pp. 33-42, Old Job was to take the same Hudson River Cruise to New York

Although he never literally "sees the Elephant" in the week and a half period covered in the nine chapters, he claims, in the letter separating chapters five and six and dated five days before the August 28 issue in which it appeared, that:

> I came to York, *green* enough in all conscience, but I have "seen the Elephant," and the old fellow has whispered many words of wisdom in my ears, and indeed, ever, even while I was being mercilessly tossed upon his tusks, hath his lessons sunk down into the depths of my memory deep and abiding, and few there are, who during a residence of not five short months in Gotham, have learned so much.[35]

This statement is anticipatory, published four weeks before the last chapter in the series appeared in the penultimate number of *Yankee Doodle*. It is important to note that plans were under way to continue the series in the aborted third volume as late as September 4.[36]

Cognizance of the elephant joke and Melville's certain knowledge of it allow some inferences. First, if Melville's use of the elephant metaphor in Chapter 66 were inspired by the reappearance of the

---

City described in Chapter 1 of "To See the Elephant." And in the third and fifth chapters, Joshua Greening, the bumpkin, encounters several of the urban phenomena long favorites of Mathews, such as the court system, the Tombs, the Park Theatre and an oyster restaurant. In the fourth chapter he is fleeced by one of the Jewish clothes merchants of Chatham Street (recall Redburn's experience in Chapter 4) in a scene similar to that Mathews had depicted in the opening chapter of *Big Abel and the Little Manhattan* (1845) and was to present again in Chapter 15 of *Moneypenny*, as well as in the "Chatham Street" section of *A Pen-and-Ink Panorama of New York City* (1853). See Herman Melville, *Redburn: His First Voyage*, ed. Harrison Hayford, Hershel Parker, and G. Thomas Tanselle (Evanston, Ill.: Northwestern Univ. Press, 1969), pp. 19-22; Cornelius Mathews, *Big Abel and the Little Manhattan*, 1st ed. (1845; rpt. New York: Garrett, 1970), pp. 2-3; *Moneypenny*, pp. 132-134; and *A Pen-and-Ink Panorama of New York City* (New York: Taylor, 1853), pp. 163-166. For some discussion of Mathews's subjects and themes see my "Foreword" to the reprint of *Big Abel and the Little Manhattan*.

35. *Yankee Doodle*, 28 Aug. 1847, pp. 201-202.

36. See for example the advertisements at the ends of nos. 46 and 48 of *Yankee Doodle*, 21 Aug. 1847, p. 200, and 4 Sep. 1847, p. 220.

joke in Mathews's new journal, as I think it probably was, then we have another piece of evidence to substantiate Professor Davis' assertions about the development and progress of the second or the romance phase of the novel. Davis speculates that Yillah, who first appears in Chapter 43, was introduced into the novel around Christmas 1847.[37] Therefore, if Chapter 66 were written in the week or so after *The Elephant* made its debut on January 22, it appears that Melville was making ordinary progress in the book even in the first month after he had begun to transform it from the travel adventure he had started. This suggests that at this time *Mardi* was developing seriatim.

Second, and perhaps more important for the quest and travelogue satire, he was drawing on a popular source as immediate as Rabelais.[38] This is not to say that the serio-comic mythology of the popular elephant joke had a greater influence than Rabelais in Melville's decision to move his narrative toward quest and travelogue satire. Rather, I suggest that the analogue in the popular literature reinforced and complemented the inspiration Melville discovered in Rabelais. Although the innocent quester Joshua Greening was more the victim in the *Yankee Doodle* series than was Taji in *Mardi*, the magazine narrative and the novel share satiric exposure of social foibles and dissimulation which leads their respective protagonists to the inevitable "disappointment of high-raised expectations" implicit in "seeing the elephant." Further, serious and careful contemporary readers aware of the elephant joke, upon reading Chapter 66, would probably have anticipated Melville's satiric intentions as well as Taji's ultimate frustration.

37. Davis, pp. 57-59, 61.
38. *Ibid.*, pp. 76-77.

Harrison Hayford

"Loomings":
Yarns and Figures in the Fabric

A linked image cluster that recurs throughout Melville's works also figures centrally in the initial chapter of *Moby-Dick*. My aim in this essay is to demonstrate how some recurrent items ("images") and topics ("motifs") in "Loomings" carry a few basic strands of thought ("themes") in the book; how these elements relate to each other; and also how they relate to syntax, rhetoric, and such larger elements as the book's characters, plot, and thought. My analysis takes up elements as they occur locally in Chapter I and relates them to similar elements in other parts of the work. The immediate effect of my discussion is to illustrate the dense imaginative coherence of *Moby-Dick*. Its images, motifs, and themes are yarns closely woven into figures in its fabric, as the chapter title "Loomings" can be taken to imply.[1]

1. On August 1, 1969. Herman Melville's 150th birthday was celebrated at Kent State University. Of course Howard P. Vincent was the organizer as he has indefatigably been, alone and with others, of so many such occasions, from the great Williamstown one in 1951, for the 100th birthday of *Moby-Dick*, to the Paris one of May, 1974. It was at his instigation that I delivered a paper at Williamstown in 1951 titled "Melville's Prisoners," in which I set out a peculiar image cluster I had found in Melville's works. It was also at his instigation that I delivered a paper at Kent in 1969 titled "Birthdays of Herman Melville," of which a razeed version of the paper now offered was substantially the central section. (A tape recording preserves the whole ebullient session at which it was presented.) I hope Howard will think it an appropriate offering, because it was worked up for him in the first place, because it may remind him of that happy Kent occasion, and because (in spite of his efforts over the years of our long association) it is the only offshoot of my larger study, the long-in-process *Melville's Prisoners*, yet to reach print.

119

Somewhat arbitrarily, I focus my discussion on the element of character. Specifically, I focus on Ishmael and on the ways in which the elements I analyze show similarities and differences between him and Ahab. My critical strategy is to take the narrative, from its opening sentence "Call me Ishmael," as altogether the work of Ishmael, its ostensible narrator, and to interpret all its elements as coming from Ishmael and hence characterizing Ishmael, not Melville. In this way the dense imaginative coherence is transferred from the book and its author to the mind of Ishmael as its ground and cause. In this perspective, the action of the work takes place in the observing and participating mind of Ishmael. His mind "contains" the tragedy of Ahab as Ishmael confronted it some years ago in experience and now confronts it once again in the telling. Of course this approach is not new, for perhaps the chief discovery criticism has made in the interpretation of *Moby-Dick* in the past generation is to recognize the presence and centrality of Ishmael. Most earlier critics had overlooked him altogether because they were so taken by Ahab and the White Whale.[2] A close corollary perception has been recognition of the thematic importance of the juxtaposition between Ishmael and Ahab. Both points are now usually taken for granted in interpretations of the book, however at odds readings may otherwise be. Neither point, though, entails taking the whole work as Ishmael's—a strategy I am adopting here provisionally and only for convenience.

2. I believe William Ellery Sedgwick, in *Herman Melville: The Tragedy of Mind* (Cambridge, Mass.: Harvard University Press, 1944), was the first critic to discuss Ishmael equally with Ahab. It was Howard Vincent who contributed as much as anyone else to this delineation of Ishmael's role, in *The Trying-Out of Moby-Dick* (1949). Others who have pursued this line of interpretation include Walter Bezanson, "*Moby-Dick*: Work of Art," Tyrus Hillway and Luther Mansfield, eds., *Moby-Dick Centennial Essays* (Dallas: Southern Methodist University Press, 1953), pp. 30-58; Merlin Bowen, *The Long Encounter* (Chicago: University of Chicago Press, 1960); Paul Brodtkorb, *Ishmael's White World* (New Haven: Yale University Press, 1965); and Edgar Dryden, *Melville's Thematics of Form* (Baltimore: Johns Hopkins Press, 1968). Most recently, the approach attributing all to Ishmael is systematically followed in Robert Zoellner's full length treatment of *Moby-Dick*, *The Salt-Sea Mastodon* (Berkeley: University of California Press, 1973), whose basic assumption is that "every word of *Moby-Dick*, including even the footnotes, comes from Ishmael rather than Melville" (p. xi).

One further bit of strategy needs a word. All along I refer to Ahab in the present tense. This is the way we usually discuss a fictional character, since we imagine him dramatically alive as we read, though the narrative is told in past tense and we may know the story ends with his death. In *Moby-Dick* Ishmael only occasionally makes any point of Ahab's being already dead and gone, and for my purposes no harm is done by my not doing so. On the other hand, since it is of more consequence that Ishmael is narrating in the present tense, I use tenses for him that distinguish between Ishmael at the time of the *Pequod's* voyage and Ishmael at the later time he is telling about it. What is involved in Ishmael-then vs. Ishmael-now is the quite unsettled interpretive problem of Ishmael's development in character and outlook.[3] It is not part of my purpose to deal with this problem here. Let me simply declare that in my reading he did not change and has not changed, from then to now, in his essential nature. Ishmael is forever Ishmael. Call him Ishmael.

I

In *Moby-Dick* Ishmael plays the role—a frequent one in Melville's writings—of sympathetic but perplexed observer. What he chiefly confronts and observes is the tragedy of Ahab in his revengeful attack upon the great White Whale. In this perspective the book's early chapters are preparation for Ahab. Before Ahab's appearance, Ishmael builds up in them the physical and conceptual worlds which make probable Ahab's character, his language, his thought, and his actions. In "Loomings" Ishmael starts on his narrative way as participant and observer. As he tells the story, his manner with words, his habitual ways of perceiving and dealing with situations, his preoccupations of thought, all reveal his character. Through these means the first chapter begins to establish the grounds both of Ishmael's sympathy with Ahab and of the differences between them that mark his dissociation from Ahab.

An initial similarity between Ishmael and Ahab is the way both of them turn every object, situation, and person they confront into a

3. For example, refer to Carl Strauch, "Ishmael: Time and Personality in *Moby-Dick*," *Studies in the Novel*, I (Winter, 1969), 468-483.

problem, one which cannot be solved, a mystery whose lurking meaning cannot be followed to its ultimate elucidation. This habit of mind
shapes the rhetorical form of the first chapter; and many later chapters also take the shape of their development from it. Chapters of exposition, especially, often treat their subjects as problematical and end
up by declaring them inexplicable. But narrative chapters, too, are
frequently constructed on a pattern of confrontation-exploration-
nonsolution of a problem.

Simply in vocabulary items, apart from context, this propensity of
Ishmael's is illustrated. In this very first chapter, for example, wonder
and mystery are constantly being evoked, at the same time that inability to solve or to understand is being declared. One running series of
words connotes wonder and mystery: *magic, enchanting, romantic,
tranced, charm, mystical, marvelous, secretly, portentous and mysterious, marvels, wonder-world, hooded phantom.* Intertwined with
these words runs another series denoting or evoking inability to solve
or identify: *ungraspable, invisible, secretly, unaccountable, unimaginable, undeliverable.* The two series continue intertwined throughout
the book, and as vocabulary items alone they imply not only a habit
of Ishmael's perception but a major thematic proposition of the book:
life—the cosmos and everything in it taken as a microcosm—confronts man as a compelling but insoluble mystery.

In the first chapter, Ishmael sets out to tell the story of this particular
whaling voyage. But no further along than his third sentence, the
narrative mode shades into exposition, as Ishmael begins explaining
his reasons not only for having gone on this voyage but for his voy-
aging in general. And then, by the end of the first paragraph, the reasons themselves have come to require explanation; the problem has
arisen of communicating some sense of his feelings toward the ocean,
feelings which, though nearly universal, are not easy for him to convey in statements. Already the narrative has generated what I take to
be a basic motif of the book: that of confronting an insoluble problem.

Why he went to sea has become, in the telling, a problem to Ishmael. Initially it is a problem in communicating just what it is that he
felt and feels, but soon it becomes something of a problem to himself.

For to Ishmael, as to Ahab, motives have lower and yet lower layers. While Ishmael is developing this problem of his motivation it splits into three successive questions: 1. Why does he go to sea? (paragraphs 1-6) 2. Why does he go as a common sailor? (paragraphs 7-11) 3. And why did he go that voyage on a whaler rather than on a merchant ship? (paragraphs 11-14)

As Ishmael deals with each of these three questions through the rest of the chapter, he shows further traits of mind and patterns of reaction which he shares with Ahab. But in his treatment of each question, and especially of the second, he also reveals traits which set him off from Ahab, and which, indeed, define a crucial distinction between them.

II

To answer his first question—why he goes to sea (initially why he went on this particular voyage)—Ishmael begins with two immediately assignable conditions, both of them negative and somewhat aimless rather than positive reasons: he had little money in his purse and nothing in particular to interest him on shore. Then he adds his general motive for going to sea not only on that voyage but at various times: he says it is a way he has of driving off the spleen—driving off spells of melancholy—and a substitute for his impulses toward violence against others or himself whenever he feels depressed. But actually his motives on that and other such occasions, he realizes, reach deeper than these personal ones, specific or general; there is something universal in them. For nearly all men, he says, share his feelings towards the ocean.

Next, to suggest that which he cannot analyze in what he declares is an almost universal feeling towards the ocean, he leaps at once (paragraph 3) from declarative statements to a series of parallel analogies couched in imperatives and interrogatives. He exhorts us to confront, and, if we can, to explain the meaning of a series of analogical situations, stated in various images. The basic motif these situations exemplify is confrontation: in each situation men are drawn toward water, gaze fixedly upon it, and meditate its mystery. They come in crowds, "pacing straight for the water, and seemingly bound for a dive." And "They must get just as nigh the water as they possibly can without falling in." This motif of confronting a mystery implies a consequent motif: that of self-destruction. For one may come too close to the fascinating object, the water—may take a dive or fall in. This implication becomes explicit in the climactic analogy of the series: "Surely all this is not without meaning. And still deeper the meaning of that story of Narcissus, who because he could not grasp the tormenting, mild image he saw in the fountain, plunged into it and was drowned." The water-gazing analogies coincide with the plot shape of *Moby-Dick*: Ahab with the crew of the *Pequod* thrusts off from land into the ocean, and in his effort to grasp a tormenting image, the White Whale, plunges in and is drowned. "But," says Ishmael, here in the first chapter commenting on the plunge of Narcissus, "that same image, we ourselves see in all rivers and oceans. It is the image of the ungraspable phantom of life; and this is the key to it all." This Narcissus analogy indeed is the "key" to a thematic argument of the book: something in man, now as throughout his history, forces him to confront the mystery of life, to pursue that phantom; but it is "ungraspable"; and the man who goes too far in the effort, who crowds too close upon the mystery, destroys himself. Such is Ahab's pursuit of Moby Dick, and such is his fate.

Ishmael, likewise, feels the attraction of the phantom. In the final words of this chapter he declares that "one grand hooded phantom, like a snow hill in the air" swayed him to his purpose of embarking on the whaling voyage. Similarly, the Spirit Spout is later a "phantom" luring the *Pequod* and her crew on and on (Ch. 51). After Ahab had revealed his purpose on this voyage, Ishmael realized, at least dimly, what the end must be. His shouts, he says, went up with the rest. "A wild, mystical, sympathetical feeling was in me; Ahab's quenchless feud seemed mine." But Ishmael "while yet all arush to encounter the whale, could see naught in that brute but the deadliest ill" (Ch. 41). And again Ishmael comments, "But in pursuit of those far mysteries we dream of, or in tormented chase of that demon phantom that, some time or other, swims before all human hearts; while chasing such over this round globe, they either lead us on in barren mazes or midway leave us whelmed" (Ch. 52).

Later Ahab shows repeatedly that he too realizes what Ishmael indicates from the beginning; that the issue of such an aggressive quest can only be self-destruction. For a single example, when Captain Boomer, who has lost an arm to Moby Dick, warns Ahab that "He's best let alone; don't you think so, Captain?" Ahab replies, "He is. But he will still be hunted, for all that. What is best let alone, that accursed thing is not always what least allures. He's all a magnet!" (Ch. 100).

Yet this first chapter makes a decisive point about Ishmael. Despite the magnetic attraction he feels towards the mystery which lures one on to destruction, he is still not by nature disposed, like Ahab, to press up so close to it as to plunge in and drown. This difference, a decisive one, between Ishmael's nature and Ahab's is manifested in several ways in the first chapter. For one thing, it is evident in Ishmael's second reason for going to sea at all, since the voyage was—as his voyages still are—his conscious substitute for aggressive action, for expressing his frustrations destructively on others or himself, either by "deliberately stepping into the street, and methodically knocking people's hats off" or by following funerals (to the graveyard) or stabbing or shooting himself. To him, going to sea is not in itself aggressive; it is rather his "substitute for pistol and ball." Even at the outset, Ishmael half-consciously recognizes death may be the ultimate goal of his journey. Omens, icons, and monuments of death attend his progress on this voyage, as they do Ahab's, and cannot swerve him from his purpose to take ship.

III

The second question Ishmael raises is why he goes to sea as a common sailor. Although, unlike his first and third questions, this question presents no problem to Ishmael, his treatment of it leads again to definition of the same distinction between himself and Ahab. In this second section of the chapter (paragraphs 7-11) the difference comes out more fully, but so does an essential similarity. Ishmael feels as strongly as does Ahab a sense of personal dignity, heightened by pride, and he too is galled by the weight of indignities which superiors impose upon his body, mind, and spirit. But from the beginning, where he tells of his custom of going to sea as a "simple sailor" rather than as an officer, he announces his habitual acceptance of subordinate positions, indeed (as if he had a choice) his settled preference for them. At the same time, he displays his feeling that this subjection is one he shares with men in general, that his lot merges with the common lot of men, all of whom, he says, are slaves or victims in one way or another and should therefore help each other endure their common lot. Ahab's parallel perception of humanity's general suffering gives him no comfort and only exacerbates his sense of outrage.

The section is couched in motifs that are recurrent in *Moby-Dick*, of which the leading and dominant one is that of the inferior-superior relationship, involving the acceptance or rejection of imposed authority. Associated motifs include money; food; bodily impairment or injury; injustice or insult; antiquity; masonry and massive objects; personal dignity; and family. All are constituents of the image cluster I referred to earlier as recurring throughout Melville's works.

When Ishmael goes to sea, he explains, he never goes as a passenger, because to do so requires a purse. Nor does he go as an officer, for he abominates all honorable, respectable posts and responsibilities and will not identify himself with them. First, the motif of money which comes in the second sentence of the chapter ("having little or no money in my purse") appears again: "you must needs have a purse, and a purse is but a rag unless you have something in it"; then the money motif is dropped until it recurs at the end of the section in the image of "paying" (paragraph 10).

Next (still in paragraph 7) the motif of food develops, in the image of Ishmael's rejecting the possibility of shipping as cook. Though a cook is "a sort of officer on ship-board," with "considerable glory," Ishmael explains that "I never fancied broiling fowls;— though once broiled, judiciously buttered, and judgmatically salted and peppered, there is no one who will speak more respectfully, not to say reverentially, of a broiled fowl than I will." Here motifs of food, authority, and bodily impairment are linked as they often are in the book. In his joshing way, Ishmael seems merely to be saying he has never cared to cook fowls, though once they are properly cooked and seasoned he has a very good appetite for them. The motifs he em-

ploys, however, carry in undercurrent the more generalized theme that
he does not take pleasure as superiors (here reductively made comic
as "cooks") do, from subjecting the bodies of inferiors ("fowls") to
radical physical impairment ("broiling")—though once the bodies so
treated have by such official and legal process ("judiciously," "judgmatically") been dignified and transformed, he is respectful, almost
reverential toward them, in a way inverting superior and inferior. In
short, he does not care to be a superior to inflict the physical hurt,
but once it has been, as it were, legally and duly done he accepts and
respects the result. He is as willing as anyone to "swallow" and "stomach" it. In a jocose second sentence, Ishmael quickly recapitulates the
same motifs: food (victimized bodies eaten), authority, reverence—
but twines them now with two further motifs, of antiquity and of
massive masonry, in a single compressed image: "It is out of the idol-
atrous dotings of the old Egyptians upon broiled ibis and roasted river
horse, that you see the mummies of those creatures in their huge bake-
houses the pyramids." The general effect of this analogy, as of those
in the earlier paragraphs, is to universalize the personal attitude Ishmael has just stated by associating it with a parallel instance in antiquity, one which (in "mummies" and "pyramids") has preserved
and monumentalized the situation through the ages.

The arc of feeling traversed in the two sentences about cooking
and eating fowl becomes thematically characteristic in *Moby-Dick*.
Ishmael repeatedly moves from opposing ("I abominate . . .") a physically threatening person, object, or situation that is somehow "superior," to reconciling himself with it ("no one will speak more respectfully . . ."). And the particular motifs that carry the theme restate it
repeatedly in the book. The motifs of food and eating are often
linked to the motif of a superior in situations which are treated in a
humorous tone, and sometimes the superior is embodied as a comic
figure in authority, or has an attendant comic figure. Such a situation
occurs in the next chapters when Ishmael confronts the cannibal
Queequeg (who might eat him!) and ends up smoking and eating
with him and even "married" to him. Another occurs when Ishmael
and Queequeg eat their chowders under the dominating eye of shrew-
ish Mrs. Hussey, who is scolding a man as the eating scene begins and

who takes away Queequeg's harpoon as it ends (Ch. 15). Another is the scene in which the mates silently eat at table with the domineering Ahab, to be followed by the savage harpooneers attended by comic Dough-Boy (Ch. 34). And still another, the most fully developed, is that in which Stubb masticates his whale steak (cooked too much for his taste) while humorously baiting Old Fleece the comic black cook into delivering a sermon to a congregation of sharks who are also devouring a whale's body (Ch. 64. Cf. also Ch. 65 on "The Whale as a Dish").

Now very likely the reading I have just given seems somewhat farfetched, particularly in its generalizing the specific imagery of broiling, salting, and peppering a fowl into a motif designated as "bodily impairment." And it would really be only a facile translation if that motif did not become a central theme in *Moby-Dick*. In Ishmael's outer and inner worlds, of whaling and of consciousness, a major theme is that living bodies, animal and human, are subjected to physical outrage, to all the possible range of injury, maiming, mangling, destruction—to the "horrible vulturism of earth." Victimizers act upon victimized bodies, superiors upon inferiors. The central instance is Ahab's dismemberment when his leg is reaped away by the White Whale's jaw; and the sustained context is the whaling world, in which bodies of men and animals are given to mutual injury and destruction in the normal course of existence, in the whole routine of chase, slaughter, and dismemberment—the hunter's and butcher's bloody work that is the whaleman's life and may be his death when the persecuted whale retaliates on his body.[4] In this destructive bodily collision of whaleman and whale the relationship of superior-inferior shifts, from one passage to another, in ways that depend as much on Ishmael's perspective and mood as on any facts of the immediate instance. He recognizes this world's general condition of mutual bodily victimization and identifies at different times either with superior or inferior, with biter or bitten. And often, as in the sentences just examined, his initial sympathy with the inferior, whose body is victimized, shifts, and he accepts the superior's victim as now transmuted into

4. Robert Lowell, in "The Quaker Graveyard in Nantucket," restated this theme accurately and magnificently.

"food." The generalized motif of such a shift in feeling can be termed reconciliation.

Despite such strategies of reconciliation with the superior, however, Ishmael is habitually and characteristically on the side of the inferior. He feels victimized and his feeling of being put upon is carried by constant bodily images in the flow of his narration. He is unusually conscious of his own body, and in the course of the first chapter he names many of his bodily parts, functions, sensations, positions, and actions. Often he expresses his feelings in images of bodily discomfort or malfunction: "driving off the spleen, and regulating the circulation," "growing grim about the mouth," "a damp, drizzly November in my soul," "hazy about the eyes," "over conscious of my lungs" —these occur with some frequency.

Ishmael's signing on as a simple sailor, he admits, entails subjection to authority and an affront to his self-respect and family pride as well as the relinquishment of his own superior authority as a schoolmaster. "True, they rather order me about some. . . . And at first, this sort of thing is unpleasant enough. It touches one's sense of honor, particularly if you come of an old established family in the land. . . . And more than all, if just previous to putting your hand into the tarpot, you have been lording it as a country schoolmaster, making the tallest boys stand in awe of you." Evidently Ishmael's sensitivity is rubbed raw on precisely the same point as Ahab's. Both resent the indignity of being ordered about, of being thumped and punched by superiors, particularly because each feels the pride of distinguished lineage and is accustomed to order tall fellows about and make them stand in awe. Ahab's sensitivity is exposed to the metaphysical thumping and punching of the gods, and the distinguished lineage he feels is not literal but the metaphysical dignity of the race of man, human dignity. Unlike Ahab, however, Ishmael has nonaggressive strategies for alleviating such indignities. Here, his first strategy is recourse to the folk wisdom of "grin and bear it," fortified by the book wisdom of Stoic philosophy; the transition from schoolmaster to sailor is a keen one requiring "a strong decoction of Seneca and the Stoics to enable you to grin and bear it." Furthermore, patience helps; for even this feeling of indignity "wears off in time."

Another jocular gambit of alleviation takes up the next paragraph (paragraph 9). Suppose some "old hunks of a sea-captain" does order Ishmael to sweep the decks (an indignity to an able seaman since this broom business is the prescriptive province of the boys, as we learn in Chapter 54)—what does this indignity amount to, weighed in the scales of the New Testament? Or does Ishmael's prompt obedience make the archangel Gabriel think less of him? And finally,

> Who ain't a slave? Tell me that. Well, then, however the old
> sea-captains may order me about—however they may thump and
> punch me about, I have the satisfaction of knowing that it is all
> right; that everybody else is one way or other served in much
> the same way—either in a physical or metaphysical point of view,
> that is; and so the universal thump is passed round, and all
> hands should rub each other's shoulder-blades and be content.[5]

In both the physical and metaphysical points of view, this recognition of universal slavery, this "thump," enrages Ahab past endurance and impels his physical attack upon the whale and his metaphysical attack upon whatever powers may stand behind the whale. But from the first, although Ishmael is as sensitive as Ahab to the indignity of physical subordination, he declares strategies, if not principles, of nonaggression: Stoic endurance, New Testament and democratic equality in suffering and slavery, fellow-feeling and mutual help—such are his remedies. Only too late does Ahab catch a glimpse, through Pip, of something resembling Ishmael's insight into the emollient effect of shared suffering, of mankind full of sweet things of love and gratitude.

Another of Ishmael's remedies, evident from the first paragraph and one which in the end may be the most important of all, is the saving practicality of his humor. From the beginning the tone of his voice has been varied and flexible. Its serious flow yields to rifts of humor which usually break the tension just when the topic has become most serious and its tone most magniloquent. In the first paragraph a swelling exaggeration of language and structure creates a sus-

---

5. In *The Salt-Sea Mastodon* Robert Zoellner calls this "universal thump" concept a "central preoccupation of *Moby-Dick*" (p. 54).

picion that ultimately he will not take altogether solemnly his own feelings and motives which are real enough but overdramatized: "Whenever . . .; whenever . . .; whenever . . .; and especially whenever . . .; then. . . ." The suspicion is at once confirmed by the next sentence where the irreverent wording of the qualifying alliterative phrase "With a philosophical flourish" reduces Cato's classical suicide to mock heroism in contrast to Ishmael's own underplayed sensible substitute, "I quietly take to the ship." In this middle section of the chapter, directly after the peroration of the first section (the series of analogies ending with the high-keyed climactic image of Narcissus which is "the key to it all"), his tone relaxes into jocularity all through the four and a half paragraphs (7-11) just discussed. As Ishmael discourses, his fluid consciousness is marked by varying tones and never settles into the monotone of a single attitude. His range does not reach the heights or the depths of Ahab's noble monomania, though it at times approaches them; he is brought back to a habitable mid-region by his humorous sense of his own practical situation, which allows him to take "a strong decoction of Seneca and the Stoics" to help him "grin and bear it." This practical humorousness is a saving quality Ishmael shares with Stubb, the second mate, a quality that distinguishes them both from Ahab in the high seriousness of his tragic nobility.

By these strategies of attitude and tone, then, the tension of the chapter's middle section is relaxed and resolved. But in diminuendo Ishmael goes on to advance two further reasons for shipping as a sailor rather than as a passenger or officer. Both of these involve the motif of inferior-superior. In each of them he now argues in consciously sophistical rhetoric that the inferior is really the superior. His tone is jocular, but, as often, its jocularity barely veils his underlying hostility to anybody in a position of social and economic superiority. Passengers, as financially superior to sailors, are dealt with in the linked motifs of money-injustice. For passengers, so his resumed argument runs, must pay when they go to sea, whereas sailors are paid—and paying is the most uncomfortable infliction the two orchard-thieves, Adam and Eve, entailed upon their descendants. "But *being paid,*—what will compare with it?" Even here, however, Ishmael turns the thought against those above him: momentarily it is he, a poor sailor, not they, enjoying the felicity of being paid. But—so his thought runs on—to receive much pay leads to wealth, and wealth leads to destruction, for money is "the root of all earthly ills," and "on no account can a monied man enter heaven." And he moralizes, "How cheerfully we consign ourselves to perdition!"

In this last line of thought two motifs are twined: that of money (coupled with injustice) and that of self-destruction, in the image of consigning ourselves to perdition. The first paired motif, that of money-injustice, comes in for fuller development in the following chapter in Ishmael's lack of money for a night's lodging and in the passage about Lazarus and Dives. The second, that of self-destruction in the image of damnation or going-to-hell, first appears as such here but will often recur. For the whole voyage of the *Pequod* is, in fact, Ahab's wilful self-consignment to perdition. Of this fact we are reminded throughout the book, both directly and indirectly, even to the final scene where the ship "sinks to hell."

Ishmael's last reason for shipping as a common sailor rather than in any position of honor is a humorously specious one that again develops the inferior-superior motif, reversing the positions. His reason is that the Commodore on the quarter-deck aft gets the air he breathes only at second hand from the forecastle sailors. The schoolmaster's learnedly indecorous joke, turning on the Pythagorean maxim to avoid eating beans, covertly vents contempt on the officers. "In much the same way do the commonalty lead their leaders in many other things, at the same time that the leaders little suspect it." At the end of the section, thus, analogizing from the sailors' station forward on the ship (of state) as she sails, Ishmael transforms the sailor-followers into "leaders" and the officer-leaders aft into "followers"—so the last shall be first and the first, last.

IV

At this point in the chapter (in the middle of paragraph 11), Ishmael by the foregoing strategies has handled two of the three questions into which he divides the problem of his going to sea. Now he takes up his final question: why did he go that voyage on a whale-ship? Why, having repeatedly smelt the sea as a merchant sailor did he then go on a whaling voyage? (Note that this is the only one of the three questions that refers solely to the *Pequod's* voyage, not to the motivations for Ishmael's voyages in general.) With this question, too, Ishmael deals in the recurrent motifs. He posits his motivation as a mystery. The dominant motif is that of the supernatural, while linked to it is that of injustice (or wrong) in the form of mystery-deception, or mystery-concealment. As Ahab characteristically does, Ishmael generalizes this particular question back into the problem of the universe—what he later calls "the universal problem of all things" (Ch. 64).

Why he took it into his head to go this time on a whaling voyage is a puzzle to Ishmael, one which is answerable only as part of the cosmic mystery, and which he deals with in a series of linked images. In the first witty image, Ishmael declares semi-seriously that he is secretly dogged and unaccountably influenced by an "invisible police-officer of the Fates," who can better answer than anyone else. His going whaling was doubtless his fate, or his predestined lot—in a second image "part of the grand programme of Providence that was drawn up a long time ago." For himself, he cannot tell (continuing the second image and showing some of his customary irreverence for high authorities over him) why it was that "those stage managers, the Fates," put him down for "this shabby part of a whaling voyage" when they assigned to others "magnificent parts in high tragedies" and to still others parts in comedies and farces. Here there lurks some irony on Ishmael's part, for on this whaling voyage high tragedy is indeed to be enacted (as well as comedy and farce), though the tragic role in it is to be Ahab's, not Ishmael's. But Ahab is a transfigured, transvaluated, common old whaleman exalted to the heights in a "democratic" tragedy. And Ahab, too, is convinced, as he cries to Starbuck, that his role was determined by the Fates: "This whole act's immutably decreed.—'Twas rehearsed by thee and me a billion years before this ocean rolled. . . . I am the Fates' lieutenant; I act under orders" (Ch. 134). Whatever motives of their own the Fates may have had in assigning Ishmael his part (Ishmael refrains from exploring that byway!), they cunningly presented to him, under various disguises, certain illusory motives as his own, into which he thinks he can now see a little way. Some of these motives, as he now recalls them in images of characteristic connotation, were: the curiosity "roused" in him by the "portentous and mysterious" monster, "the overwhelming idea of the great whale himself"; the "undeliverable, nameless perils" and "attending marvels" of the whale; the "torment" of his own "everlasting itch for things remote." These images associate the coming voyage with the motif of confrontation—the numinous fascination of the mysterious, here, as often, embodied in the massive and associated with the perilous (the danger of destruction from approaching it too close). Ishmael, like Ahab, like all men in their degree, feels this attraction. He feels, too, its frequently associated quality of forbiddenness. Paradoxically, to move toward the region where all these qualities coalesce is to respond actively to an attraction which is at the same time forbidden; he says (in active verbs), "I love to sail forbidden seas and land on barbarous coasts." But unlike Ahab, Ishmael by his characteristic strategy again dissolves into sociality the aggressive, implied motive of invasion. To his sociality of feeling the barbarous horrors themselves will turn out to be just fellow "inmates" of this prison world: "Not ignoring what is good, I am quick to perceive a horror, and could still be social with it—would they let me—since it is but well to be on friendly terms with all the inmates of the place one lodges in."

So far as Ishmael can see into his motives when he confronts them as a problem, the foregoing were his reasons. "By reason of these things, then, the whaling voyage was welcome." But there is a still lower layer—for he realizes that these felt motives only "cajoled" him into "the delusion that it was a choice resulting from my own unbiased freewill and discriminating judgment." The climactic and final image of the chapter reasserts Ishmael's conviction that his motives were somehow imposed upon him as a passive receiver: "The great floodgates of the wonder-world swung open, and in the wild conceits that swayed me to my purpose, two and two there floated into my inmost soul, endless processions of the whale, and, midmost of them all, one grand hooded phantom, like a snow hill in the air." By the syntax of this sentence Ishmael becomes the passive recipient of conceits that "float" into his "inmost soul" from some exterior source; he is "swayed" by them rather than being their active originator. This image of something "floating" into the mind is one more metaphor (perhaps for an experiential sensation, perhaps for a metaphysical concept) to explain the same process Ishmael alluded to above in the theatrical image as a cleverly deceitful casting operation of the stage-managing Fates: "the springs and motives which being cunningly presented to me under various disguises, induced me to set about performing the part I did."

Here, indeed, the imagery brings up one of the major themes of *Moby-Dick*. In most general terms the theme may be defined as the problem of free will, of responsibility for one's actions. Already in this chapter the theme has been broached in three different metaphors, or concepts. First it was introduced as discussed above, under the image of "magnetic virtue," the attraction of water. Then it appeared under the loosely equivalent image or concept of "the Fates" and "Providence," with supplementary allusion to an "invisible police-officer of the Fates," who is evidently a sort of special daemon or supervisory angel put into modern dress and so comically demeaned as a petty official who "dogs" one. Finally, it is restated here in terms of the sensation of a psychological process, of something "floating" into the consciousness from outside—a metaphor evidently derived from a conceptual system of "atmospheric influences" frequently invoked elsewhere in *Moby-Dick* (and at great length in *Pierre*, where the etiology of motivation is examined with great intensity). Of all three images—magnetic influences, Fates or Providence, and "atmospheric influences"—the common denominator is their postulation of exterior forces determining the action of the mind. The mind is essentially their passive instrument, and its subjective sense of "a choice resulting" from "unbiased freewill and discriminating judgment" is only a "delusion" cunningly contrived and made pleasant by invisible superior powers.

The syntax of many sentences in the chapter supports the tenor of these metaphors in the motif of active-passive, and it here bears out Ishmael's explicit declaration that he has no free will. Many passive

verb constructions and dissociations of self occur. In the opening paragraph, for example, a kind of struggle goes on in Ishmael between
what he feels happening independently in him ("I find myself growing grim about the mouth"; "it is a damp, drizzly November in my
soul"; "I find myself involuntarily pausing"; "hypos get such an upper hand of me") and his assertive will opposing it ("a way I have of
driving off the spleen"; "it requires a strong moral principle to prevent me"). In this sentence, the syntactical structure declares the control of Ishmael's active will in the struggle, for that assertion is placed
in the main clause; but the declaration is only that he must get away
to sea "as soon as I can," and "quietly take to the ship." The forces are
still working upon him, even in his supposition that he "chose" this
evasion of the aggression and suicide towards which they are driving
him; for in passively ("quietly") taking to ship, as in welcoming
the whaling voyage, he is actually shipping on Ahab's aggressive mission, which leaves him in "abandonment" at the end (in the last words
of his epilogue), "another orphan."

V

This discussion of "Loomings" has, I hope, illustrated what I called
at its beginning the dense imaginative coherence of *Moby-Dick*, the
close weaving of yarns in the figures of its fabric. I suppose readers
have been at least as uneasily aware all along as I have of the limitations of some of my strategical assumptions, and especially do I sense
the artificiality of my main working assumption that everything in the
book is coming to us from its narrator Ishmael. When one should
ascribe such elements as imagery, syntax, rhetoric, and their implications for thought and character in *Moby-Dick* to the fictional narrator Ishmael and when to his creator Melville is, I suspect, perhaps
more a matter of critical strategy and relevance than of inherent propriety. If readers have noticed points in the discussion where taking
such linguistic elements to characterize Ishmael seems unusually arbitrary, such points may indicate where it might have been better to as-
sign them to Melville instead. Ultimately, this must somehow be done
if sense is to be made of such recurrent images, motifs, and themes

as I have been most concerned with displaying, especially since those which figure centrally in "Loomings" and the rest of *Moby-Dick*, where Ishmael is narrator, also permeate the whole of Melville's work from *Typee* to *Billy Budd*, where of course he is not. The total imaginative coherence of these works must have as its ground the mind of Melville, as author of them all.

Sanford E. Marovitz (signature)

Old Man Ahab

Oh, what quenchless feud is this, that Time hath with the
sons of Men!

Melville, *Pierre*

The enormous amount of interpretive criticism regarding *Moby-Dick*
makes it difficult for a devotee of Melville's classic to remember that
apart from all the philosophical, religious, and psychological layers
and strands, its initial impact is principally attributable to an absorb-
ing sea narrative and the characters who participate in the action.
Ahab is the aging captain of a whaler before he is the symbol of
philosophical rebellion or anything else; Ishmael is a common sailor
and the narrator of a long, complex tale before he is the incarnation
of some abstract quality or thing; the whale is a living, swimming,
diving, extraordinarily large and powerful cetacean before he is the
representation of any force or Being, natural or supernatural; each of
the crew members and artifacts aboard the *Pequod* serves an express
purpose within the structure of the narrative. The reader coming to
Moby-Dick for the first time visualizes the ship and the adventures of
its crew before he turns a microscopic lens upon them for the purpose
of critical analysis, whereupon the strands do come apart, revealing
the complexity of the palimpsest that bears the title of its central
figure, the great humped white whale himself. But a part of that com-

An earlier, shorter version of this essay was read before a conference of the
Northeast MLA, April 6, 1974, at the Pennsylvania State University (University Park).

plexity lies in the fact that the major characters are people with very real human qualities; they are not simply clothed abstracts—and here I admittedly adapt Melville's descriptive term for the *Pequod*'s carpenter.

I

When Ishmael sets forth upon the *Pequod* he is a relatively young man, still inexperienced enough to make his whaling voyage an educative one. His captain, however, is nearly sixty, tyrannical, violent, defiant, and as mortal a being as the rest of us. He is well aware of his increasing age, of his graying hair and his weakening limbs; and he is not one to wish himself young again simply to endure another round with destiny. But Ahab is defiant, thoroughly so. For nearly sixty years he has lived, but in all that time he has found no meaning in his life. What has been its purpose? What is behind it all? Year after year he has plunged through the seas, but the time passes and no answer is forthcoming. As he approaches three score, he begins to realize that death may overtake him before he learns what he must, and the unsatisfied quest makes him frantic as time inexorably moves on. Ahab does not fear death, which could have come upon him suddenly and unexpectedly since the beginning of his whaling days some forty years earlier. Perhaps a violent death would of itself provide the answers to his questions; possibly they are answered in his final gasping moments as he is towed through the depths by his conquering white nemesis. Such knowledge as he might have gained we can surmise but not confirm. No, until the instant he is jerked "voicelessly" from his boat by a loop of his own harpoon rope, he fears not death itself but its coming in a natural way, through the ordinary course of living out his years; this, indeed, is a fearful possibility to Ahab, for the horror of the unanswered questions, then, would remain with him to the end. The inscrutability of mortal human life is intolerable to Ahab; he cannot comprehend it, and without comprehension there is no acceptance. There is only confrontation, defiance, denial: "No, in thunder!"

But what is it exactly that the whale means to Ahab? We know that he sees and abhors Moby-Dick as an incarnation of "outrageous strength" and "inscrutable malice"; he also regards him as a barrier —a "wall" and a "mask"—through which he must strike for answers to metaphysical and epistemological questions that he cannot otherwise hope to obtain. Yet there is the "little lower layer" still that Ahab does not touch upon, for the whale represents more than the detested sea-monster impeding his philosophical quest. Like other cetaceans, the whale is a migratory animal, nature-bound to wander instinctively in predestined hence predictable paths throughout his years,[1] and it is only because of such charted migrations that Ahab is certain the snowy leviathan himself can be traced and found in a given spot at a specific time amid an oceanic wilderness. To a large extent, then, Ahab sees the white whale not only as the ferocious, malicious sea-beast that nearly killed him and as the septum he must penetrate to confront a questionable underlying reality; but still more significantly, to him, the reputedly unassailable and allegedly immortal Moby-Dick appears as an embodiment of the time continuum itself operating within and upon the processes of nature.[2] For crazy Ahab, to stop leviathan, to slay him—be he "principal" or "agent" —would mean correspondingly to check the heretofore inexorable and malign passage of time, thereby nullifying the relevance of questions of mortality and initiating for himself a new unconditional existence in a state of idealized stasis. That he may die in his attempt to kill the whale does not deter him for a moment; indeed, in his egocentricity, which virtually divorces him from the mundane reality of the whale oil, the *Pequod*, and its crew, he believes that the white whale's death and his own would have the same effect, for the self-motivated destruction of his mortal being would be but secondary to the ideality that would evolve from it. Here, then, is the ultimate and fatal result of the narcissism described by Ishmael in the first chapter. Essentially, self-destruction—consciously or unconsciously motivated—may be

1. See Robert Zoellner, *The Salt-Sea Mastodon: A Reading of Moby-Dick* (Berkeley: University of California Press, 1973), p. 258.

2. That this temporal theme was already in Melville's mind at the time he was writing *Mardi* is suggested by William B. Dillingham, *An Artist in the Rigging: The Early Work of Herman Melville* (Athens: University of Georgia Press, 1972), pp. 135-36.

seen as Ahab's "technique for controlling nature and preventing change"; he exemplifies those suicidal individuals who Avery Weisman believes "are self-destructive in order to *preserve* themselves and to *triumph* over death."[3] Either way, through killing the whale or himself, Ahab narcissistically anticipates a kind of apotheosis through death, achieving neither heaven nor hell but a state of permanent ideality; and his quest for, his struggle with, leviathan, regardless of its earthly outcome, will leave him—in his own eyes—victorious.

Hence whirling at the center of *Moby-Dick* is the maelstrom of Ahab's combined fear of, despair over, and defiance against humanity's—and particularly his own—mortality, a limitation largely manifest for him in the nature-bound, migrating white whale. How or why Melville himself, while still a young man in his early thirties, became despondent over the thought of death is not known, but evidently he was already brooding upon it by the time he began writing *Moby-Dick*;[4] and several clues indicate that the question continued to weigh heavily upon him for the remainder of his days. Indeed, the mortality theme in *Moby-Dick* is introduced even before the narrative begins. On one of the preliminary pages, the etymology of *whale* allegedly has been provided by "a late consumptive usher to a grammar school," a teacher who "loved to dust his old grammars; it somehow mildly reminded him of his mortality."[5] Thus early in the novel, then, the reader is—or should be—aware of the possibility that

3. "Self-Destruction and Sexual Perversion," in *Essays in Self-Destruction*, ed. Edwin S. Shneidman (New York: Science House, 1967), pp. 294, 298. Also, Karl A. Menninger has written that one way "the life instinct finds satisfaction, paradoxically, [is] in self-inflicted death. It depends upon that deadliest of erotic investments, narcissism" (*Man Against Himself* [New York: Harcourt, Brace, 1938], p. 70).

4. For a superb essay on Melville's nearly lifelong brooding over death, see Edwin S. Shneidman, "The Deaths of Herman Melville," in *Melville and Hawthorne in the Berkshires*, ed. Howard P. Vincent (Kent, Ohio: Kent State University, 1968), pp. 118-43.

5. Herman Melville, *Moby-Dick; or, The Whale*, ed. Luther S. Mansfield and Howard P. Vincent (New York: Hendricks House, 1952), p. xxxvii. Hereafter all references to *Moby-Dick* will cite this edition by chapter (in Romans) and page (in Arabics), and notes will be incorporated parenthetically in the text.

man's earthly impermanence may be a subject of some speculation in the pages to follow.

As melancholy as the usher but not nearly as secure, Ishmael broods over the memorial stones gracing the inside walls of Father Mapple's church, the Whalemen's Bethel in New Bedford, shortly before the sermon begins: "It needs scarcely to be told, with what feelings, on the eve of a Nantucket voyage, I regarded those marble tablets, and by the murky light of that darkened, doleful day read the fate of the whalemen who had gone before me. Yes, Ishmael, the same fate may be thine. . . . Yes, there is death in this business of whaling—a speech-lessly quick chaotic bundling of a man into Eternity" (VII, 36). Here Ishmael uncannily anticipates Ahab's being "voicelessly" jerked into the sea; but as disturbing to him as the sudden, unexpected death of the whaleman is the fact that the memorials he is reading have been dedicated to seamen whose bodies were never recovered from the deep, the bodies of men who sailed onto the wild unknown of the sea and remained there forever, with no final resting place and no spe-cial grave above which their loved ones may stand and mourn. "What bitter blanks in those black-bordered marbles which cover no ashes! What despair in those immovable inscriptions! What deadly voids and unbidden infidelities in the lines that seem to gnaw upon all Faith, and refuse resurrections to the beings who have placelessly per-ished without a grave" (VII, 35). Ishmael, of course, has already iden-tified himself as a "simple sailor" (I, 4) with "an everlasting itch for things remote" (I, 6); his journey on the *Pequod* is neither his first nor his last ocean voyage, and despite his melancholy brooding before the marble tablets, death at sea can be no uncommon phenomenon to him. An "*Isolato*" himself, having no strong social bonds with friends or family ashore, and, as far as we know, foreseeing none, Ishmael may well be subconsciously anticipating his own death at sea; for, as he explains early in the first chapter, signing up as a common sailor before the mast enables him to subdue his "hypos"—i.e., his depres-sion—and to suppress at least for a time his latent inclination to use "pistol and ball" (I, 1).

Ishmael's meditations often set the stage for Ahab's and harmo-nize with them. The two men are not as different as they often appear to be; both are brooders, both are fatalists, and, strangely, both do a good deal of pondering over the questions and conditions of senescence. Exactly when Ishmael and Ahab become fatalists is impossible to determine, though the monomaniac's fatalism is most strikingly evident on the second day of the chase, whereas Ishmael's is clear from the opening chapter, where he admits: "the springs and motives . . . cunningly presented to me under various disguises, induced me to set about performing the part I did, besides cajoling me into the delusion that it was a choice resulting from my own unbiased freewill and discriminating judgment" (I, 5-6). Does he become a fatalist during the journey? That is a question not to be answered, for the voyage occurred many years before Ishmael's narrative actually begins; and therefore the entire account is necessarily offered from the fatalist's point of view. From beginning to end a fatalistic current underlies the novel, fostered not only by such overt manipulations as the accurate predictions of Elijah and Fedallah, but, also, more profoundly and subtly, by the occasional comments of Ahab and Ishmael; their thoughts implicitly constitute an indirect dialogue on the questions of necessity and the inevitability of death, if not by violence, then through the natural process of aging.

It is on this theme of mortality that the rhythmical correspondence of their meditations is most suggestive. Ishmael's attention is first directed to Ahab's age by Captain Peleg, who provides him with a vague thumbnail biography of the "grand, ungodly, god-like man"; Ahab is a personage of widely diversified experience who "has a wife —not three voyages wedded—a sweet, resigned girl. Think of that," Peleg asserts; "by that sweet girl that old man has a child: . . . stricken, blasted, if he be, Ahab has his humanities!" (XVI, 79-80). Not long afterwards, Elijah's ominous remarks reinforce Peleg's description of Ahab as a man who has spent many years at sea (XIX, 92); and Ishmael himself notes when it is time for the pilot to leave the *Pequod* on her outbound voyage that Bildad seems loath to go, for Ahab is "a man almost as old as he, once more starting to encounter all the terrors of the pitiless jaw" (XXII, 103). This metaphor of "the pitiless jaw" has already been used more concretely by Ishmael to emphasize age and approaching death in the Spouter-Inn scene, where beneath "the vast arched bone of the whale's jaw, . . . in those jaws of swift destruction, . . . bustles a little withered old man" who sells rum, "deliriums and death," to the sailors at the bar (III, 12). What is the impression, then, that Ishmael forms of his new captain as a result of hearsay and surmise even before viewing him for the first time? It is the image of a Protean wanderer, an old man with a young wife; his impression leads him to infer (as he is unable to see for himself) that Bildad is reluctant to leave the *Pequod* because Ahab's age is so near his own, and Bildad retired at sixty—though how many years that was prior to the *Pequod*'s sailing, we are not told.

This impression is confirmed when Ishmael first observes Ahab on the quarter-deck. The captain is described as robust and statuesque, as though "made of solid bronze"; but there is a suggestion, too, that his limbs are "aged," and a striking scar courses down from "among his grey hairs" (XXVIII, 120). Further, Ahab's age seems to be in Ishmael's mind when he indicates that an "old Gay-Head Indian . . . superstitiously asserted that not till he was full forty years old did Ahab become that way branded . . . in an elemental strife at sea" (XXVIII, 121). Assorted comments soon to follow render more indelible the impression of Ahab's advanced age. Each night, for example, when all is quiet on deck, "the silent steersman would watch the cabin-scuttle; and ere long the old man would emerge, griping at the iron banister, to help his crippled way" (XXIX, 124). Stubb considers Ahab to be "about the queerest old man [he] ever sailed with. . . . A hot old man!" (XXIX, 125); and Ahab himself, immediately before tossing his lighted pipe into the sea, soliloquizes: a pipe "is meant for sereneness, to send up mild white vapors among mild white hairs, not among torn iron-grey locks like mine" (XXX, 126). Although many such allusions to Ahab as the "old man" can be taken as applications of the conventional figurative epithet often employed in reference to the leader of an enterprise—be he chief executive, general, or captain of a ship—certainly not all or even most instances of its appearance in *Moby-Dick* can be explained away thus easily. At times, the term is clearly descriptive and meant to be taken literally.

Indeed the image of Ahab as an aging man, already old and growing older, should qualify any vision we have of him, and yet how easily and often this aspect of his portrait is overlooked because of the glaring nature of his monomaniacal defiance. Ishmael sees him as a "grey-headed, ungodly old man"; "God help thee, old man," he muses, "thy thoughts have created a creature in thee; and he whose intense thinking thus makes him a Prometheus" (XLI, 184; XLIV, 200). How many are the readers who have caught the Promethean element of Ahab's character—and how few are those who have looked upon him as a fearful old man, grizzled and partly infirm![6] Yet the latter view is as significant as the former, and certainly it is as consequential for students of Melville himself, who exposed his looming fears and despondencies through the portrait of his monomaniacal captain.

Ahab could have aged like Emerson, who learned by the time he wrote "Fate" that man must come to terms with time and circumstance; he must align himself with his destiny and not attempt to counter it. He could have enjoyed a "ripe, old age," as Captains Peleg and Bildad enjoy theirs; or he could have left the sea and become a lone traveler amid a world of other lone travelers. After all, Ishmael implies, is the world not filled with Isolatoes, each man a continent unto himself? (XXVII, 118). He suggests this option for an aging man by analogizing him with the male sperm whale, which he compares whimsically with a Turkish sultan in his harem (cf. that "certain sultanism of [Ahab's] brain" [XXXIII, 144]), but in no way does he seem bitter or despondent over the natural mortality of beast and man. Eventually,

> as the ardor of youth declines; as years and dumps increase; as reflection lends her solemn pauses; in short, as a general lassitude overtakes the sated Turk; then a love of ease and virtue supplants the love of maidens; our Ottoman enters upon the impotent, repentant, admonitory stage of life, forswears, disbands the harem, and grown to an exemplary, sulky old soul goes about all alone among the meridians and parallels saying his prayers, and warning each young Leviathan from his amorous errors. (LXXXVIII, 391)

Despite the whimsy, Ishmael's portrait here of the aging, once-amorous, and once-potent cachalot is rich with suggestions in its parallels to normal human senescence, but whereas the whale aligns him-

6. The most extensive discussion of the Promethean element in Melville's fiction appears in Richard Chase, *Herman Melville: A Critical Study* (New

self with his destiny, albeit instinctively, the abnormal Ahab confronts it, defies it, and battles it before he finally succumbs. The whale lives according to natural schedules and cycles, but Ahab does not; left an orphan when only a year old, he first went to sea at eighteen and did not wed until "past fifty" (XVI, 80; CXXXII, 534). Like Hawthorne's Chillingworth, who suffers similar consequences, Ahab has stepped outside the natural order—i.e., the normal rhythms of nature —by taking a "young girl-wife" to bear his child (CXXXII, 534); outside the natural order, he defies and attempts to overrule it, but he is himself being slowly, steadily quashed by his own ineluctable mortality—and he realizes it. Whether taken down by the white whale or by the natural order, which in part it represents,[7] Ahab is well aware that his end is only a matter of the inexorable passage of time, an implacable circumstance that will not retreat before the fiercest defiance and antagonism—unless, that is, it can after all be stopped by his effectually striking "through the mask!" (XXXVI, 161-162). Like the retiring "schoolmaster" whale (note the affinity here with the "late consumptive usher to a grammar school"), Ahab is "in his advancing years . . . a solitary Leviathan"; but unlike the aging cachalot, he does not take "Nature . . . to wife in the wilderness of waters" (LXXXVIII, 392). Instead, with his special harpoon he thrusts forth not love but the hell-fired phallus of death, and nature's reaction is swift—and final.[8]

To be sure, Ishmael is not the only observer to envision Ahab as a grizzled old sea captain, a kind of patriarchal authority on the deep by virtue of his many years and sundry experiences. Fedallah, Ahab's Jungian shadow figure—himself portrayed as "the white-turbaned old man" because of the "living hair braided and coiled" around his

York: Macmillan, 1949). Also see Thomas Woodson, "Ahab's Greatness: Prometheus as Narcissus," *ELH*, 33 (September, 1966), 351-69.

7. Zoellner, p. 258.

8. In his rich and fascinating Introduction to *Pierre*, Henry A. Murray suggests that Melville's attitude in writing *Moby-Dick* might be stated thus: "I see that I am to be annihilated, but against this verdict I shall hurl an everlasting protest!" (*Pierre; or, The Ambiguities*, ed. Henry A. Murray [New York: Hendricks House, 1949], pp. xiv-xv.)

head—addresses his monomaniacal captain as "old man" when repeating his prophecies of doom (XLVIII, 215; CXVII, 492). The story
of Perth the blacksmith is analogous to Ahab's: an excellent but aging artisan, he "embraced a youthful, daughter-like, loving wife," who
listened with her children "to the stout ringing of her young-armed
old husband's hammer" (CXII, 480).[9] But alcohol made the hammer
arm impotent, as Moby-Dick had sundered Ahab's leg, and beyond
the age of sixty, Perth became an Isolato and took to the sea as a blacksmith: "the houseless, familyless old man staggered off a vagabond
in crape; his every woe unreverenced; his grey head a scorn to flaxen
curls!" (CXII, 481). Old men both, Ahab and Perth are sea-going
Isolatoes; both have left behind young wives with offspring (though
Perth's family is dead); both have lost the potency of a limb, and in
both this loss came during their late years. As Fedallah is a psychic
shadow incarnate, so Perth is a reflected image. The doubloon is not
the only mirror in *Moby-Dick.*

But of all the crew members other than Ishmael who respond to
Ahab's age, perhaps the most strikingly significant comment is uttered
by Starbuck, who confronts the unfathomable captain in his cabin and
pleads with him to repair an oil leak in the hold. Ahab's refusal metaphorically reveals his preoccupation with his own ephemerality; he
replies: "Let it leak! I'm all aleak myself. . . . Yet I don't stop to plug
my leak; for who can find it in the deep-loaded hull; or how hope to
plug it, even if found, in this life's howling gale?" (CIX, 470).[10]
One can, I suppose, convert Ahab's response into an irrelevant *double-
entendre*, but taken as a metaphor for the inevitable ebbing of life
with time, the statement once again suggests that Ahab cannot evade
an overpowering concern with his own mortality. For him, as Zoell-

9. Zoellner's complementary discussion of Perth is illuminating in this context. See pp. 101-02.

10. Melville's probable source for this metaphor is Enobarbus' assessment of
Antony's plight after his first loss to Caesar at sea; in an aside he says: "Sir,
sir, thou'rt so leaky, that we must leave thee to thy sinking" (William Shake-
spear, *Antony and Cleopatra*, III, ix. 63-64). Melville marked these lines in
his edition of Shakespeare.

ner suggests, "living is only dying."[11] His reply to the first mate is worth remarking for that reason, but far more telling than his own words is Starbuck's warning in response to the brief argument between them which ensues. Ahab asserts his authority, and Starbuck admonishes him: "[L]et Ahab beware of Ahab; beware of thyself, old man" (CIX, 471). This line clearly echoes Kent's warning to Lear after the vain and foolish old king has given away Cordelia's rightful share of the domain to his two bitch daughters; Kent pleads with Lear to be reasonable and reconsider what he has done, but the unmoved king threatens the earl, who replies in turn: "Be Kent unmannerly/When Lear is mad. What wilt thou do, old man?" (I, i. 147-148). Melville's borrowing here foreshadows the method Eliot was to employ more than half a century later, for seen in the context of old Lear's blind folly and Kent's implication of senility in his warning, Starbuck's admonition to Ahab suddenly evokes the vision of a stubborn, graying, and partly senile tyrant prepared at any cost to retain his authority even to the grave.

Another, more surprising and equally pertinent echo of *Lear* occurs shortly before the three-day chase begins. In a revealing monologue, Ahab's "humanities" predominate; he drops a tear into the sea and relates to Starbuck a nostalgic account of his past, his forty years at sea, his young wife and child: "[W]hat a forty years' fool—fool—old fool, has old Ahab been! . . . Here," he whispers, "brush this old hair aside" (CXXXII, 534-535). It seems for the moment that Ahab's memories have regenerated his soul, extirpated his monstrous pride, and restored his "humanities"; there appears to be newfound humility in Ahab akin to Lear's when the dying king requests of a bystander: "Pray you, undo this button: thank you, sir" (V, iii. 309). All the pyrotechnics of Lear's earlier raging are blown away by the quiet spendor of this one marvelous line in which the helpless king acknowledges his inability to perform the most mundane task for himself, unhesitantly "Pray[s]" for assistance, and reveals through

11. Zoellner's discussion of Ahab as entropic and auto-consumptive is brilliant, and my own observations on the mortality theme are meant to complement rather than contradict his views. See p. 194.

these whispered words how absolute the transformation from his earlier self has been. As with Lear, so with Ahab—we expect. But we
are wrong because Melville has shrewdly seduced us into accepting the
likelihood of an immediate and radical shift in character. Later, in
The Confidence Man (Chapter XIV), Melville would specify that
inconsistencies in fictional characters are no less realistic than they are
in the flesh-and-blood people around us; but Ahab's character has
been developed along one line for too long to permit so drastic and
quick a change. Lear is dying as he pleads for help with opening a
collar button, but he has no spectral figure hovering beside him drawing him on toward the fulfillment of a mad quest. Ahab's immense
pride remains essentially untouched, however, and Fedallah's influence is fatal. Hence Ahab necessarily reverts before the chapter ends,
and the remaining pages of the novel are devoted to the catastrophic
chase.

II

The Shakespearean ties are fascinating, but they only darken the
lines that have already been drawn to limn the configuration of an
aging Ahab. The highlights come through Ishmael's observations—
if, for the moment, they may be distinguished from the rest of the
narrative—his inferences, and, most particularly, from Ahab's own
thoughts and utterances. Some confusion is inevitable in any attempt
to analyze Ahab's speculations apart from the shading that Ishmael,
as omniscient narrator, probably applies to them. Implausible as it
may be, we must be satisfied for now to assume that Ishmael is able
to know and tell all, though this ability is not clearly marked until
shortly after Ahab has made his initial appearance on the quarter-
deck. Meditating generally on the question of mortality, Ishmael
shifts into specificity by focusing particularly upon Ahab's plight:

> Old age is always wakeful; as if, the longer linked with life, the
> less man has to do with aught that looks like death. Among sea-
> commanders, the old greybeards will oftenest leave their berths
> to visit the night-cloaked deck. It was so with Ahab; only that
> now, of late, he seemed so much to live in the open air, that truly

speaking, his visits were more to the cabin, than from the cabin to the planks. "It feels like going down into one's tomb,"—he would mutter to himself,—"for an old captain like me to be descending this narrow scuttle, to go to my grave-dug berth."

(XXIX, 123)

From his own observation and meditation, Ishmael has moved directly into the mind of his troubled captain; and from this point on, the reader becomes aware of what Ahab feels and thinks through revelations of the monomaniac himself as provided by a seemingly omniscient teller rather than by way of the original limited first-person narrator.

In *Moby-Dick* and elsewhere, Melville associates age with moss.[12] The small packet schooner that ferries Ishmael, Queequeg, and others to Nantucket is named the *Moss*; this is possibly a coincidence, but the name achieves more than passing significance when Ishmael, standing on its deck, muses over the shoreline vista as they glide along the river and shifts from describing the wharves to philosophizing upon the implications of the scene: all of the activity, he says, betokens that "new cruises [are] on the start; that one most perilous and long voyage ended, only begins a second; and a second ended, only begins a third, and so on, for ever and for aye. Such is the endlessness, yea, the intolerableness of all earthly effort" (XIII, 59). The *Moss*, then, becomes a vehicle for speculation on the ephemeral nature and value of human life. Ahab himself specifically mentions moss at least twice in his meditations, once as, Hamlet-like, he apostrophizes the head of a sperm whale hanging alongside the *Pequod*: "Speak, thou vast and venerable head . . . which, though ungarnished

---

12. For a few examples of Melville's use of this image, see: the "venerable moss-bearded Daniel Boone" (LXXXVIII, 392), the moss-covered backs of the tortoises from the Encantadas (Sketch 2, p. 57), the "mossy old misanthrope" of a narrator watching his "mossy old chimney" of "I and My Chimney" (pp. 407-08), and a curtain of cobwebs hanging "like the Carolina moss in the cypress forests" in "The Apple-Tree Table" (p. 411). All references to Melville's short fiction are from the Modern Library edition of *Selected Writings of Herman Melville* (New York: Random House, 1952); hereafter references to this edition will be cited as *Sel. Wr.* and incorporated parenthetically in the text.

with a beard, yet here and there lookest hoary with mosses" (LXX, 309). Here he seeks the wisdom of experience and age from the "Sphinx," which of "all divers . . . hast dived the deepest." The cachalot head, like Perth the blacksmith and the doubloon, should be seen as another reflective device for Ahab; it not only draws him out, but it also conveys a kind of image of the mad captain through their mutual association with mossy age.

Ahab's most revealing utterances regarding his mossy affinities, however, appear on the third and final day of the chase as he clings to the masthead for the last time. The nostalgia, the "humanities," the resignation, the sense of impending doom, the moss, and the unconcealed realization of his aging mortal being are all brought together in his last contemplative soliloquy. Peering at the endless sea around him before descending from the masthead, Ahab says:

> An old, old sight, and yet somehow so young; aye, and not changed a wink since I first saw it, a boy, from the sand-hills of Nantucket! The same!—the same!—the same to Noah as to me. . . . But good bye, good bye, old mast-head! What's this?—green? aye, tiny mosses in these warped cracks. No such green weather stains on Ahab's head! There's the difference now between man's old age and matter's. But aye, old mast, we both grow old together; sound in our hulls, though, are we not, my ship? Aye, minus a leg, that's all. By heaven this dead wood has the better of my live flesh every way. I can't compare with it; and I've known some ships made of dead trees outlast the lives of men made of the most vital stuff of vital fathers.[13]

Lowered to the deck a moment later, he tells Starbuck:

> For the third time my soul's ship starts upon this voyage. . . .
> Some ships sail from their ports, and ever afterwards are missing. . . .
> Some men die at ebb tide; some at low water; some at the full of the flood;—and I feel now like a billow that's all one crested comb, Starbuck. I am old. . . . (CXXXV, 557-558)

13. Zoellner notes Ishmael's paradoxical association of greenness and death, but he does not deal with moss as a pervasive symbol for age in Melville's work. See p. 214.

After a handshake and Starbuck's final plea that the mad chase be forgotten, Ahab's boat is lowered to the sea, and he is gone, a long life behind and death in the offing.

III

Ahab remarks that he and the *Pequod* are both "sound in [their] hulls," but that assessment does not altogether correspond with the impression we have gained of him as a result of several seemingly contradictory descriptions. In fact, by the time we have reached this point in the novel we should no longer envision an heroic Prometheus or an anti-heroic Satan: Ahab is an aging, raging, defiant old madman who is physically crippled to the point of being unequal to the herculean task of slaying the white whale and psychologically crippled to the point of being intellectually incapable of reaching a reasonable decision concerning the chase, the ship and crew, Moby-Dick, or his own future. Many descriptive statements made by Ishmael, the mates, and even Ahab himself document this point of view. Equally important to the descriptions, however, are the highly charged Freudian images and symbols that pervade the novel, all of which should be fully explained in the context of the passages and sections in which they appear or in the context of the entire novel when they are continuously mentioned.[14] These symbols and others, in conjunction with

14. Some of the more important of these Freudian allusions are: Ahab's leg, of course, the natural limb and the ivory ones made by the ship's carpenter; the pivot hole; the lances and harpoons, especially the latter, Ahab's own and those heaved by the massive hyper-masculine non-Caucasians; the mastheads (as the corposants burn, Ahab tells his mates, "all that sperm [from the oil] will work up into the masts, like sap in a tree . . .[so to] be as three spermaceti candles" [CXXIX, 499]; the sharks that bite the oars of Ahab's whaleboat as it plunges after Moby-Dick; the association of senescence, impotence, physical deterioration, and death with blindness, especially with Ahab's words among his final cries: "I grow blind; hands! stretch out before me that I may yet grope my way. Is't night?" (CXXXV, 563); Ahab's broad-brimmed hat, plucked from his head by a passing bird and dropped far away into the sea; the evasive spirit-spout; the spermaceti; the cassock and the organ from which it is cut; etc.

For an elaborate Freudian reading, see: David Leverenz, "Moby-Dick," in *Psychoanalysis and Literary Process*, ed. Frederick C. Crews (Cambridge,

the many implicatory allusions to the sexuality of the sea, the air, and the whale (its members and *in toto*), are not simply there to give another, separate, dimension to the novel, for they serve a very definite and vital function with regard to Ahab himself. When considered in the light of that most illuminating chapter (CVI), "Ahab's Leg," the Freudian references point to Ahab's overwhelming fear of losing his sexual power; and it is no desire on his part to sire a large family and an endless string of progeny that stirs him so but the fact that the loss of his sexual potency is a clear though subtle indication of his life's approaching end, of the inevitable close to an existence that has proved thus far to be inscrutable, meaningless, and, to him, unacceptable in its mortal brevity.

The mysterious injury that occurs to Ahab not long before the *Pequod* leaves Nantucket clearly yokes the Freudian symbolism of his artificial leg with the reproductive function of the phallus and the "groin." Ahab was found one night lying unconscious on the ground, and in some unfathomable manner "his ivory limb [had] been so violently displaced, that it had stake-wise smitten, and all but pierced his groin; nor was it without extreme difficulty that the agonizing wound was entirely cured" (CVI, 460). The physical wound has healed, but a psychic scar remains; his potency has been touched. Oddly, but appropriately enough, the paragraph describing this bizarre mishap follows the opening one of the chapter, detailing the effects of Ahab's sudden flight from the *Samuel Enderby*—where he had crossed ivory limbs with Captain Boomer. Having hurriedly left Boomer's ship, Ahab lands hard on his ivory leg and then twists it with a wrench in the pivot-hole, weakening it so that although "it still remained entire, and to all appearances lusty, yet Ahab did not deem it entirely trustworthy" (CVI, 460). Instead, Ishmael says, Ahab "did at times give careful heed to the condition of that dead bone upon which he partly stood," and the description of Ahab's injury follows immediately. To all appearances healed, there is something yet in Ahab's mind that

Mass.: Winthrop, 1970), pp. 87-88, 91-92, 102. Leverenz suggests that the pervasive "phallicness" in *Moby-Dick* "ends" for all alike in "mute mortality" (p. 102).

keeps him from altogether trusting the "lusty"-looking ivory leg and the nearly pierced "groin." What is this agent of distrust? What else but the gnawing truth of mortality! As Robert Zoellner suggests, "Life for Ahab is not a process of regeneration or renewal or rebirth. It is instead a steady declension into nothingness and annihilation."[15] Unlike Queequeg, who is certain that "whether to live or die [is] a matter of his own sovereign will and pleasure" (CX, 476), Ahab vainly defies his imminent and inevitable doom. But Starbuck foretells what Ahab himself refuses consciously to acknowledge; echoing the "Tomorrow and tomorrow and tomorrow" lines that Macbeth utters upon learning of his wife's death, Starbuck muses as he looks at a furious Ahab lurching along the deck: "I have sat before the dense coal fire and watched it all aglow, full of its tormented flaming life; and I have seen it wane at last, down, down, to dumbest dust. Old man of oceans! of all this fiery life of thine, what will at length remain but one little heap of ashes!" (CXVIII, 495).

The last few chapters bear out Starbuck's prophecy, though, to be sure, Ahab's life ends more suddenly than the slow waning of a coal fire. Of principal importance in this context, however, is not the manner of Ahab's actual death but the way he reacts to his nearly three score years, over which he is constantly brooding, especially as the first day of the climactic chase draws near. Emphatically repeating to Starbuck that he has spent forty years a-whaling, Ahab admits to his "desolation of solitude," and his "weariness! heaviness!" (CXXXII, 534). "Locks so grey," he says, "did never grow but from out some ashes" (CXXXII, 535), foreseeing for himself, perhaps, the same "little heap of ashes" that Starbuck anticipates for him. "But do I look very old, so very, very old, Starbuck?" he asks:

> I feel deadly faint, bowed, and humped, as though I were Adam, staggering beneath the piled centuries since Paradise. God! God! God!—crack my heart!—stave my brain! . . . mockery of grey

15. Zoellner, p. 193. In a long "Editorial Essay," Hale Chatfield effectively presents Ahab as a "fertility figure" whose "masculinity is in some kind of disrepair"; see: " 'The Step-Mother World': One more Reading of *Moby-Dick*," *Hiram Poetry Review*, No. 11 (Fall-Winter 1971), p. 32.

hairs, have I lived enough joy to wear ye; and seem and feel thus
intolerably old?

· · ·

But it is a mild, mild wind, and a mild looking sky . . . they have
been making hay somewhere under the slopes of the Andes,
Starbuck, and the mowers are sleeping among the new-mown
hay. Sleeping? Aye, toil we how we may, we all sleep at last on
the field. Sleep? Aye, and rust amid greenness; as last year's
scythes flung down, and left in the half-cut swaths. (CXXXII,
535-536)

Here Ahab not only reveals his own melancholy sentiments about
mortality, but he also echoes Ishmael's philosophizing aboard the
Moss when the young sailor comments upon "the intolerableness of
all earthly efforts."[16]

Ahab's portrait, then, clearly depicts him as a man who is physically deteriorating. On the first day of the chase, Moby-Dick wrecks
Ahab's boat, and the floundering captain is dragged into another,
"the white brine caking in his wrinkles; the long tension of Ahab's
bodily strength did crack, and helplessly he yielded to his body's
doom" (CXXXIII, 543).The next day Ahab's boat is again stove in,
and his ivory leg is "snapped off, leaving but one short sharp splinter."
In response to Stubb's asking him if he has broken any bones, Ahab
replies, "Aye! and all splintered to pieces, Stubb!—d'ye see it.—But
even with a broken bone, old Ahab is untouched" (CXXXIV, 552).
Ah, but he is not "untouched." Still highly spirited, he calls for his
crew to stand around him and tells them: "Ye see an old man cut down
to the stump; leaning on a shivered lance; propped up on a lonely
foot. 'Tis Ahab—his body's part; but Ahab's soul's a centipede, that
moves upon a hundred legs. I feel strained, half stranded, as ropes
that tow dismasted frigates in a gale; and I may look so. But ere I
break, ye'll hear me crack; and till ye hear *that*, know that Ahab's
hawser tows his purpose yet" (CXXXIV, 554). Physically Ahab is

16. Zoellner makes a strong case for Ishmael's sharing Ahab's fear of "nothingness behind phenomena and at the heart of noumena—a haunting fear of
the *void*." See p. 135.

degenerating, and he knows it. Nevertheless, he remains furious, dynamic, and defiant to the end, fully expecting to go out with a bang, a "crack," but ironically being yanked voicelessly by his own "hawser" —in this case, his harpoon rope—into the sea and down, down, down perhaps to the very treadle of God's loom where Pip has been before him. But for Ahab, as for all of us, there is no return.

IV

To see Ahab as a mere man resenting and defying his mortality offers a confessedly limited perspective from which to view *Moby-Dick* as a whole, but it is a peculiarly appropriate point of view nevertheless because it so well comports with Melville's own concern over aging and death, which appears at times to have been almost obsessive. Several of his stories of the 1850's, for example, including "The Encantadas," "I and My Chimney," "The Apple-Tree Table," and "Jimmy Rose," emphasize the value of things that are old, not especially for the sake of tradition but for the almost palpable esteem attributable to the amassing of years in themselves. In "I and My Chimney," which Leon Howard has called "the most intimately personal of all Melville's magazine sketches that summer [of 1855],"[17] the narrator, diametrically opposed to his wife, is most impressed with age: "Old myself, I take to oldness in things" (*Sel. Wr.*, 386). One would think that the story were being written by a man past the age of retirement, the Melville, perhaps, of the late 1880's rather than the youngish author of thirty-five who still should have been anticipating a long career ahead. When the narrator complains to his wife that she is too readily attracted to newness and youth, she responds: "Oh, don't you grumble, old man (she always calls me old man), it's I, young I, that keep you from stagnating" (*Sel. Wr.*, 387). Not unexpectedly, Jimmy Rose, the title figure of another story Melville wrote the same summer, also frets: "[M]y wife, . . . I fear, was too young for me" (*Sel. Wr.*, 243). Surely, the same fear was not justifiable in Mel-

17. Leon Howard, *Herman Melville: A Biography* (Berkeley: University of California Press, 1951), p. 224; hereafter references to this biography will be cited as *HM* and incorporated parenthetically in the text.

ville, whose wife, Elizabeth, was less than three years younger than he. Again in "I and My Chimney," when his wife complains that the huge chimney is settling, the narrator admits, "As for its settling, I like it. I, too, am settling, you know, in my gait. I and my chimney are settling together [cf. Ahab and the mast], and shall keep settling, too, till, as in a great feather-bed [cf. the sea], we shall both have set-tled away clean out of sight" (*Sel. Wr.*, 401). The ambience here is lighter, of course, than that of the melancholy philosophizing of both Ishmael and Ahab musing over the same subject of mortality, but the salience of that theme in both works, and in several other contempo-rary sketches confirm its predominance in Melville's mind during these crucial years as he was descending from the apex of his career.

Even more telling than the published work, however, are the out-pourings of his deepest self to Hawthorne in letters written during the composition of *Moby-Dick* and shortly thereafter, especially the long, intimate missive of, presumably, June 1, 1851. This letter is al-ready so well known that I hesitate to quote from it at all, but in it Melville's plaintive comments on senescence and mortality are too cru-cial to overlook; he writes:

> [A] presentiment is on me,—I shall at last be worn out and perish, like an old nutmeg-grater, grated to pieces by the constant attrition of the wood, that is, the nutmeg. . . . My development has been all within a few years past. I am like one of those seeds taken out of the Egyptian Pyramids, which, after being three thousand years a seed and nothing but a seed, being planted in English soil, it developed itself, grew to greenness, and then fell to mould. So I. Until I was twenty-five, I had no development at all. From my twenty-fifth year I date my life. Three weeks have scarcely passed, at any time between then and now, that I have not unfolded within myself. But I feel that I am now come to the inmost leaf of the bulb, and that shortly the flower must fall to the mould.[18]

18. *The Letters of Herman Melville*, ed. Merrell R. Davis and William H. Gilman (New Haven: Yale University Press, 1960), pp. 128, 130; hereafter references to this collection will be cited as *Letters* and incorporated paren-thetically in the text.

Later in the year, clearly in response to Hawthorne's appreciation for *Moby-Dick*, Melville wrote again, and once more the feeling of impending death pervades the letter: "Lord, when shall we be done changing? Ah! it's a long stage, and no inn in sight, and night coming, and the body cold. . . . I shall leave the world, I feel, with more satisfaction for having come to know you" (Nov. 17?, 1851; *Letters*, 143). And after nearly a year had passed, he appended to another letter to Hawthorne: "If you find any *sand* in this letter, regard it as so many sands of my life, which run out as I was writing it" (Oct. 25, 1852; *Letters*, 162). Having read most of Melville's work and received such correspondence from him over an extended period of time, is it any wonder, then, that Hawthorne spoke of things mortal and immortal with him when the two men met in Liverpool late in 1856, in the midst of one of Melville's most somber periods? Hawthorne's oft-cited journal entry for November 12 of that year reads in part: "Melville, as he always does, began to reason of Providence and futurity, and of everything that lies beyond human ken, and informed me that he had 'pretty much made up his mind to be annihilated.' "[19] Melville was a man of faith who found nothing to put his faith in, and Hawthorne realized this of him. Unlike Hawthorne, however, Melville could not be comfortable with his skepticism; life for him seemed to be growing intolerable—as if he had burned his way through it in a relatively few years and become an old man before his time.

He would recognize the early loss of his sea legs, for example, not long after his sojourn in England and the Continent had ended; on May 30, 1860, two days out at sea aboard the *Meteor* on his way to California—an abortive journey for him—Melville wrote in his journal: "Quite sea-sick at night." Even as late as June 18, he added: "Not yet completely settled in my stomach" (*Log*, II, 618, 619).[20] More-

19. Quoted by Jay Leyda, *The Melville Log: A Documentary Life of Herman Melville,1819-1891* (New York: Harcourt, Brace, 1951), II, 529; hereafter references to this source will be cited as *Log* and parenthetically incorporated in the text.

20. Many years later on his final sea voyage, to Bermuda and Cuba during the spring of 1888, the journey was so rough at times that Melville had to

over, his psychological condition even then was already that of a man preoccupied with the coming of death. With a sense of resignation in early October of the same year, he had checked and underscored the opening line of Chapman's concluding verses in his translation of Homer's *Batrachomyomachia*: "The work that I was born to do is done!" (*Log*, II, 627). Clearly, by then Melville saw his career finished as an author in the public eye. Some two years later, in November 1862, he was thrown from his carriage; he broke his shoulder, bruised several ribs, and was generally shaken up. He was also suffering from neuralgia at the time, and this, combined with the injuries from his mishap—none of which were of prolonged seriousness—led to his being strangely afflicted for an inordinately long period; according to Leon Howard, Melville "seems to have spent much of his time in bed meditating death" (*HM*, 273). By the late 1870's, his observation that "life is short" had become "habitual"; and in his final years, while planning *John Marr and Other Sailors* (1888), one of his "major interests" was the "thoughts of sailing men just before they dropped anchor in their last port" (*HM*, 313, 321).

Taken by themselves, these biographical facts are suggestive but no more than that. In the context of the attitude toward life betrayed in his prose of the 1850's, however, from *Moby-Dick* through the final depressing scene of *The Confidence Man* (1857), these data become highly significant because they manifestly confirm the immediate correspondence between Ahab's brooding over his mortality and Melville's own enduring deep-seated preoccupations with the same disturbing questions. Simultaneously, of course, they help to document a novel perspective from which to view Ahab's character and the whole of *Moby-Dick* as an exploration into the limitations of mortality through the extensive implications of the acceptance or denial and defiance of them.

What it was precisely that set the still-young author morosely pon-

crawl on his hands and knees to move from one part of the ship to another (*HM*, 324). That the debilitating effects of age had come to him as they do to Ahab can be inferred from a description worth repeating in this context: "the old man would emerge, griping at the iron banister, to help his crippled way" (*Moby-Dick*, XXIX, 124).

dering fate, futurity, and the Void will probably remain a subject of speculation for many years to come, but a small book purchase that he made early in 1851 connotes that his innermost thoughts were well focused, indeed, on these vast subjects as he drove toward the completion of *The Whale*. On March 6 of that year, he acquired an inexpensive reprint of *The New England Primer*, on pages 12 and 13 of which appear the following couplets:

> Rachael doth mourn
> For her first-born.
>
> . . .
>
> Time cuts down all,
> Both great and small.
>
> . . .
>
> Whales in the sea
> God's voice obey.
>
> Xerxes the Great did die,
> And so must you and I.
>
> Youth forward slips,
> Death soonest nips.

$$(Log, \text{ I, } 407)$$

Like sharp knives, these spare couplets cut through to the heart of Melville's great novel. They tell us, as he did: Others abide the sentence; so, too, must thou.

Ah, Herman. Ah, humanity.

Nilson L. Heflin

Sources from the Whale-Fishery
and "The Town-Ho's Story"

*"So help me Heaven, and on my honor the story I have told
ye, gentlemen, is in substance and its great items, true. I
know it to be true; it happened on this ball; I trod the ship;
I knew the crew; I have seen and talked with Steelkilt since
the death of Radney."*

—Chapter 54, *Moby-Dick*

I

I should like to propose that Chapter 54 of *Moby-Dick*, "The Town-Ho's Story," had its origins in five unusual incidents of the whale-fishery in 1842 and 1843 which Herman Melville could have heard about directly from the principals or eyewitnesses or through the scuttlebutt of the fleet.[1]

First, a brief summary of "The Town-Ho's Story" will better establish its relationships with the historical incidents to follow:

Cruising the Pacific Ocean, the *Town-Ho* of Nantucket sprung a leak, having been rammed, it was supposed, by a swordfish. When the amount of water the craft was taking greatly increased, orders were given to sail for the nearest island. Among foremast hands of the *Town-Ho* was a seaman named Steelkilt, "a Lakeman and desper-

1. Years ago at a Melville Society meeting in New York City, Howard Vincent and I convivially discussed the possible relationship of the story of Luther Fox and that of Steelkilt in *Moby-Dick*. Since then further research has turned up the four additional relevant incidents recounted here.

163

ado from Buffalo," a mariner of heroic proportions. Taking his turn
at the pumps one day, he jestingly made remarks about Radney, the
mate of the ship, a Vineyarder "ugly as a mule; yet as hardy, as stubborn, as malicious."[2] Radney, overhearing Steelkilt, determined to
sting and insult him. He commanded the Lakeman to sweep down the
deck and remove some excrement from it. Such duty being menial,
Steelkilt refused to obey. Seizing the cooper's club hammer, Radney advanced on the Lakeman and repeated his command. Steelkilt
retreated round the windlass, declaring his determination not to obey
and warning the mate not to touch him with the hammer. But, writes
Melville, "the fool had been branded for the slaughter by the gods.
Immediately the hammer touched the cheek; the next instant the
lower jaw of the mate was stove in his head; he fell on the hatch
spouting blood like a whale."

In the ensuing turmoil, Steelkilt and nine followers took refuge behind a group of large casks. The Lakeman addressed his indignant
captain, declaring that he and his allies would all willingly return
to duty and man the pumps, but only upon the promise that no one
would be flogged. The captain would make no such agreement. To
his repeated order "Turn to!" Steelkilt replied, "treat us decently, and
we're your men; but we won't be flogged."

"Down into the forecastle then, down with ye, I'll keep ye there till
ye're sick of it. Down ye go."

After the men went below, the captain padlocked the hatchway.
Twice a day for three days, he summoned the prisoners to work. On
the fourth morning, four men burst from the forecastle. Three more
revolters surrendered the next day. Steelkilt then proposed a frantic
plan to his remaining two allies. They would arm themselves with
mincing knives, rush forth at the next summoning, and if possible
seize the ship. The men agreed to his proposal, but that night they betrayed him. As he slept they bound and gagged him and called at
midnight for the captain. The three men were seized into the mizzen
rigging and left there until morning.

At sunrise all hands were called to witness punishment. The cap-

2. Quotations from "The Town-Ho's Story" are from *Moby-Dick*; *or*, *The
Whale*, ed. Luther S. Mansfield and Howard P. Vincent (New York: Hendricks House, 1952), chapt. 54.

tain began with the two traitors, violently laying the rope on their backs. When he turned to Steelkilt, the Lakeman warned him: "What I say is this—and mind it well—if you flog me, I murder you!" To the surprise of the whalemen, the master of the *Town-Ho* threw down his rope.

Radney was not similarly reluctant. He grasped the rope and flogged Steelkilt, after which the men returned sullenly to their duty. Steelkilt advised them to remain peaceful, then to jump ship as soon as the ship reached land. Meanwhile he privately and systematically built a plan of revenge against Radney. On his watches below he was observed carefully braiding with twine "an iron ball, closely netted." He knew that Radney on night watches was in the habit of dozing off. Steelkilt, therefore, planned to take his revenge at the first opportunity during a mid-watch. But, Melville writes, "by a mysterious fatality, Heaven itself seemed to step in to take out of his hands into its own the damning thing he would have done."

Moby-Dick breached within fifty yards of the *Town-Ho*. In the frenzied chase, Radney's boat pulled well ahead of the others. His boat struck Moby-Dick, and Radney spilled upon the White Whale and then into the water. Seizing the Vineyarder between his jaws, Moby-Dick reared high up and plunged headlong into the sea.

After the *Town-Ho* reached a savage island, most of the foremast hands deserted, sailing away in a double war-canoe. The captain of the ship called upon natives for assistance in heaving down his whaler and repairing the leak. Once the work was done, he set out with one man in his best whaleboat for Tahiti, hoping there to procure additional mariners for his ship. On passage he met with the war-canoe led by Steelkilt. Boarding the whaleboat, the Lakeman made the master of the *Town-Ho* swear to land on a nearby island and remain there six days. Thus the deserters "for ever got the start of their former captain."

II

There is a remarkable similarity between the nautical mishap of the fictional *Town-Ho* of Nantucket and that of the actual *London Packet* of Fairhaven, Captain Jabez Howland. Melville and Toby

Greene at Nukahiva, while still in the crew of the *Acushnet*, saw the *London Packet* on July 7, 1842, "put in leaky having been run through by a Billfish."[3] The *London Packet* continued to leak during her next cruise for whales, with Toby Greene, recently escaped from Taipi Valley, aboard her as a foremast hand. In January, 1843, the ship "was run on shore at Whahapoa, Bay of Islands . . . to be repaired, the blade of a sword fish having passed through her bottom."[4]

The open boat journey of the *Town-Ho*'s captain to Tahiti suggests a nearly parallel event connected with the loss in August 1842 of the whaler *Cadmus* of Fairhaven. After this ship was wrecked on a lagoon island, Captain Edwin L. Mayhew, his first mate, and four seamen took the only whaleboat left and sailed more than a thousand miles to Tahiti for assistance. They arrived on August 21, and Captain Mayhew chartered the schooner *Emerald* to go to the scene of the accident. (The master of the *Town-Ho* chartered at Tahiti "a small native schooner.") Finding eighteen destitute survivors of the *Cadmus*, Captain Christopher Hall brought them in the *Emerald* to Tahiti on September 30,[5] shortly after Herman Melville had cast his lot there with ten revolters from the barque *Lucy Ann*.

III

Now let us consider three somewhat longer incidents, from which Melville seems to have taken the essential ingredients for human conflict in "The Town-Ho's Story" of *Moby-Dick*.

The first incident occurred on a New Bedford whaler. The *Nassau*, Captain Hiram Weeks, cruised on April 11, 1843, not far from 30° South latitude and 117° West longitude. Captain Weeks was on deck when Charles G. Cleavland, second mate of the ship, gave or-

3. Logbook of the *Potomac* of Nantucket, Captain Isaac B. Hussey (owned by Mr. Peter Black), entry for July 7, 1842.

4. Boston *Courier* of July 20, 1843.

5. "Report of the loss of the American Ship Cadmus on a Lagoon Island in the South Pacific on the 4th of August at midnight 1842," in Tahitian Records, Foreign Records of the Department of State, the National Archives, Washington, D.C. (hereafter FR-NA).

ders to loose the main topgallant sail. Luther Fox, a foremast hand, climbed aloft of his own accord and while he was carrying out the command, Mr. Cleavland told him to light the foot rope of the sail over the stay.

"Damn the foot rope to Hell," Fox called out in a loud voice.

"Stop that swearing aloft," Captain Weeks shouted.

When Fox came down on deck, Captain Weeks reprimanded him severely. Fox made no reply. The master of the *Nassau* then ordered his first mate, Jepitha Jenney, to punish Fox by making him scrape down the topmasts and topgallant masts. Next morning Fox was ordered to tar the bobstay and the rigging about the bowsprit. He commenced work early in the day but stopped to go below when his watch was called to breakfast.

Some time later Mr. Jenney went to the top of the forecastle gangway and called out, "Fox, turn to."

"I shall not come up till after dining," Fox replied. "It is my watch below." He added that he would sooner die than come up.

Mr. Jenney went to Captain Weeks, who was in the fore topgallant crosstrees on the lookout for whales, and reported Fox's failure to obey his order. The time was about eight o'clock.

"Fox has not got command of the ship quite yet," Captain Weeks said. "We'll get him out of the forecastle at some rate."

Mr. Jenney returned to the scuttle and repeated his order, but again Fox insisted upon what he deemed his rights.

"It is my watch below and I will not come up alive unless the whole watch comes up."

Mr. Jenney started down the forecastle gangway just as Frank Joseph, a seaman, was climbing to the upper deck with his tin pan and pipe. Joseph jumped quickly aside, and a scream rang out over the ship. Joseph turned around at once and saw Fox sitting on his sea chest, his mincing knife in his hand. There was blood on the knife.

The third mate and several of the crew ran forward upon hearing the cry and found Mr. Jenney holding to the coaming of the gangway, crying, and trying vainly to throw himself out of the forecastle. They lifted Mr. Jenney to the deck and placed him on the larboard side of the scuttle. His right leg appeared to be nearly shorn from his body.

Bones from the part of his leg attached to the body were protruding. They pushed together the severed parts of the leg.

Captain Weeks hurried down from his lookout post and asked the first mate what had happened.

"Fox has cut my leg off with a mincing knife."

Mr. Jenney was carried aft, and since there were no surgeons aboard American whale ships, Captain Weeks examined the wound. He found that the blow had been struck with such force that the leg bone had been completely cut through, and the leg was hanging by a small piece of flesh on the inner part of the thigh. He applied a tourniquet, stopped the flow of blood from two or three of the main arteries, cut off the leg, and took up the remaining arteries. Mr. Jenney was placed on a bed in the cabin and rendered as comfortable as possible.

About a half-hour later, Captain Weeks ordered James Hackett, the cooper, to go forward and see Fox. Hackett found him in the forecastle, still sitting on his chest with a mincing knife across his legs. When the cooper asked him if he knew what he had done, Fox replied that he could not help it, and burst into tears. He said that he had warned Mr. Jenney not to come into the forecastle.

Hackett asked for the mincing knife but Fox refused to give it up.

"If they come after me I shall defend myself and sell my life as dear as I can," he said.

Hackett, insisting that no one would attempt to force him on deck, attempted to persuade Fox to give himself up. After a while Fox handed his mincing knife to the cooper. Later that day when Mr. Cleavland ordered Fox to go aft, he left the forecastle without hesitation and was put in irons.

At three o'clock Jepitha Jenney died. On the following noon orders were given to bury the head, and his body was cast into the ocean.

The *Nassau* came to anchor at Honolulu on May 26, 1843.[6] By order of William Hooper, United States Vice Commercial Agent, Luther Fox was imprisoned in the fort, and two witnesses, Joseph Dutra and Manuel Deauvilla, Portuguese members of the crew of the *Nassau*, were left at the Agency.

6. Journal of Stephen Reynolds, Volume 6, Peabody Museum, Salem, Massachusetts.

Three days after his ship made port, Captain Weeks, his third mate, two boatsteerers, the cooper, and two seamen appeared before Hooper and gave sworn testimony that Luther Fox had killed Jepitha Jenney.[7] Samuel H. Goodhue, seaman, produced the fatal mincing knife, marked "J. Durfee, cast steel," pointed to gaps in the weapon, and told of the blood he had seen upon it. He declared: "The business of mincing blubber had been allocated to Fox during the voyage and it was his Custom to keep the Knife in his possession—it was also usual for him to grind the Knives always after cutting in a whale."

Luther Fox remained imprisoned in the Honolulu fort until July 22, when he and the two Portuguese witnesses, the mincing knife, and the depositions of the men of the *Nassau* were delivered aboard the United States frigate *Constellation*, Commodore Lawrence Kearney commanding.

Less than two months later, while the *Constellation* was lying off port of Monterey, California, Fox escaped. It was supposed that he had jumped through one of the portholes of the frigate and had swum toward shore.[8]

Herman Melville must have heard this story. Only a few days after he came to Honolulu, the *Nassau* entered the harbor, and of the five American whalers which were in port during the period of Melville's stay in the town, she arrived under the most dramatic circumstances.

Jepitha Jenney's murder was recounted in a Honolulu newspaper under the headline "Bloody Affray at Sea," and Fox was described as a "native of Renselaerville, Albany Co. N.Y."[9] To Melville the fate of a whaleman whose home was so near Lansingburgh should have been a matter of especial interest. One might even speculate that Melville went to the Honolulu fort, during the some fifty-eight days of

7. Depositions of Captain Hiram Weeks, Third Mate Michael Griffin, Boatsteerers Edward Alvood and Robert Eldridge, Cooper James Hackett, and Frank Joseph and Samuel H. Goodhue, seamen, May 29, 1843, in Consular Letters, Department of State, the National Archives (hereafter CLDS), Honolulu II. The foregoing account of the murder of Jepitha Jenney is based on these documents.

8. Captains Letters, September 1843, in Old Navy Records, the National Archives (hereafter ON-NA).

9. *Temperance Advocate and Seaman's Friend* of June 27, 1843.

Fox's imprisonment there, and listened to Luther Fox's own story of murder aboard the *Nassau*.[10] It is possible, too, that Melville heard of Fox's escape at Monterey. For the frigate *United States* in which he served and the *Constellation* from which Fox escaped were together in Callao harbor in January 1844, a few months after Fox had disappeared.[11]

* * *

The second relevant episode commenced one day in late October 1842, when Isaac Collier, carpenter of the ship *Vineyard* of Edgartown, then in the second year of a whaling voyage, noticed that Benjamin Brown, a seaman, was making a slung shot out of a whale's tooth as long as a man's finger and grafting it with twine. When a shipmate in the forecastle asked what he was doing, Brown replied that he was fashioning the weapon for possible use should he desert from the whaler. Later Brown was seen making another slung shot, this time using a piece of lead.

About ten days later Benjamin Brown and John Thompson began fighting at the wheel of the *Vineyard*. The first mate intervened and struck Brown, who immediately hit back. Captain Silas R. Crocker, upon hearing the row, came quickly on deck. He ordered Brown and Thompson to be tied together and gave them a "cat" each "to whip one another and have it out." Afterwards, when some of the men had gone below decks, Daniel Blackett and George Walker angrily remarked that they were sorry they "hadn't jumped into the mate." Soon resentful members of the crew were evolving a plan of revenge.

During the day seamen who lived in the forecastle sought to enlist the aid of crew members who berthed in other parts of the ship. Daniel Blackett approached Isaac Collier, the carpenter, asking whether he intended to visit the forecastle that night.

"What for?"

10. In *Omoo*, Melville remarked significantly: "No sailor steps ashore, but he straightway goes to the 'Calabooza,' where he is almost sure to find some poor fellow or other in confinement for desertion, or alleged mutiny, or something of that sort" (*Omoo: A Narrative of Adventures in the South Seas*, ed. Harrison Hayford, Hershel Parker and G. Thomas Tanselle [Evanston & Chicago: Northwestern University Press and Newberry Library, 1968], p. 159).

11. Logbook of the frigate *United States*, in ON-NA.

"We're going to have a cattle show."

"What are you going to do?"

"We're going to have a fight among ourselves," Blackett said. "Timothy Sargeant is going to start, and if the Captain or any of his officers comes down we'll drive 'em out of it [the forecastle], and if he presents a pistol at me, I'll run a lance through him."

When he went aloft to relieve Sargeant, James Walsh heard about the plan "to have a sham fight and . . . kick the officers out of the forecastle." Sergeant told Walsh that he, Ichabod Davis, George Walker, and Daniel Blackett were the ringleaders. James Harvey, who bunked in the steerage, was visited by a Portuguese seaman and asked to participate in the plot. When Harvey came on deck, he found Sargeant, Blackett, Walker, and Domingo sitting together forward of the mainmast. He joined them and learned the details of their plan.

In the forecastle Domingo and several other seamen asked Levi Lee, the regular cook who was lying sick in his bunk, what would be the consequences of the plot. "I told them," Lee later testified, "they'd either be tried for their neck, or put in prison, and tried to suade 'em from it. Sargeant told 'em they couldn't do nothing with 'em for it and coaxed 'em into it."

Daniel Blackett prepared openly for the "cattle show." From the mast-head Second Mate Edward Osborn saw him "cut off a length from a stick of wood about the size of a small heaver, go round the galley, show it to Sargeant, and then commence whittling on one end of it apparently making a handle." Other seamen took pieces of wood into the forecastle, shaped them into clubs, and hid them in their bunks.

Shortly after sundown the men were ready. Lee pleaded with them not to start anything until Third Mate Ansel Fuller could dress his blisters. They said they would wait five minutes. Mr. Fuller came into the forecastle, examined Lee, and applied new bandages.

As soon as the third mate had returned to the main deck, Benjamin Brown stood up and began swinging his slung shot menacingly about his wrist. Then someone shouted, "You stole my molasses." The men started yelling, striking against the bunk boards, and pushing one another about.

"Get off of me. Let me alone."

"Give it to him."

"Don't kill me!"

Mr. Fuller ran forward and sang out twice to the men to stop the noise. When they ignored him, he became riled and made for the scuttle. He had taken three steps down the forecastle gangway when someone caught him by the shoulder.

"No go down there a kill you."

The third mate drew back quickly to the safety of the deck. Looking down into the forecastle, he saw a Portuguese named Bill hopping about and striking his fist against his hand. Mr. Fuller then went aft to report the disturbance to Captain Crocker and to make ready his arms. All lights in the forecastle were put out except that in Levi Lee's bunk. Captain Crocker went forward with his second mate.

"What's the matter, men?"

In reply there was only a derisive hoot, something which sounded like "Wow, wow, wow!"

Down into the darkened forecastle went Captain Crocker, followed by Second Mate Osborn. The master of the *Vineyard* was immediately surrounded by a group of the men. Daniel Blackett and then George Walker struck him. They hauled him about and threw him down on a chest, making jeering remarks when he ordered them to quit.

Second Mate Edward Osborn, who jumped into the group around Captain Crocker, was hit by Blackett. Then Benjamin Brown struck him a violent blow with a weapon. (Some of the witnesses later said that it was a club; Levi Lee insisted that it was a slung shot.) Mr. Osborn fell unconscious to the forecastle deck. Apparently satisfied with their revenge, the men let Captain Crocker escape to the upper deck.

"When I came to," Mr. Osborn later testified, "I found Brown clinched to me, hauling me to get me off the chest. I kicked him away from me. I afterwards got on deck as quick as I could with the loss of part of my shirt and one leg of my trousers." There was blood on his face and his head was split open.

When Captain Crocker ordered the men on deck, they mocked him. Then he called them by name. Some of the group came up; the others defied him, insisting that they would stay below until the *Vineyard* made port. Captain Crocker said he would give them until morning to think it over. He barred down the scuttle.

Every day thereafter he came to the forecastle hatch and ordered the men to come up and go in irons. Again and again they refused. Testimony differs as to the length of their endurance, but several of the depositions of witnesses suggest that the ringleaders remained below until the *Vineyard* reached Tahiti. One of the witnesses, however, said that on the Friday after the "cattle show" the rebellious mariners came up and were locked in irons.[12]

Herman Melville was already at sea in the *Charles and Henry*, the Nantucket ship he had joined at Eimeo in early November, 1842, when the *Vineyard* anchored on November 12 at Papeete.[13] He was not nearby to hear of the trial of the mutineers before Consul S. R. Blackler. There was, however, opportunity later for him to learn from eyewitnesses this story of violence aboard an Edgartown whaler. During eight of the days Melville spent at Lahaina in May, 1843, the *Vineyard* lay at anchor in the roadstead.[14]

* * *

A few days after the whaler *Mercury* of Stonington, Captain Simmons L. Gray, had left Tahiti, the third historical analogue took place. The decks were cleared on February 18, 1843, and while the crew, including a blacksmith named Ishmael Guyer,[15] looked on, George Washington, a black seaman was seized into the rigging and flogged. Washington had attempted to desert at Tahiti but had been apprehended. He was being punished as an example to the crew. While the lash was being administered, Joseph Smith, a foremast hand aboard

12. "Depositions of Mates and Crew of Ship Vineyard November 16th 1842," in "Accounts, Mutinies, Surveys, Estates, 1841-1870," Tahitian Records, FR-NA. In making quotations from these documents I have expanded abbreviations and corrected a few scribal errors.

13. Boston *Daily Advertiser* of May 9, 1843.

14. She was recruiting at Lahaina during May 8-23, 1843; in "Consular Return," Lahaina, in CLDS-NA, Honolulu.

15. The crew list of the *Mercury* is in the Treasury Department records in the National Archives Regional Annex at Dorchester, Massachusetts.

the *Mercury*, walked onto the quarter-deck and spoke menacingly to Captain Gray.

"The man has been flogged enough," Smith said.

Angered at impertinence from a common seaman, Captain Gray drove Smith to the forward part of the ship. When Smith reached the forecastle, he turned to the master of the *Mercury* and, in the hearing of officers and crew, told him that no man should again be flogged on board the vessel. He had the support of ship's company, he said. And he would be the death of any officer who attempted to lay hands upon him. He had murdered one mate before, Smith declared, and he would kill again if anyone tried to correct him.

Thus the matter rested, and there was no more flogging. On March 21, when the *Mercury* was nearing the island of Maui, Captain Gray called Smith into his cabin and asked him what he thought of his past conduct. Smith admitted that he had behaved rashly and that he had been in a passion at the time Washington had been flogged. But as the talk went on, Smith again became angry and insolent. When he called Captain Gray "a damned liar," the latter caught up a bayonet. Smith retreated to the upper deck, with Captain Gray following and ordering him forward.

Upon reaching the forecastle, Smith called out: "Captain Gray, there you are on the starboard side of the quarter deck, and I am here on the forecastle. I tell *you now* that the sailors shall do their duty. *I* will see that they do. And I will see that *you do yours*. And I will see that no man is punished on board this ship. If any of the men do wrong, you shall keep them on bread and water according to the Marine Law."

On the following day when the *Mercury* cast anchor at Lahaina Roads, Smith was ordered to enter one of the boats which was to go ashore. He refused to do so until Captain Gray agreed to let men of Smith's own choosing get into the boat with him.

That day the master of the *Mercury*, his third mate, two boatsteerers, the cooper, and two seamen appeared before John Stetson, United States Vice Commercial Agent at Lahaina. Captain Gray said that his life was not safe nor was it consistent with the interest of the voyage for Smith to remain on board the *Mercury*. He accused Smith of using mutinous language and threatening a captain and his officers. Third Mate Henry S. Comstock witnessed his affidavit, and members of the crew took oaths in substantiation of his statements.[16]

Stetson was new at the business of being a vice commercial agent and had never before had a case like this one. He decided, however, in favor of Captain Gray and had Smith imprisoned in the fort at Lahaina. Later Stetson was chided by his senior at Honolulu for having discharged Smith as a mutineer rather than as "a troublesome fellow."[17]

Available records do not tell what eventually happened to Joseph Smith. Perhaps he was still at Lahaina in late April and early May 1843 during the twenty or so days that Melville spent there. At any rate, the story of Smith's impertinence and daring is one that Melville might well have heard, for it was of a sort to be told frequently by whalemen in port.[18]

IV

The documentary evidence veritably speaks for itself. It seems clear that Melville found the essential ingredients for human conflict in "The Town-Ho's Story" in the foregoing *Nassau*, *Vineyard*, and *Mercury* incidents. Both Melville's Steelkilt and the actual Luther Fox hailed from New York, the one a native of Buffalo, the other from Rensselaerville. Each of them was ordered by the mate of his ship to perform a humiliating task, a punishment hardly commensurate with the behavior which provoked it. Both men reacted with violence. Although he never, like Fox, used a mincing knife as a weapon, Steelkilt referred menacingly to "those mincing knives down in the fore-

16. The foregoing narrative is based on the affidavit of Captain Simmons L. Gray, made before John Stetson, March 22, 1843, in "Miscellaneous Letters," Honolulu, FR-NA.

17. William Hooper to John Stetson, in "Miscellaneous Letters, Honolulu, FR-NA.

18. I should remind the reader that a modern researcher can acquire the details of these stories with much greater particularity than Melville could have remembered them when he was composing *Moby-Dick*.

castle," and he planned to arm himself and his followers with such knives and run amuck from bowsprit to taffrail.

Benjamin Brown of the *Vineyard* suffered humiliation, too, and he found his vengeance, striking the second mate of his ship with just such a weapon as Steelkilt planned to use against Mate Radney. There are further parallels to "The Town-Ho's Story" in the *Vineyard* revolt of 1842. The rebellious whalemen of the Edgartown ship were locked in the forecastle by their indignant master. To Captain Crocker's command that they return to duty, a few of the less hardy of the disaffected complied, but others continued day after day to shout scornful refusal. Steelkilt, like Joseph Smith of the *Mercury*, defied his captain and threatened violence or even murder if anyone were flogged.

Here the basic similarities of fact and fiction end. "The Town-Ho's Story" differs considerably in its details from any of its factual counterparts. Melville motivates, in terms of a well-established personal antagonism, the violence of his story. (There is nothing in the record to indicate a prolonged dislike between Luther Fox and Jepitha Jenney or between Benjamin Brown and the mate of the *Vineyard*.) Melville has Steelkilt build a plan of private revenge against Mate Radney. (Fox's murder of Mr. Jenney seems to have been the result of an impulse of anger rather than deliberate planning, and Benjamin Brown's revenge was achieved by group, not private planning.) And Melville has an external agency kill Radney. In the climax of "The Town-Ho's Story," Radney dramatically meets his death, not from a blow with a blubber knife or a slung shot, but in the grinding jaws of the White Whale—in what seemed to be, Melville wrote, "a certain wondrous, inverted visitation of one of those so called judgments of God which at times are said to overtake some men."

Marjorie Dew

Black-Hearted Melville:
"Geniality" Reconsidered

In prose and in poetry, in early works and in later ones, Melville lacerates his persistently genial men. With few exceptions, he dissects them for the laughter, or the contempt, or even the pity of discerning readers. That is not to say he does not permit moments of congeniality, pipes, wines and suppers, to all his characters. Moods vary; not even Ahab lives in unalleviated blackness, although he tries. One wants to discover an un-ironic geniality in Melville's characters, admirable and admired men, genial men in the sense of cheerful, kind, pleasant, even joyful, or "affable, comradely, even fraternal."[1] Melville rejects geniality, however, always and ultimately when geniality is his subject (or his narrator's or his mediator's). Melville was not, I think, willing to pay the price for geniality, and especially not for the spurious sort, as Merton M. Sealts concludes he *was*.

I contend that geniality to Melville is nearly always of the spurious sort. And, in later writing, he is increasingly savage with his genial men. One must deal with the priest Derwent of *Clarel*, finally, that late and most fully developed genial character.[2] Because *Clarel, a*

1. Melville's sense of the word according to Merton M. Sealts, Jr., "Melville's 'Geniality,' " *Essays in American and English Literature Presented to Bruce Robert McElderry, Jr.*, ed. Max F. Schulz, with William D. Templeman and Charles Metzger (Athens: Ohio University Press, 1967), p. 5.
2. Professor Sealts points out only that the word "genial" occurs "nearly a dozen times" in *Clarel*, "notably in the characterization of Rolfe." But certainly Rolfe is not *the* genial man in *Clarel* (nor does Professor Sealts imply that he is).

Poem and Pilgrimage in the Holy Land (1876) represents Melville's final full statement of geniality closest in time to the debated *Billy Budd*, that book and the early, presaging *Mardi* (1849), with its many images of felicity, will be considered most fully here.

In Melville, only those "pledged" to geniality remain genial for more than a moment in time, and they are not sympathetic characters. For example, the "palmy" King Abrazza of Bonovona "vows he'll have no cares" (*Mardi*, 179.589).[3] Stubb "takes oaths that he has always been jolly!" (*Moby-Dick*, Ch. 114). Amasa Delano of "Benito Cereno" has determinedly been of "singularly undistrustful good nature"; and the attorney-narrator of "Bartleby" "from his youth upward" has plighted himself to "the easiest way of life." Finally, Derwent is "pledged to hold the palmy time / Of hope" (*Clarel*, II.xxi. 110-111).[4]

The best philosophy is a "free and easy sort of genial, desperado philosophy," says the narrator of "The Hyena" chapter of *Moby-Dick* (Ch. 49): in desperate times the whole universe is to be taken as a practical joke, at one's own expense, to be sure, and the joker is God; but one laughs to live. In such moods death and destruction, all round, can be viewed with contentment and tranquility. Ishmael says that "nothing dispirits, and nothing seems worth while disputing." As God elbows him in the side, Melville-Ishmael laughs genially. "There are certain queer times and occasions in this strange mixed affair we call life" when one must laugh like a hyena. But the perceptive man knows the laughter for what it is, a momentary stay against chaos—stoic laughter. In the lost whale boat with Ishmael and Starbuck, Queequeg has sat holding up his lamp, his "imbecile candle, in the heart of that almighty forlornness," the uncaring ocean-universe, expecting of course not to be found. But trust is no less for all

3. *Mardi and A Voyage Thither*, ed. Harrison Hayford, Hershel Parker and G. Thomas Tanselle (Evanston, Ill.: Northwestern University Press, 1970), ch. 179, p. 589. Subsequent citations will follow this form.

4. *Clarel: A Poem and Pilgrimage in the Holy Land*, ed. Walter Bezanson (New York: Hendricks House, 1960), Part II, section xxi, lines 110-111. Subsequent citations will follow this form.

that. It takes something like the "perils of whaling" to raise a what-the-hell confidence and easy-heartedness, says Ishmael.

In *Mardi*, Taji had found the need for congeniality, cast away in a whale boat with Jarl. In certain moods Taji deplores Jarl's taciturnity. The Norseman, "dear, dumb Jarl," is never a genial man. And "upon occasion" does not everyone need a "sprightly fellow, with a rattle-box head," "a lively loon, one of your giggling, gamesome oafs whose mouth is a grin?" (*Mardi*, 11.35). With his rhetorical questions Taji-Melville defines the genial man: has not Providence given us such men to fill up vacuums "in intervals of social stagnation relieving the tedium of existing?" Do they not keep up our good opinions of our-selves? If they drive to suicide "ungenial and irascible souls"—"let us not be hard upon them . . . but let them live on for the good they may do." No Melvillean hero, however, is such a man; the genial souls are "them," not "us." In more characteristic moods, Taji's needs are not for genial company. But Jarl, is he not forever intent upon minding his own business, a project so many neglect? And does he not stick to it without any likelihood of "winding up [his] moody af-fairs, and striking a balance sheet?" Taji is admiring; but he reverses himself again: "at times . . . I longed for something enlivening; a burst of words; human vivacity of one kind or other." He enjoys no such conviviality with Jarl. Then, his thoughts turning upon themselves, Taji sums up Jarl: "He had little but honesty in him (having which, by the way, he may be thought full to the brim)" (11.36). Finally comes the calm, when the reader infers that, had Jarl been a genial man, Taji *would* have been brought to suicide. They are becalmed four days and four nights.

> [On the third day] sullenly we laid ourselves down; turned our backs to each other; and were impatient of the slightest casual touch of our persons. What sort of expression my own counte-nance wore, I know not; but I hated to look at Jarl's. When I did it was a glare, not a glance. I became more taciturn than he. I can not tell what it was that came over me, but I wished I was alone. I felt that so long as the calm lasted, we were without help; that neither could assist the other; and above all, that for

one, the water would hold out longer than for two. I felt no re-
morse, not the slightest, for these thoughts. It was instinct. Like
a desperado giving up the ghost, I desired to gasp by myself.
From being cast away with a brother, good God deliver me!
(16.49-50)

Genial Media, king of the island Odo, with whom Taji next throws
in his lot, is not at all the "lively loon" either. Unquestionably,
though, through most of the book Media is of genuinely genial cast.
Early on, bringing forth the wines and the pipes and setting the suppers provide Taji's party with good-feeling aplenty. But each occasion is incremental; men grow. Consider several scenes of existential
accretion. In one, "demi-gods" Media and Taji drink with twenty and
five kings summoned by hedonist, satyriacist (but effeminate and
palely lethean) King Donjalolo, whose orgies are "relapses of desperate gayety invariably following his failures in efforts to amend his life"
(84.254). "Drink, Taji. . . . Drink deep; drink long. . . . Drink forever," raves the "jovial" Donjalolo. And "grape-glad": "ha, ha, ha,
roared forth the five-and-twenty kings . . . holding both hands to their
girdles, and baying out their laughter from abysses" (84.257-258).
Wine is, ironically, a "glorious agrarian." Unwavering democrat, Melville means "leveler" here. The sentimentality and good-heartedness
induced by the grape make all men brothers. Wine, raising spirits
and dulling senses bring "all hearts on a level . . . even those of kings,"
who, rascals on the throne, are vinous good fellows in their cups, their
"frankness exceeding that of base-born men." "If ever Taji joins a
club, be it a Beef-Steak Club of Kings!" (84.259).

But, Taji reckons, "Who may sing for aye? Down I come, and light
upon the old and prosy plain" (84.256). The drinking is a "frenzied
lyric to the soul." As Taji, Media, and their fellows leave him, Donjalolo, temples throbbing, acknowledges wine his captor: "Oh,
treacherous, treacherous friend! . . . Yet for such as me, oh wine, thou
art e'en a prop, though it pierce the side; for man must lean" (85.
261). Of winy geniality Taji learns from Donjalolo.

As Ishmael fades in and out of *Moby-Dick*, so Taji of *Mardi*. In
a later scene of quaffing, of striking celestial and worldly cups and
heads together, Media, who, like Taji and Babbalanja, is another Mel-

ville avatar, learns of wine's inefficacy and good-fellowship's limitations. Try as he will to be merrily drunk, pretend as he does, Media's counterfeit king-in-his-cups act is finally not well done, as old Mohi points out. Crying "Be we sociable," even King Media cannot flood the lees often enough to genialize Babbalanja's philosophy. "A wise man can not be made drunk"; and, possessed by his devil Azageddi, the philosopher contends that what men *say* they trust, their actions belie. "When I die, the universe will perish with me," says Babbalanja. Considering that pronouncement, Mohi hopes Babbalanja comes of a long-lived race: "I have many little things to accomplish yet" (151. 489). And Media *pretends* drunkenness. Only so far can wine settle doubts, political, social, or religious.

Like all mortals, Babbalanja's levity is only occasional. Media has advised him, to little avail, to meditate as much as he wants, "but say little aloud, unless in a merry and mythical way," a precept followed by all "gay, sensible Mardians, who desire to live and be merry" (120. 369). (That precept an ironic Melville will hold to in his esoteric writing of the 1850's, in "Benito Cereno," for instance.)

And so, desiring to live and be merry, the undeveloped but developing Media and Taji turn to the conviviality of the pipe. As they smoke, Yoomy lyricizes:

> For care is all stuff,
> Puffed off in a puff:—
> Puff! Puff!

" 'Ay, puff away,' crie[s] Babbalanja, 'puff, puff, so we are born and so die.' " And, forgetting he is a demi-god, and thus immortal, Media gives directions: "Subjects, hear,—when I die, lay this spear on my right, and this pipe on my left, its colors at half mast; so shall I be ambidexter, and sleep between eloquent symbols" (121.377). Thus a cheery chapter beginning with Media's glad cry—"Ho! Mortals! mortals! . . . Go we to bury our dead? . . . Cheer up, heirs of immortality! . . . Bring forth our pipes: we'll smoke off this cloud"—ends with hints of death. "Vee-Vee! haul down my flag." With or without companions, a wise man can no more puff away than drink away his doubts. Media sleeps as he will die, alone.

Near the end of their journey through Mardi, the wanderers meet the most genial and the most "sinister, hollow, heartless" (181.603) of all Mardians, King Abrazza, who regales them at supper. Although neither the word "genial" nor its cognates, except for "uncongenial," appear in the Abrazza chapters (179 to 182), some thirty near-synonyms do, all ironic, a concentration of geniality rivaling that of *The Confidence-Man* (1857): *amiable, kind, placid, jocund, pleasant, carefree, social, bright, glad, calm, content, snug, ship-shape, jolly, free*, for example, plus an essay on bachelors "sitting out life in the chimney corner, cozy and warm as the dog." Abrazza's "genial" neutrality in the face of his own inhumanity leaves no doubt about Melville's ironic attitude here toward joviality, sociality, and contentment. Snugness and amiability are wicked in this marred world. Melville condemns the easy-heartedness of Abrazza, who says, "What one can not see through, one must needs look over." Conversely, Lombardo-Melville's joy as a writer was "jolly woe"—"amazing jolly!" (And if, when Melville speaks of Lombardo's *Kostanza* he speaks of his own *Mardi*, as almost surely he does, then, as I shall attempt to show later, there is ample biographical evidence for black-heartedness.)

The supper episode ends ironically. Abrazza has been insulted by both Babbalanja and Media. And yet, says the wide-eyed narrator at the chapter's end: "Now, thus, for the nonce, with good cheer, we close. And after many fine dinners and banquets—through light and through shade; through mirth, sorrow, and all . . . meet is it that all should be regaled with a supper" (181.609). Small surprise to the reader that, by morning, King Abrazza has lost his conviviality; he sends "frigid word" that he will be indisposed and that of course the travelers will want to be sailing on.

From a genial spring-morning beginning to autumn-evening and finally to a "midnight of despair" ending, metaphors gradually change in *Mardi* from light to dark. Early there are brightly terrible images associated, for example, with fish (akin to the crowing cock Beneventano of "Cock-a-Doodle-Doo!") who swim under the sun desperately gay, "ten times merrier than ever" after the raid of the voracious sword-fish, singing in their "fishy glee": "Let him drop, that fellow

that halts. . . . Let him drown, if he can not keep pace" (48.150).
If there is "something under the surface," swordfish to devour or
seaweed to entangle and drown, swim away from any unfortunate
fellow—evade, be deluded, be anesthetized. Somewhat later come
sweetly, ribald images of the young poet, Yoomy, who wistfully sings
of the Muse's charms (discomfiting old Mohi):

> Her bosom! Two buds half blown, they tell;
> A little valley between perfuming;
> That rove away,
> Deserting the day,—
> The day of her eyes illuming;—
> That roves away, o'er slope and fell,
> Till a soft, soft meadow becomes the dell. (156.510)

Oops! "Thy muse's drapery is becoming disordered," exclaims the
wriggling Mohi: "no more!"

"Then no more it shall be. . . . But you have lost a glorious sequel,"
says Yoomy serenely. Perhaps the sequel would not have been glorious; Melville avoids sequels.[5] But no matter. What is evident is the
temporary efficacy of evasion and humor's detachment. As metaphors
darken in *Mardi*, Yoomy later sings of "perished warblings." (Min-
strels are not, he says, so "gay of soul" as the world believes). And as
he sings, the gamesome bowsman joins him, merrily, and "too glee-
fully reaching forward," falls into the black lagoon. "Blindly," says
the narrator, "we groped back," reversing canoes, as "deep Night
dived deeper down in the sea." The only sound was the wind's moan,
as he "with a song in his mouth," was lost to the sea. The last image
is of "hoarse night-winds" and black lagoon as Taji, seizing the helm,
darts alone to the "realm of shades." The only "light" is of "ghost-
white" breakers and his white wake in which three murderous spec-
ters (retribution) pursue him.

5. Cf. Yoomy's refusal to provide an ending to a later song about Yillah (one
that he wrote, he says, much earlier), a song full of light—sun, flare, flash,
rays, shining; and consider the tentativeness of the endings of most of Melville's books, which seem to promise sequels, *The Confidence-Man* being only
the most obvious.

To be sure, laughter images abound in *Mardi*: the hurricane laughs, the blue skies smile, hyenas and jackals yell, Rabelais roars, and the sun laughs over all. But, except in Serenia, neither in exterior nature nor in men does a laugh express joy or a smile betoken serenity or acceptance. Perhaps contradictory to my thesis is that Taji and Media are the only characters to choose annihilation. The philosopher, the poet, and the antiquarian find a haven in Serenia, and surely each of these is, to some extent, a Melville avatar. They have accepted as Melville *wishes* he could accept, the great Oro (God) and his sovereign son, Alma (Christ)—a kind of simple, unorthodox, unchurchlike Christianity. And, as the good old man of Serenia has told the wanderers, here on Serenia we laugh: "And when we laugh, [it is] with human joy at human things,—*then* do we most sound great Oro's praise" (187.628). Melville, however, flies on like Taji, pursued and possessed, "over an endless sea" with "eternity in his eye" (195.654).

The restriction of space allows me barely to indicate facts of Melville's life during 1847 and 1848 and some conjecture about them that might help explain his black-heartedness during the writing of *Mardi*. Several extenuating forces operated on Melville at this time: the limitations and the demands of Herman's and Elizabeth's residence in the newly set up family commune in New York; the financial pressures;[6] Herman's lack of time for seeking out intellectual conversation to externalize his "chartless" voyages through the mind; his anxiety that *Mardi* be a popular book; and the apparent restiveness of his young bride, homesick, purposeless, even listless, "no more than a satellite revolving around Herman."[7] All this and more is supported by Melville's letters of that period and by Jay Leyda's *Log*.[8]

6. Jay Leyda, *The Melville Log: A Documentary Life of Herman Melville* (New York: Harcourt Brace, 1951), I, 263; II, 615. Young, proud, forced to borrow money from his father-in-law, Judge Shaw, Melville could not have borrowed with equanimity.

7. Leon Howard, *Herman Melville: A Biography* (Berkeley: University of California Press, 1951), pp. 109-121.

8. *The Letters of Herman Melville*, ed. Merrell Davis and William Gilman (New Haven: Yale University Press, 1960), pp. 65-72; Leyda, *The Melville Log*, I, 263-278.

Melville, a new husband, would have been disturbed by his bride's unhappiness and by their understandable communication lag. Nothing in Elizabeth's letters indicates that she might have enjoyed philosophical discussion. Each day, after having written for hours, he chatted with her for an hour or so and sometimes read to her from the day's writing.[9] Internal evidence in *Mardi* implies a loss of conjugal felicity during this first year of marriage. Newton Arvin says that the Yillah-Hautia allegory "is strongly suggestive of the passage from an idealized courtship to the fleshly realities of marriage."[10] "The dream begins to fade" in Chapter 51: "As our intimacy grew closer," the narrator tells us, "in the sight of Yillah, I perceived myself thus dwarfing down to a mortal. . . . And now, at intervals, she was sad" (51. 158-159). Henry A. Murray expresses that bleakness when, from his evidence, he postulates Melville's saying: "I made it clear enough (in *Mardi* and in *Pierre*), for any knowledgeable reader, that passionate love for my gentle, innocent little wife dissolved within the first month of marriage."[11]

Herman Melville's compulsion was to reveal those things he knows to be in every man—sadness, great sadness, and yes, delight, too, and love and compassion—and to reveal them as no one had done before in American literature. But Melville's greatest compulsion is to "out" with the sadness, to speak fully what his nineteenth century readers refused to hear spoken. He is that man Hawthorne saw in 1856 and described in his journal: "He has persisted ever since I knew him, and probably long before—in wandering to and fro over these deserts." Reading Melville confirms Hawthorne's feeling that Melville "will never rest until he gets hold of a definite belief"; and I am convinced that Melville never, after his twenty-fifth year, rested. He never believed, and he never became "comfortable in his unbelief." To him long-enduring comfort seemed out of reach for all men. One of life's greatest pitfalls seemed the temptation to settle for easy jocular-

9. Leyda, *The Melville Log*, I, 266-267, a letter from Elizabeth Melville to her step-mother, 23 December 1847.

10. *Herman Melville* (New York: William Sloane, 1950), p. 96.

11. "Bartleby and I," *Bartleby, the Scrivener: A Symposium*, ed. Howard Vincent (Kent, Ohio: Kent State University Press, 1966), p. 18.

ity, for the joy of good company, good food, good drink, and easy belief, even in the face of ignorance, insensitivity, deception, and man's
fall from grace. Truly such an author, able to speak from his depths
to some few men of his time and to many men of the later century,
possessed the "high and noble nature" Hawthorne recognized as making him "better worth immortality than the rest of us."[12]

The treacherously genial men in the writings of the 1850's, benign
bachelors like Bartleby's snug employer and Benito Cereno's "com-
forter," Amasa Delano, of whom I've written elsewhere,[13] I will pass
over lightly here. "Christian" and loving, they are like Derwent in
Clarel; in avoiding confrontations they somehow do harm to their
fellow beings.

In "The Paradise of Bachelors" (1855), from its beginning where
the mediating narrator finds the genial templars of his time reveling
in their "genialness," no longer in "glorious battle" but content "to
fall in banquet [rather] than in war," bachelors are "hypocrites and
rakes," although always decorous. "The Templar is to-day a Lawyer,"
like Bartleby's employer, allowing "nothing loud, nothing unman-
nerly, nothing turbulent" in his life. A passage there consciously parallels an "untrueness" spoken by a bachelor in *Moby-Dick* (Chapter
115): "Pain! Trouble! . . . No such thing.—Pass the sherry, sir."[14]
The parallel passage in *Moby-Dick* occurs when the *Pequod* meets
the homeward bound whaler the *Bachelor*. Ahab: "Hast seen the
White Whale?" "No; only heard of him; but don't believe in him at
all," says the good-humored *Bachelor* commander, hoisting glass and
bottle. "Come aboard!" With wit and precision, Professor Bezanson
describes the condition of the bachelors of Melville's 1855 story—
they have fallen "from grace to graciousness" and their portrait is
"relevant to Derwent."[15]

12. Leyda, *The Melville Log*, II, 529.

13. "The Attorney and the Scrivener," *Bartleby, the Scrivener*, ed. Howard
Vincent, pp. 94-103; "*Benito Cereno*: Melville's Vision and Revision of the
Source," *A Benito Cereno Handbook*, ed. Seymour Gross (Belmont, Cali-
fornia: Wadsworth, 1965), pp. 178-184.

14. "The Paradise of Bachelors," *Selected Writings of Herman Melville*
(New York: Random House, 1952), pp. 193-194.

15. *Clarel*, II, i, 30n.

In creating Derwent in his narrative poem, *Clarel*, Melville demonstrates his pervasive and ongoing disapproval of easy geniality as a way of life. The "skimmers," Walter Bezanson points out, that is, the men of determined cheer, the avoiders of doubt and dark, are chiefly five in the long poem: the Man of Lesbos "stands midway between the young pleasure-seekers (the Cypriote, Glaucon, the Lyonese) and the meliorist Derwent."[16] On the long pilgrimage through Israel's drear desert, Derwent, seldom sidetracked, merrily darts in and out of most of the cantos (II.i.-IV.xxxii). Melville characterizes him in a Chaucerian key line: "Lightly he in the saddle sat" (II.viii.44). Derwent is never dejected (II.i.18) (never finds more of woe than of joy in this life and is, therefore, presumably "untrue" or "undeveloped").[17] Although he is middle-aged, the priest Derwent remains immature (II.i.17-56). He is a faddist in that he follows the "last adopted style" (in Melville's America, bright optimism) and refrains as far as possible, says the narrator, from thinking about such men as sorrowful Solomon and Job.

Rhetorically, Melville underlines Derwent's easy cheer when, for instance, Rolfe's bleak words characterize the tormented Mortmain, and Derwent replies in a lilting, lulling voice. Mortmain, says Rolfe:

> No cloister sought. He, under ban
> Of strange repentance and last dearth,
> Roved the gray places of the earth.
> And what seemed most his heart to wring
> Was some unrenderable thing . . . (II.iv.129-133).

When Rolfe's sad tale of the wrecked Mortmain trails off, Derwent trills soothingly:

> . . . One fine day
> I saw at sea, by bit of deck—
> Weedy—adrift from far away—
> The dolphin in his gambol light

16. "The Characters: A Critical Index," *Clarel*, p. 539. Bezanson valuably describes and interprets the poem's characters in an alphabetized appendix, pp. 529-549.
17. *Moby-Dick*, Ch. 96: "That mortal man who hath more of joy than sorrow in him, that mortal man cannot be true—not true, or undeveloped."

Through showery spray, arch into sight:
He flung a rainbow o'er that wreck. (II.iv.151-156).

In dialogue with solemn Rolfe, Derwent always tinkles a light reply. At one point he shrinks from the saintly, demented Nehemiah's
Sisyphean task, moving stones to change the stony world (II.x.195-
209), and for solace turns to Mortmain, who questions where a man
can turn in this sharkish world (II.x.218-227). But—

Hardly that chimed with Derwent's bell:
Him too he left. (II.x.228-229)

Derwent is, indeed, as Mortmain has characterized him—"Brass, / A
sounding brass and tinkling cymbal!" (II.iii.103-104)

The Pilgrims, Rolfe (close to Melville-man as Clarel is to Melville-
boy),[18] Clarel, and Vine, confront the desert, that stony infinite from
which man sprang and on which "he falls back at need," the desert
they cross like bleaker Chaucerian pilgrims. Rolfe meditates upon
the half-crazed Mortmain, upon his wild plunge into the desert night
in spite of roving bandits, insisting that there is nothing to fear "if
God but be." Who is so secure, Rolfe wonders, that he might not,
like Mortmain,

[Burst] through every code and ward
Of civilization, masque and fraud,

18. Benzanson describes Rolfe, the "central figure among Clarel's companions," as a self-projection of Melville, intro., viii. He sees Rolfe as "a thoroughly sociable being." "Biographical data on the *younger* Melville generally parallels this image, and there is evidence that *even* in his middle years he still
occasionally flowered in social interchange. We have seen, however, in the two
decades after *Moby-Dick* his descent into self . . .: the sense of defeat, willful
isolation, unmanageable moods, fear of death, and anxiety over his own physical and mental health. Rolfe knows of such things, but he does not exhibit
them" (emphasis added). But Bezanson says that Rolfe "leans toward the
monomaniacs (Mortmain, Agath, and Ungar) and away from the varied as-
surances of a Nehemiah, a Margoth, or a Derwent. . . . In the long run Rolfe
is sure . . . that the tragic view is the only tenable one" ("The Characters,"
p. 545). Bezanson's conclusion is not inconsistent with mine or that of Richard
Chase (*Herman Melville: A Critical Study* [New York: Macmillan, 1949]),
who says that one danger to the tragic-hero quester is the denial of Man's Fall,
represented by a Derwent or a Captain Delano.

[Take] the wild plunge. Who so secure [?]
. . .
What any fellow-creature bides,
May hap to any.

Derwent changes the subject, as usual turning to nature to reinforce geniality:

Yon moon in pearl-cloud: look, her face
Peers like a bride's from webs of lace. (II.xvi.126-127)

Interrupted, rebuked, discouraged, Rolfe says:

My earnestness myself decry;
But as heaven made me, so am I.

Vine (Hawthorne) breaks his habitual silence to return to the subject: "You spake of Mortmain." Here Rolfe begins where he left off:

. . . In gusts of lonely pain
Beating upon the naked brain—

It is too much for the genial Derwent:

"God help him, ay, poor realist!"
So Derwent, and that theme dismissed. (II.xvi.141-142)

Just so does Derwent dismiss all themes ungenial.

In "The Priest and Rolfe" canto (II.xxi), as in other parts of the poem, Rolfe, like Babbalanja (and Melville), regrets his earnestness, but he is "as heaven made me." He will keep turning away from darkness, striving for joy; but only

Where's no annoy
I too perchance can take a joy—
Yet scarce in solitude of thought:
Together cymbals need be brought
Ere mirth is made. (II.xxi.46-50)

Dedicated to geniality, Derwent tries persuasion: "There's many a merry man." And "by all means" find your laughter in good company, he says:

> . . . O ye frolic shapes:
> Thou dancing Faun, thou Faun with Grapes!
> What think ye of them? tell us, pray. (II.xxi.53-55)

Rolfe, dryly: "Fine mellow marbles." And when Derwent persists, Rolfe babbles almost like Babbalanja possessed. God is dead, the "genial" God: "Whither hast fled, thou deity/ So genial?" There was once Unfallen Man. No more. His "last and best avatar" brought a dream to earth. "But it died." And men have made earth worse for Christ's coming, have perverted His love. Nothing remains but "dubious dregs." Be honest and admit, he says to Derwent. And then, exactly like Babbalanja babbling:

> Cut off, cut off! Canst feel elate
> While all the depths of being moan [?]

But, still like Babbalanja (who often repents of *his* earnestness and "revives" momentarily), Rolfe pulls himself up short:

> ". . . Nay,"
> Starting abrupt, "this earnest way
> I hate. Let doubt alone; best skim
> Not dive." (II.xxi.102-105)

Derwent exults; liking Rolfe he

> . . . fain would make his knell a chime—
> Being pledged to hold the palmy time
> Of hope—at least, not to admit
> That serious check might come to it. (II.xxi.109-112)

Wise Vine "sidelong regarded him":

> As 'twere in envy of his gift
> For light disposings: so to skim! (II.xxi.119-120)

And Clarel, listening, learning, vows no longer to shrink from Rolfe's painful thoughts.

> [He] surmised the expression's drift,
> Thereby anew was led to sift
> Good Derwent's mind. (II.xxi.121-123)

In the following canto, Clarel is further repelled by Derwent's coziness, seeing his faith "an over-easy glove" (II.xxii.147).

But, yes, Rolfe would *prefer* conviviality to dark "solitude of thought." Moods change, however. Rolfe, again and again, enjoying Derwent's good temper, drops seriousness. Let us drink:

> . . . Yon mule
> With pannier: Come, in stream we'll cool
> The wine ere quaffing. . . . (II.xxvi.191-193)

And (herein lies some support for Professor Sealts' theory of balanced darkness and light) Clarel wonders: Can Rolfe be true?—how reconcile his "forks of esoteric fire,/ With common-place of laxer mien?" Can Derwent be honest?—can one be "half-way"? Can all have partial truth?

> . . . But if in vain
> One tries to comprehend a man,
> How think to sound God's deeper heart!
> (II.xxxii.117-119)

At the saintly Nehemiah's death, Derwent, "his genial spirits" jarred, holds back, "pained, dispirited—/ Was dumb." Here he momentarily is too troubled for unfeeling cheer; here he cannot easily evade (II. xxxix.41-53).

In Parts Three and Four, the seeking Clarel and the "sociable" Rolfe, however, find it increasingly difficult to accept Derwent's quick evasions of life's pain. Similarly, Derwent grows impatient of conversations that depress his high spirits. The two Melville counterparts, Clarel and Rolfe, scorn the priest with increasing intensity, empathize with the dark Mortmain, Agath, and Ungar. Mortmain, overwhelmingly monomaniac, haunts Derwent. Derwent retaliates with cheerful retorts, lighthearted advice. As priest, he answers Mortmain's plea for priestly solace for "a sinking heart . . . when every hope lies flat": "Well, *if* such one—nay!" No solace, he tells Mortmain, *if* such a person exists; Derwent does not, however, believe that hopelessness can come to "that last degree."

> Assume it though: to him I'd say—
> "The less in hand the more in store,

> Dear friend." . . .
> Closing with cheerful Paul in lore
> Of text—*Rejoice ye evermore.* (III.vi.43-49)

At this easy answer, Mortmain droops as if a hump has fallen on him. Rolfe comes to his support. Derwent goes on, "afresh, well pleased, and leisurely," to answer Rolfe's question: "But the Jew? . . . How with the Jew?" Ah, says Derwent, they're happy now; the genial Greeks and Hillel have come, and "ay, [Christ] comes: the lilies blow!"

> I do avow He still doth seem
> Pontiff of optimists supreme! (III.vi.137-138)

Derwent "trying to cheerfulize Christ's moan" (III.vi.143) astonishes the Swede and Rolfe. Derwent saddens for a moment; but the habit of cheer, joy, hope, total trust in God and in men prevails. All's well.

Melville's America, as he wrote *Clarel* (and earlier, of course), was ideologically disturbed by religious and secular controversy generated by Darwinists, zoologists, botanists, geologists, astronomers; religious apologists, scientific materialists, utopians; and such individualists as Emersonian transcendentalists, hedonists, and nihilists. *Clarel* contains them all. Melville's travelers—taken out of history, out of Western culture to wander deserts in the East—follow all paths, "to and fro," "hither and thither." Closely related to Melville, the chief questers, Clarel and Rolfe, are central. They are sometimes genial and sometimes joyless, depending on circumstance and mood. Clarel differs only in that he remains the spectator-student, the early Melville, passing through innocence toward experience. His passage, the pilgrimage, is his rite of initiation as the whaling voyage is Ishmael's. The older Rolfe, experienced, congenial when he can manage it, has learned many of life's hard lessons but, like the older Melville, continues to learn more, with a fair amount of control. A third main character is Vine, self-protectingly enigmatic, silent, quiveringly perceptive and sensitive—Hawthorne.

The fourth of the central biographical characters, the norm, is the Druze, Djalea. Seemingly having looked into the fire not too long but long enough, he will not be defeated by the world nor by the universe. He prevails. His heart, his head, his hand are always ready; he is the guide and the guard of the pilgrimage and the expedition to the pelvis of the world. As Bezanson has termed him, he is "one of the ideals which Melville set himself in his middle years."[19] But Djalea is not genial; he is an isolate of "temperate poise," "moderate mind" (IV. xvi.7-8); considerate, prudent, passionate but sedate (IV.xxix.25-30), he stays apart—

> In patient self-control high-bred,
> . . . his arms at hand for use. (II.ix.43-46)

He keeps to himself and to his purpose. When the holy Nehemiah insists that men are merciful to men, Djalea "bowed, but nothing said." Like other Orientals, says the narrator, he pays homage to "men demented," like Nehemiah. And, just then, as Djalea bowed, over the ridge can be seen prowlers, their spear points "like dorsal fins of sharks" (II.ix.72,80,98).

If there is anything approaching balance between sorrow and joy, between solitariness and conviviality in Melville's outlook here, then it must lie in the characterization of Clarel, Rolfe, Vine, and Djalea. Of these, only Rolfe approaches geniality, and he only with a singular determination, attaining cheer infrequently, evanescently.

Another group, the joyless men, includes the holy Nehemiah (compare the Old Man of Serenia in *Mardi*), the outcast Celio, the Job-like Agath, the self-destructive unbeliever Mortmain, and the darkly religious Ungar. For these dark-hearted men, Melville has great liking, great compassion.

Men of joy, besides Derwent, include the careless youths: the Cypriote (like Yoomy of *Mardi*), Glaucon, the Smyrniote, and the Lyonese (like Donjalolo). The Arnaut, the Lesbian, and the misanthropic but jolly Mexican complete the group of "genialists." None is admired by his author. Derwent is sometimes (seldom) an exception as I have shown. But, finally, Clarel perceives that Derwent's "happiness seems paganish" (iv.xxvii.36). The poem's epilogue is as unconvincing as the epilogue of the Book of Job. Its consolation denies the

19. "The Characters," *Clarel*, p. 537.

whole of the poem. "Keep thy heart, . . . Clarel," says the mediating narrator. But Clarel's last words have been: "Never comes to me/ A message from beneath the stone" (IV.xxxiv.52-53). He has found his Ruth (ruth?) dead, and he is "alone, for all had left him so."

Space does not allow dealing substantially with *Billy Budd* here.[20] A final apotheosis-Melville, the perceptive Vere chooses to act out a part in the charade of an ordered human society, but, in so doing, he goes so far against the instincts of his human heart that he lives in hell. Melville, by the evidence of *Billy Budd*, had not at the time of this last composition "accepted" the world as a place to feel at home in.

20. See my "The Prudent Captain Vere," *American Transcendental Quarterly*, 7 (Summer, 1970), 81-85; reprinted in *Studies in the Minor and Later Works of Melville*, ed. Raymona Hull (Hartford: Transcendental Books, 1970).

Part Four

Text:
Orca, Part Two

Paul Metcalf

Orca

Part Two

Scammon discovered the lagoon in the Baja,
Scammon Lagoon,
where the California gray
foregathered for foreplay
and mating.

Scammon waited.

the harpooned whale lob-tailed, thrashing,

breached, leapt clear,
crashed back,
        snowing foam on the whaleboat;

writhed, sounded and
somersaulted, breaching behind,
              "he went clean rampageous loony"
lashed the waters into a pink foam,

crashed the whale-boat into
the ship's side,
        or breached at night, the sky blue-black, the
water falling from his flanks in green columns, the foam phos-
phoric,
        and wrapping himself in whale lines, splintering the boat,
rolled over and over and over

197

"Then the bow actually touched the animal. The Lieutenant leaned forward and thrust in his lance quite near the eye, about a yard from the spot where the harpoon was fixed. After the thrust he began to shake the weapon, twisting it with a rotating movement, as if he meant to enlarge the wound. Red blood appeared on the brown body . . ."

"He thrust in the second lance, farther back this time, and stirred it in the wound. The blood came gushing as if from a tap."

"They also launce the whales near their privy-parts, if they can come at it; for if they are run in there, it doth pain them very much; nay, even when they are almost dead, if you run in your launce thereabout, it causes the whole body to tremble."

. . . the whale enters his flurry, turning on his side, swimming in a circle, slowly, at first, then faster, and faster,

                           head above

water, jaws clashing;

                 there is a hissing sound, then a fountain

of steam, first pink, then red,

                    floods of blood spurting from the

blowhole:

        enters his flowering, blows his blood . . .

                        "Some whales

blow blood to the very last," says Scammon, "and these dash the men in the long-boats most filthily, and dye the sloops red . . ."

   ". . . the very sea is tinged red . . ."

                    There is a low

groan, growing to an echoing bellow—the lungs last heavings through bloodclogged tubes

               the bloodfountain dies to a few

drops, a gurgle . . .

            "Those whales that are mortally wounded

heat themselves, that they reek while they are alive, and the birds sit on them, and eat on them . . ."

". . . long and white maggots grow in their flesh,
they are flat,
like unto worms that breed in men's bellies,
and they smell worse
than ever I smelt anything in my life.
The longer the whale lies dead in the water,
the higher he doth swim above it;
some swim a foot high above the water,
others to their middle,
and then they do burst easily,
and give a very great report.
They begin immediately to stink,
and this encreases hourly,
and their flesh boils and ferments
like unto beer or ale,
and holes break in their bellies,
and their guts come out."

————————

"My dear Wife and Mother,
     Saturday of the 7 I got a whale that made 80 bbls after great del of
trouble. He was one of the knowing kind. I strok him to my boat.
The whale went off a little way and then came for the boat. He stov
the boat very bad so he seam to be contented with that and lade clost
to me as the other to boats was off about 4 miles from me in chase of
other whales. Finly the Mate came to me. I told him never mind me
but get the whale if he cold. He went and struck him and the whale
stove his boat wost than mine, and heart 3 of the men. He nock the
Mate as hie as our house. Well I began to think that fish was not for
me. Her war to stoven boats and 12 men swimming in the sea and the
Ship and other boat long way off."

     . . . rogue whale,
     biting whale, fighting
     whale . . .

. . . Payta Tom, New
Zealand Tom, Timor
Jack . . .

". . . I observed a very large spermaceti whale, as well as I could judge about eighty-five feet in length; he broke water about twenty rods off our weather-bow, and was lying quietly, with his head in a direction for the ship. He spouted two or three times, and then disappeared. In less than two or three seconds he came up again, about the length of the ship off, and made directly for us, at the rate of about three knots. The ship was then going with about the same velocity. His appearance and attitude gave us at first no alarm; but while I stood watching his movements, and observing him but a ship's length off, coming down for us with great celerity, I involuntarily ordered the boy at the helm to put it hard up; intending to sheer off and avoid him. The words were scarcely out of my mouth, before he came down upon us with full speed, and struck the ship with his head, just forward of the forechains; he gave us such an appalling and tremendous jar, as nearly threw us all on our faces. The ship brought up as suddenly and violently as if she had struck a rock, and trembled for a few seconds like a leaf. We looked at each other with perfect amazement, deprived almost of the power of speech. Many minutes elapsed before we were able to realize the dreadful accident; during which time he passed under the ship, grazing her keel as he went along, came up alongside of her to leeward, and lay on the top of the water (apparently stunned with the violence of the blow) for the space of a minute; he then suddenly started off, in a direction to leeward. After a few moments reflection, and recovering, in some measure, from the sudden consternation that had seized us, I of course concluded that he had stove a hole in the ship, and that it would be necessary to set the pumps going. Accordingly they were rigged, but had not been in operation more than one minute before I perceived the head of the ship to be gradually settling down in the water; I then ordered the signal to be set for the other boats, which, scarcely had I despatched, before I again discovered the whale, apparently in convulsions, on the top of the water, about one hundred rods to leeward. He was enveloped in the foam of the sea, that his continual and violent thrashing about in the water had created around him, and I could distinctly see him smite his jaws together, as if distracted with rage and fury. He remained a short time in this situation, and then started off with great velocity, across the bows of the ship, to windward. By this time the ship had settled down a considerable distance in the water, and I gave her up for lost. I, however, ordered the pumps to be kept constantly going, and endeavoured to collect my thoughts for the occasion. I turned to the boats, two of which we then had with the ship, with an intention of clearing them away, and getting all things ready to embark in them, if there should be no other resource left; and while my attention was thus engaged for a moment, I was aroused with the cry of a man at the hatchway, "Here he is—he is making for us again." I turned around, and saw him about one hundred rods directly ahead of us, coming down apparently with twice his ordinary speed, and to me at that moment, it appeared with tenfold fury and vengeance in his aspect. The surf flew in all directions about him, and his course towards us was marked by a white foam of a rod in width, which he made with the continual violent thrashing of his tail; his head was about half out of water, and in that way he came upon, and again struck the ship. I was in hopes when I descried him making for us, that by a dexterous movement of putting the ship away immediately, I should be able to cross the line of his approach, before he could get up to us, and thus avoid what I knew, if he should strike us again, would prove our inevitable destruction. I bawled out to the helmsman, "Hard up!" but she had not fallen off more than a point, before we took the second shock. I should judge the speed of the ship to have been at this time about three knots, and that of the whale about six. He struck her to windward, directly under the cathead, and completely stove in her bows. He passed under the ship again, went off to leeward, and we saw no more of him."

"I began to reflect upon the accident, and endeavoured to realize by what unaccountable destiny or design (which I could not at first determine) this sudden and most deadly attack had been made upon us: by an animal, too, never before suspected of premeditated violence, and proverbial for its insensibility and inoffensiveness. Every fact seemed to warrant me in concluding that it was anything but chance which directed his operations; he made two several attacks upon the ship, at a short interval between them, both of which, according to their direction, were calculated to do us the most injury, by being made ahead, and thereby combining the speed of the two objects for the shock; to effect which, the exact manoeuvres which he made were necessary. His aspect was most horrible, and such as indicated resentment and fury. He came directly from the shoal which we had just before entered, and in which we had struck three of his companions, as if fired with revenge for their sufferings."

Did a whale grasp a loose sailor? . . . sound with him? . . . and, breaching, spit him out?

Is the spermaceti gorge too narrow to admit a man? . . . but a 10′ shark? . . . a 35′ squid?

Was a man swallowed, and recovered, later, dead? . . . the chest crushed? . . . the skin eaten, by gastrin and pepsin?

Was another swallowed, and lived, 24 hours, in a whale's stomach? . . . and when released, on the deck of *Star of the East*, was he revived with a bucket of sea water? . . . was he then a raving lunatic, two weeks, before recovering his senses?

And another, did he remember a great darkness? . . . slipping along a smooth passage? . . . his hands touching a slimy substance . . . and was the heat terrible—not scorching or stifling, but seeming to draw out his vitality through opened pores? . . . and were face, neck and hands changed to parchment—bleached by cetacean juices?

The killer whale, *orca*, with truly falcate flukes, and an enormous dorsal fin—so slender that the tip turns over like the ear of a dog—

—the killer, though barrel-shaped and bulky, is capable of bursts of immense speed. Knife-edged, recurved, interlocking teeth line his jaws, and he swims in ranks five abreast, heads and tails turned downward, backs elevated all in one instant, with great sabre-formed fins

a shoal of killers, spouting as one, renders the ocean a plain of waving geysers.

Orca eats anything: seal, porpoise, penguin, salmon, a finback or humpback whale,

and will, in packs, attack the great blue:

the school dividing, some attack the flukes, biting in,
                                                    and the
great blue, fighting, hurls killers aloft,
                                    descending flukes and
orcas resounding on the seasurface,

while others of the school swim to the head, nipping the muzzle,

but all, all killers, working from the sea side, driving the
quarry to the shallows.

When the tail is nailed to the seasurface, more killers plunge
for the head, the eyes, the lips, while others leap over the
blowhole, to smother,
                            while one, lashing flukes, thrusts his snout
between the lips, pushing against the horny strips, reaching for
the tongue.

the great blue writhes, lunges clear of the foam, the clinging
killers borne aloft,

and the one orca reaches the tender great blue tongue, bites in,
begins to eat;

       the great jaw relaxes, goes slack, the tongue lolls
out,
    while others churn for the eyes, the belly, the teats,
                    working
always in an arc, pushing the blue to the shallows, to the surf,
to the beach

one killer sinks his teeth in the genitals,

and the great blue whale, insane with pain, brain flooded with fouled
blood—thrashes, lunges inland—free, now, of *orca*—rolls in the
breakers, comes to stillness in the backwash, the ripple, near the dry
sand

---

with an arm-length razor-knife the man stabs the sperm whale's
head—the tough, spongy cells, the whitehorse—and lets the spermaceti flow

    clean and clear,
    clear as water,
    barrel after barrel,
    bubbling

    a film forms on the surface, and the stuff
slows to a trickle, cools to ropy strings, icicles, frozen waxy
waterfalls

    spermaceti, sperm

---

    the blubber-room men are bathed in oil,
    slipping with the ship's roll,
    rolling in blubber . . .

. . . on the butchering deck, piled high with meat, bones, steaming
intestines, the men work . . . in the clatter of the bone saws, steam of

the boilers, stench of guts . . . cables and winches, meat hooks, whale
oil and bone dust

    and spread their legs,
    the wasted meat lumps,
    bone hunks,
    thickets of gut,
    sliding away

and after—a warm bath, a balanced meal, a show in the on-board
movie theatre,

and every year, in the long antarctic summer, some will lose their
reason.

———————

out comes the fatty tongue, two tons, soft as a cushion
                                    seven
strong men, or perhaps a steam winch, drag the half-ton head
across the oily deck
        and the blood pours, and pours, and pours
                                       the
intestine, relaxed, measures twelve hundred feet
                          the balls weigh
a hundred pounds, each
        and the prick is a thin, hard rope—like a
bull's, a ram's, a goat's, or a stag's—ten feet long and a foot
thick

or, from inside the cunt, out come the ovaries, sixty-five pounds,
each
    and within, there may be an ovum—visible to a man's naked
eye

———————

the beached great blue,
alone and helpless,
heaves,
struggling to breathe

but the water-molded muscles,
the soft, spongy bones,
will not lift the
unsupported carcass,
for ventilation,

and the whale
begins to suffocate,

heaving in convulsions,
bellowing.

the scientist,
alerted to the prize,
stands aside,
appalled,

as the writhing dwindles,
the bellows soften to a wail—

until the man can stand it no longer,
puts a bullet through the great blue brain,
gets him out of his suffering,

and then goes about his work

Part Five

"Indirect Egoists":
Some Versions of the Modern

Emily Dickinson
and the Right of Way to Tripoli

All science, Emerson says, has only one aim, "to find a theory of nature." His view is no holdover from his spiritual forbears: an accepted "theory" of nature was a central part of their response to 1,500
years of Christian symbology. Emerson's statement specifically points
to the dilemma of Emily Dickinson, who also attempts to define a
"theory" of nature, and without the comfort of a system of symbols
sanctioned by Christian tradition. Anne Bradstreet's reading of nature
is predetermined by the structure of faith she brings to the act of
viewing. The heavens declare the glory of God. In one sense, they
exist in and for themselves; in a more meaningful way, however, external nature is an emblem, an intimation, of the central reality of God,
knowledge of Whom may begin but does not terminate in the senses.
Bradstreet exists within the comforting dual vision of the religious:
external reality is in part created in the act of perception, but created
from the *a priori* assumptions of the pietistic. Meaning is always, at
once, everywhere present. Thus, in her emblematic reading of the light
of the sun in "Contemplations," its "glory," "shining rays," and
"splendid throne erect" shadow forth "that Majesty" of the glorious
Creator. The sun has an independent existence; its significance,
though, is determined by its place in a universe completely under the
control of the Almighty.

Nature also has objective reality for Edward Taylor; but only rarely, and then incidentally, does that reality impinge upon his *Meditations*. His mind is so steeped in biblical cadences and images that his
meditative psalms exist in a world in which external phenomena have

been—prior to the act of poetry—transmuted into the world of the Hebrews. There are a few rocks and rivers and seas in his poetry; but his rock is Horeb's in the Sinai, not the granite outcroppings of the Berkshires; his rivers are not the Connecticut or Westfield branch, but the Jordan; his sea is the Red Sea, not the Atlantic; and his wilderness is not studded with firs and covered with snow but filled with wandering tribes and heavenly manna. The intermediate step which exists in Bradstreet, and which is the poet's "leap of faith" beyond the physical and temporal to the spiritual and eternal, has already been taken by Taylor before the poetic act begins. There are a few bogs and meadows and fog-pits, of course, but, in general, nature is of little consequence. In Taylor's poetry the external world has been largely internalized; however much his blottings may jar and jumble, it is not because Taylor wrestles with the ambiguity of physical reality:

> I cannot see, nor Will thy Will aright,
>   Nor see to waile my Woe, my loss and hew
> Nor all the Shine in all the Sun can light
>   My Candle, nor its Heate my Heart renew.[1]

In relation to Jonathan Edwards, however, the central ambiguity of the Calvinistic response to physical phenomena defines his view of the natural world. On the one hand, the natural universe has been degraded by the Fall; nature is physical, carnal, an emblem of mortality and death. For the regenerate, however, the "new sense" which accompanies the reception of God's grace provides a means for coming to know nature beyond its material and temporal significance. For the regenerate, "the works of God are but a kind of voice or language of God to instruct intelligent beings in things pertaining to Himself."[2] Hence the meaning of the physical exists not so much in its emblematic quality (which is also available to the unregenerate), though it exists there as *exemplus*. True meaning exists in the re-

1. *The Poems of Edward Taylor*, ed. Donald E. Stanford (New Haven: Yale University Press, 1960), p. 28.
2. *Images or Shadows of Divine Things*, ed. Perry Miller (New Haven: Yale University Press, 1948), p. 61.

deemed mind's act of perceiving; for the truly re-born, natural phenomena are intimations of the immortal mind. "Before" his conversion, Edwards notes, "I used to be uncommonly terrified with thunder
. . . but now, on the contrary, it rejoiced me. I felt God . . . and used to
take opportunity . . . to fix myself in order to view the clouds, and see
the lightnings play, and hear the majestic and awful voice of God's
thunder."[3] For the converted, then, the ambiguity of the world of
nature is partially resolved; the "whole outward creation . . . is so
made as to represent spiritual things."[4] This is not to say that God's
Works have supplanted his Word; natural phenomena are still "shadows" of the ultimate reality of the Godhead; but, Edwards insists,
if "we look on these shadows of divine things as the voice of God . . .
it will abundantly tend to confirm the Scriptures."[5] In the mind of
God's Elect, then, nature and Christ—the "light of the world"—are
fused in the unified and redeemed consciousness.

Hence, Bradstreet, Taylor, Edwards—and the Puritans generally—
exist within a definable and defined universe. Although individualis-
tic readings of natural phenomena occur, the central meaning of
events and objects is essentially—and arbitrarily—established by the
absolute nature of the Godhead. Their response to the world around
them exists within an orthodox structure of belief; God's actions cannot be excluded from His "Handywork not made by hands." Such
absolute certainty does not characterize the Puritan's internal geography. He can always be certain that natural events take place within
the limits of God's Providence; but the significance of these events
is not always comprehensible—the finite mind, however regenerate,
is still finite. The Puritan consciousness, then, is suspended between
personal doubt and eschatological certitude. Doubt is not despair, for
doubt is the state of the religious: life in this world is incomplete and
unfulfilled. God assuredly speaks to them through the images of nature, although His voice might only be dimly heard. Within this in-

3. "Personal Narrative," *Jonathan Edwards: Representative Selections*, ed.
Clarence H. Faust and Thomas H. Johnson (New York: Hill and Wang,
1962), p. 61.

4. *Images*, p. 63.

5. *Images*, pp. 69-70.

complete state there exists an absolute assurance that meaning in even its limited aspects is attainable. Uncertainty, where it exists, is not attributable to the Creator; it is the consequence of the imperfect perception of the finite. Although the Puritans' soul-searching is genuine, the expressions of their fallen state and insufficiencies sincere, these are imbedded within a construct where even the sparrow does not fall without God's knowledge. Final revelation lies in the future; in the interim, however, there is no doubt that such revelation is possible, that it will come about, however unclear its present meaning may be.

On July 1, 1750, Edwards preached his farewell sermon in Northampton; one hundred years later, almost to the day, the Honorable Mr. Edward Dickinson had "hopefully been converted" in the spring revival in Amherst. Much had changed in that century, but Squire Dickinson's Emily was to spend much of her life preoccupied with the matters which concerned Edwards and his predecessors. And her search would seem all the more intense, for the "images and shadows of divine things" of her spiritual ancestors were not so readily available to her. Nature no longer existed in partnership with the divine Word; nature was now tested in relation to the poetic word, to the words of a poet loosed from the moorings that gave hope in adversity and release in suffering to an Anne Bradstreet.

The young Emily Dickinson was not as conscious of the ambiguities of nature as she was later to become; her response to it was traditional, if slightly arch, and her awareness of nature's benign countenance was gilded with the sense of a simple, devout faith:

> Summer—Sister—Seraph!
> Let us go with thee!
>
> In the name of the Bee—
> And of the Butterfly—
> And of the Breeze—Amen![6]

Her increasing puzzlement, not to say disillusionment, with the ambiguity of natural phenomena was temporarily assuaged by a flirta-

---

6. *The Poems of Emily Dickinson*, ed. Thomas H. Johnson (Cambridge: Harvard University Press, 1955), I, 21. Poem numbers refer to Johnson's numbering in this edition, and will be entered in the text.

tion with what appears to be her understanding of Emerson's transcendental gospel, the good news indeed to the waif of Amherst. Speaking, as Emerson suggests the poet should, with the "intellect inebriated with Nectar," the "Debauchee of Dew" does in fact "reel" through apparently endless summer days. There is about many of the poems of the late 1850's an exuberance and aura of flight and soaring distinctly Emersonian in cast. At the same time, however, and increasingly central, is the debilitating effect on the poet of the vastness and apparent impersonality of the Creator, especially as revealed in images of nature:

> Grand go the Years—in the Crescent—above them—
> Worlds scoop their Arcs—
> And Firmaments—row—
> Diadems—drop—and Doges—surrender—
> Soundless as dots—on a Disc of Snow—(J216)

For Emily Dickinson, at any rate, the limitless space in which the Divine Force moves—no threat in Taylor's cosmos—becomes more and more oppressive. The difference is "internal," of course, for that is—in a universe which is no longer a decipherable sign of a spiritual reality—"Where the Meanings, are—" (J258).

It is not that she does not wish to hear "his voice as the sound of many waters," but that the images of nature which so clearly spoke to the Puritan sensibility do not speak to her. He moves, "Soundless as dots—on a Disc of Snow"; even the "Landscape listens" and "Shadows—hold their breath." But there is no utterance. The same universe which for the Puritans hieroglyphically broadcasted the images of the Divine becomes increasingly difficult for Emily Dickinson to fathom because the impulse of meaning has shifted. For her there is no structure of faith to provide the framework in which meaning is established. Whatever may be His character, He was—to the Puritans—the I AM, the central sound of the universe. But when ultimate reality has shifted from the Alpha and Omega to the finite point of the poet's "internal differences," the voices babble, if voices there are. In her assertion of identity—the voice of the Amherst poet saying I am—the symbolic drama that played for the Puritans in the images and shadows of external nature has been internalized, and the Puritans' corresponding internal new sense does not exist for her. Meaning must therefore be derived from the poet's consciousness imposing upon the object the poet's reality, not the reality attainable when the heavens declare—unequivocally—the glory of God.

For the Psalmist—and his spiritual descendants—"Day unto day uttereth speech, and night unto night sheweth knowledge. /There is no speech nor language where their voice is not heard." Such a revelation, in relation to the scriptural Word, was, of course, imperfect. But the world of nature as the hieroglyph of the world of Spirit was relatively intelligible: the heavens' declaration went "out through all the earth, and their words to the end of the world." Nature dimly veiled the Divine; the Puritan poet responded, domesticating the Infinite in natural images and defining the unity that exists between the Creator and His created. The heavens also spoke to Emily Dickinson; too often, however, the sound is unintelligible, ringing ceaselessly, ambiguously:

> As all the Heavens were a Bell,
> And Being, but an Ear,
> And I, and Silence, some strange Race
> Wrecked, solitary, here—(J280)

And so the exuberance associated with the elevation of the self, the transcendental surge, ceased to provide the foundation upon which meaning could be erected.[7] "This World" may not be "Conclusion," as she asserts in a poem written early in 1862:

> A Species stands beyond—
> Invisible, as Music—
> But positive, as Sound—

Yet the confidence of that assertion leads directly to the admission that "Narcotics cannot still the Tooth/That nibbles at the soul—" (J501). Hence, a number of poems during these years focus upon images of sound that hover at the edge of consciousness.

7. Cf. in this connection Albert J. Gelpi's comment that Dickinson's "Peculiar burden was to be a Romantic poet with a Calvinist's sense of things" (*Emily Dickinson: The Mind of the Poet* [Cambridge: Harvard University Press, 1966], p. 91).

Unfortunately, however, it is not the unequivocal voice of God that speaks through the medium of nature. For between the object and its Creator the poet's self has intruded, and the vagaries of consciousness introduce an ambiguity that did not exist for Jonathan Edwards' regenerate soul. The traces of the Divine in external objects could be perceived in the mind of Edwards' regenerate man because a new sense had been created in the consciousness. For that mind, "To hear an Oriole sing" was both a "common thing" and a "divine." In Emily Dickinson's case, however, the determination of the significance of the bird's song rests squarely upon the divided self:

> The Fashion of the Ear
> Attireth that it hear
> In Dun, or fair—(J526)

The problem is not that meaning does not exist and therefore the mind is trapped in absurdity, but that nature's ambiguity results from the defining quality of the poetic act: "Nature is what we know—/Yet have no art to say—" (J668). And the saying is an act of faith which seems to be beyond the poet's grasp.

The dilemma is described in one of the best of her poems, "A Light exists in Spring" (J812). The poem rests on the assumption that nature's revelatory message may be abstracted, although the light, so the poet says, exists beyond a rational determination of significance: "That Science cannot overtake / But Human Nature feels." And the scene is pregnant with meaning; the light "waits upon the Lawn, / It shows the furthest Tree / Upon the furthest Slope. . . ." Whatever expectations she has had of perceiving the sign of the spirit in the physical object are frustrated: the light "almost speaks"—almost, but not quite. Instead it is absorbed in the vastness and abstractions of space:

> Then as Horizons step
> Or Noons report away
> Without the Formula of sound
> It passes and we stay—
>
> A quality of loss
> Affecting our Content

> As Trade had suddenly encroached
> Upon a Sacrament.

Nature has not changed in any significant or observable way. The light will still exist in spring; it will still wait upon the lawn. But the state of mind attuned to transcribing meaning from the Creator's physical manuscript, and reenforced by the tenets of faith, no longer exists.

Nature, in one sense, is a sacrament: an outward, physical sign of a higher, spiritual reality. But any sacramental act involves a mind capable of moving beyond the *signe* to the *signatum*. Further, coming to know what the object signifies is an act of faith, of totality. The light passes "Without the Formula of sound" because the splintered self does not possess the order of a tradition which distinguishes between the thing and the thing signified. Without that order, the consciousness can only be reduced to ambiguity—or silence. The "Consciousness that is aware / Of Neighbors and the Sun" is also aware that "itself alone / Is traversing the interval / Experience. . ." (J822). For Taylor, the light is the emblem of revelation; it shadows forth the reality of the Divine; it exists in the sun/son construct of Christian symbology. For Emily Dickinson, as she shifts the metaphor, the "Light" may be "His Action," yet He remains "A Force illegible" (J820).

" 'Tis a dangerous moment," she once wrote, "for anyone when the meaning goes out of things and life stands straight—and punctual —and yet no signal comes."[8] Prepared to respond to the signal she expected from natural phenomena, she is condemned to the snares of definition when no signal comes, or when what does come is so garbled that without a structure of faith, the "dangerous" moments are imminent. To be unable to define through the poetic act the reality with which she must deal, however, leads not to the conclusion that all is void, that meaning itself is a will-of-the-wisp of the finite mind. The light of Spring still exists:

8. "Prose Fragments," *The Letters of Emily Dickinson*, ed. Thomas H. Johnson and Theodora Ward (Cambridge: Harvard University Press, 1958), III, 919.

I cannot meet the Spring unmoved—
I feel the old desire—

. . .

A Competition in my sense
With something hid in Her. (J1051)

The ultimate "language and lesson" of nature, in Edwards' phrase, is to emphasize the finite limits of the human mind. Yet Dickinson's view of the vastness of the cosmos does not result in despair or a lasting sense of defeat. Quite the contrary. The ungraspable in nature—in contrast to the definable in man—is amplified. When man begins to think that he comprehends the actions of nature, when he "shuts" his observation, then nature extends her "practices" to "Necromancy and the Trades / Remote to understand" (J1170). The actual and central meaning of the world of nature is in fact that she cannot be unriddled, that nature's show cannot be reduced to the finite scale:

A little Madness in the Spring
Is wholesome even for the King,
But God be with the Clown—
Who ponders this tremendous scene—
This whole Experiment of Green—
As if it were his own! (J1333)

At this point Emily Dickinson is closest to the Puritan sensibility. Man's true response to nature is not to create God in man's own images, to reduce the "bronze and blaze" to human symbols. Such attempts lead only—and inevitably, in her view—to the "mystery" which still "pervades a well!" (J1400). Those patterns in nature—the grass standing next to the well and the sedge standing next to the sea—that sense of Emersonian correspondence, may point to an aspect of Spirit: "Related somehow they may be." But the relationship, suggestive as it is of the Creator's total design, remains a mystery still. For to try to define the world of natural mystery in human, or poetic, terms, is to attempt to reduce the unknowable to the frame of quantification. And to find that Nature or God or Being is graspable and

definable, is to shrink the vision of the universe to a simple reflection
of the self. That, to Emily Dickinson, would be despair. For that
would diminish her quest for meaning to the vagaries of the ego. Her
universe, however, cannot be reduced:

> But nature is a stranger yet;
> The ones that cite her most
> Have never passed her haunted house,
> Nor simplified her ghost.
>
> To pity those that know her not
> Is helped by the regret
> That those who know her, know her less
> The nearer her they get.

Hence, in her own way, Emily Dickinson adopts the voice and
stance of her Puritan predecessors. To the mystery which resides in
nature her response is the Christian sense of "what is awe to me."
The attachment to the world of beauty, as Edwards notes, is why most
men are so reluctant to shut out the life of the senses:

> . . . the reason why almost all men . . . love life, [is] because they
> cannot bear to lose sight of such a beautiful and lovely world.
> The ideas, that every moment whilst we live have a beauty that
> we take not distinct notice of, brings a pleasure, that, when we
> come to the trial, we had rather live in much pain and misery
> than lose.[9]

However temporal and transitory our presence in the world, however frustrating and incomplete our attempts to decipher its meaning,
natural beauty draws the finite mind to it in awe and wonder: "Estranged from Beauty—none can be— / For Beauty is Infinity—"
(J1474). And in its magnetic pull upon human sensibilities, however
indirectly, the poetic act that images natural phenomena is an act of
praise, a response to that which is larger than the self and which, unlike the self, need not be defined in order to live with. It is the eternal presence, the I Am, in the robes of the senses. And even if the mystery continues to mystify, if the mind cannot encircle and grasp it,

9. *Images*, p. 137.

> Better an ignis fatuus
> Than no illume at all—(J1551)

In this stance rests the basis of Emily Dickinson's humility, her acceptance of that which she cannot know. The active pursuit—the breathless waiting for sounds that do not come—is supplanted by the passive identification of self with external mystery, of an inner peace and active acceptance of the reality of color and motion, the "Route of Evanescence":

> The pedigree of Honey
> Does not concern the Bee,
> Nor lineage of Ecstasy
> Delay the Butterfly
> On spangled journeys to the peak
> Of some perceiveless thing—
> The right of way to Tripoli
> A more essential thing. (J1627)

Vivian Pemberton

Hart Crane's Heritage

*I Arthur E. Crane being of sound mind and memory . . . do
publish this my will and testament as justly as I can to dis-
tribute my interest in the world to those who succeed me.*

. . .

*And I leave to them the poetry of Burns, Shakespeare,
Wordsworth, Whittier, Riley, and others . . . .*
Arthur E. Crane, "Diary" (27 November 1923)

What heritage thou'st signalled to our hands!
Hart Crane, "Cape Hatteras"

More than three decades after the death of her gifted nephew,
Elizabeth Crane Madden ("Auntie Bess") gripped the arms of her
wingback chair, leaned forward and remarked indignantly to me, "If
Harold had *not* been artistic, *then* he would have been a mutant."[1]
But Harold Hart Crane's family legacy—of aesthetic taste, talent, and
temperament—has virtually been overlooked or neglected, and yet it
was an inheritance which influenced Crane from his earliest years.

1. Pertinent details have been supplied by family members through interviews,
correspondence, and telephone conversations from March 1966 to May 1974.
I acknowledge my gratitude for their cordial and invaluable assistance. In
identifying them, the following abbreviations have been used: ECM: Elizabeth
Crane Madden; BCM: Betty Crane Madden; BCH: Bessie Crane Hise, the
former Mrs. C. A. (Clarence) Crane, Hart's step-mother; HHH: Helen Hart
Hurlbert; FCL: Fredrica Crane Lewis; HCS: Helen Crane Sherwood; LW:

221

Of the numerous writers who have dealt with Crane or his poetry, his latest biographer, John Unterecker comes closest to revealing that heritage when he devotes two short paragraphs to the Crane family's cultural interests. He mentions Crane's father, Clarence's, "flair for drama" and "fondness for literature and literary games," his Uncle Fred's large book of his own poems, and the family's interest in literature and music.[2]

Hart Crane was a member of a family in which the propensity for music, literature, dramatics, and art was unusually strong, a sensitive family composed of artists in various fields. That this knowledge has been overlooked is attributed by the Cranes, in part, to the influence of the poet's mother on several important early books. Unterecker reveals that Grace Hart Crane, after her son's death, devoted her remaining years to the "perpetuating of his memory, working with Sam Loveman and Waldo Frank [selecting Frank as editor herself] on the manuscripts that went into *The Collected Poems*" published in 1933, and later with Philip Horton who published the first biography in 1937, as well as "gathering together copies of Hart's letters, assembling the nucleus of the material Brom Weber eventually drew on for the volume of letters he edited in 1952" (*V*, pp. 17, 765). Unfortunately, these early books were produced without the benefit of significant recent materials which present a more equitable view of Crane's father and his family.

Throughout his book, Unterecker attempts to alter the former image of the poet's father, summarized by Jethro Robinson who wrote, "Tradition, mistakenly arising from the first biography, makes Clarence Crane [also called C.A.] the poet's legendary devil: passionately commercial, sneeringly hostile towards art." Robinson continues, "That book, as it happens, was written under his mother's thumb and had to contend with her half remorseful desire to settle with her dead, including both the poet, who . . . severed himself from her . . .

Loring Williams. Permission to quote from Frederic Crane's poetry was granted by his daughter, Fredrica Crane Lewis.

2. *Voyager: A Life of Hart Crane* (New York: Farrar, Straus and Giroux, 1969), p. 6. Hereafter *V*, with page numbers parenthetically inserted in the text.

and the father whom she had divorced years before."[3] This tradition can also be attributed to Waldo Frank's "Introduction" to *The Collected Poems of Hart Crane*, in which the poet's father is described as "a man of turbulent and twisted power, tough-fibred and wholly loyal to the gods of Commerce . . . sincerely outraged by the jest of fortune which had given him a poet for a son,"[4] a description which appears in even the most recent edition of *The Bridge*.[5]

In his introduction to *The Letters of Hart Crane, 1916-1932*, Brom Weber says "Crane was in great part responsible for creating the time-worn legend of a hard-hearted father. During the years from 1917 to 1925, less so afterward, he wrote or informed countless friends of the brutality of his father's behavior, his lack of kindness and generosity, and the suffering this caused." He also writes, "However, it seems unwarranted . . . to perpetuate Crane's own misconceptions of the older man's values and attitudes in relation to his son prior to 1927. From an early date, the elder Crane was apparently profoundly interested in his son's choice of a literary career and anxious to have him prepare for it."[6] Although Unterecker, like Weber, tries to modify the view of Clarence Crane, his summary of the family's aesthetic interest is inadequate, and he wholly neglects its probable influence on Crane's intellectual and literary development.

I

Unfortunately, the details of Crane's early years are uncertain, for "documents are scarce and memories—sixty years faded—untrustworthy" (V, p. 4). Because many clues to Crane's artistic development lie in his relationship with his father's family during those formative years, they are doubly important. But additional problems have obscured our view of the family's effect on Crane. One difficulty is

---

3. "The Hart Crane Collection," *Columbia Library Columns*, 4 (February 1955), 4-5.

4. (New York: Liveright, 1933), p. xii.

5. (New York: Liveright, 1970), p. xxii.

6. (New York: Hermitage House, 1952), pp. x-xi. Hereafter *Letters*, with page numbers parenthetically inserted in the essay.

that Crane's three biographers—Horton, Weber,[7] and Unterecker—
have discounted family influence, knowing the poet lived in Garrettsville near his Crane relatives for only a short time. According to Unterecker, "Of Garrettsville, all that remains in Crane's works is a reference to an aria Grace sang" there (*V*, p. 19). In fact, however,
there is a good deal more of the town than this in his poetry. One section of *The Bridge* ("The Dance") depicts area sites: the mill-race,
not more than five hundred yards from Crane's birthplace and his
grandfather Crane's house next door; the portage climb (Portage
County received its name from the portages in the region); the village
itself; and the hills and waterfall nearby. Because they were unaware
of the considerable time the youth spent with his father's family, these
places were all mistakenly located by Horton (pp. 21-22) and Unterecker (p. 21) in the Warren, Ohio, area. It is true that Clarence
Crane moved his family from Garrettsville to Warren "before the
boy's legs were long enough to permit independent sorties into the
village,"[8] but to their former home the boy returned, and often.
Throughout Hart's most impressionable years of childhood and early
adolescence, *The Garrettsville Journal*[9] carried accounts of his repeated
and extended visits to the homes of his Crane relatives there. And
Betty Madden, the poet's cousin, recalls the summer of 1915 when
Arthur Crane, several years after both he and Clarence had moved
their families to Cleveland, rented his old Garrettsville home and
gathered his family there for a long vacation, commemorating the
event with a family photograph which included the sixteen-year-old
Hart among his Crane relatives.[10]

7. Philip Horton, *Hart Crane: The Life of an American Poet* (New York:
Norton, 1937), and Brom Weber, *Hart Crane: A Biographical and Critical
Study* (New York: Bodley Press, 1948). Hereafter Weber, *Hart Crane*, with
page numbers parenthetically inserted in the text.

8. Horton, *Hart Crane*, pp. 14-15.

9. *The Garrettsville Journal*, from 1900-1920. Hereafter *GJ*, with dates parenthetically indicated.

10. Crane family photograph and "Poem to Alice" first appeared in Vivian
Pemberton, "Some Family Figures behind Hart Crane" (Kent State University MA thesis, 1966), pp. 6, 69 respectively. Both later appeared in Alfred

Most of the Cranes could have been characterized as was Elton Crane, the poet's great uncle, in his obituary as "possessed of a keen appreciation of the best in art and literature" (*GJ*, 10 December 1914). All seem to have been active, publicly and privately, in cultural activities. From Crane's earliest years, family musicales and operas with the "Crane Jubilee Singers," dramatics, charades, and poetry readings were the social events the young boy participated in or witnessed, often in the music room of his grandparents' home. One such event probably furnished the memory he recorded of having heard his mother sing Mignon's song:

> 'Connais tu le pays. . . ?'
> Your mother sang that in a stuffy parlour
> One summer day in a little town
> Where you had started to grow.[11]

In that "little town," also, the youngster climbed to the loft of his grandparents' big carriage house where his grandmother and Auntie Bess had their studio. Both were talented amateurs, painting in the romantic and impressionistic traditions. Here under their guidance he painted his own first canvases and developed an interest in art (ECM) that Unterecker considers "completely serious," describing one of Crane's early works as an "impressionistic oil painting which he produced in his ninth year [that] reveals a fine sense of muted color" (*V*, p. 25). Art was indeed a family tradition. Unterecker writes that Clarence Crane had a "sometimes profitable side-line, the large-scale reproduction of famous oil paintings" (*V*, p. 14). This is true; what is also true, however, is that Crane reproduced works from his own sizable collection *only*, lithographing perhaps a dozen of the close to forty works he possessed (BCH). That the poet was not enthusiastic about his father's acquisitions can be deduced from a letter he wrote a friend in which he described Canary Cottage, his father's imposing

Cahen and David French, "Newly Discovered Poem by Hart Crane," *American Weave*, 30 (December 1966), 1-3.

11. *The Complete Poems and Selected Letters and Prose of Hart Crane*, Brom Weber, ed. (New York: Liveright, 1966), pp. 145-146. Hereafter *Complete Poems*, with page numbers parenthetically inserted in my essay.

combination home and inn, saying, "you'd be delighted by some of the early American pieces though rather embarrassed by some of the paintings" (*V*, p. 641). Although Maxfield Parrish is frequently mentioned in connection with the poet's father, who packaged his famous "Victoria" and "Mary Garden" chocolates in containers decorated with Parrish prints, Clarence Crane's collection was by no means limited to that painter. Most of the works—seascapes, landscapes, and genre paintings—reflect his romantic taste and were created by European and American artists of the last three centuries, many of whose works are found in such distinguished museums as the Corcoran Gallery and the Louvre.[12] While Hart was abashed at his father's taste in paintings, his initial interest in art was stimulated and nurtured by his aunt and grandmother in Garrettsville. Unterecker, emphasizing the importance of Hart's response to art, writes, "from the time he was sixteen until the end of his life, painters were among his closest friends; in discussions with them he evolved many of his most valuable aesthetic theories" (*V*, p. 25). Carl Schmitt, an artist friend from Warren whose patron had been Hart's aunt, Zell Hart Deming, was the first professional painter to influence the poet. He summarizes his teachings with, "Of course you know I taught him aesthetic balance; both Horton and Unterecker wrote about that, but I also taught him to

12. For example: Hans Dahl and Fritz Thaulow: State Museum of Norway; Percy Moran: Plymouth Museum; Franklin DeHaven: The Brooklyn Museum of Art and The National Gallery; Ridgeway Knight: Brooklyn Institute Museum; Emil Marcke: Metropolitan Museum of Art; Robert Levrac Tournieres: Musee des Beaux-Arts, Louvre, Versailles and Nantes Museums; Montague Dawson: British National Maritime Museum; and the collection of H.M. Queen Elizabeth II and H.R.H. the Duke of Edinburgh. Crane shared his father's enthusiasm for two clipper-ship paintings by Dawson, a contemporary marine artist (BCH). This affection for the paintings can probably be explained by the poet's own fondness for such vessels: *The Thermopylae, Leander, Flying Cloud, Black Prince, Rainbow, Nimbus, Taeping* and *Ariel* were all used by Crane in the "Cutty Sark" section of *The Bridge*. He wrote Otto Kahn, "It was a pleasure to use historical names for these lovely ghosts. Music still haunts their names long after the wind has left their sails" (*Letters*, p. 308). In his personal copy of the Black Sun edition of *The Bridge*, he affixed a label of his favorite Scotch whiskey, Cutty Sark, and inscribed it for a bookplate.

be more *aware*. When he came first to me in New York, he relied too much on rhythm and rhyme. I taught him to be more unconscious of himself, to let his unconscious work for him,"[13] a statement that approximates a paraphrase of Emerson's "Merlin," a poem with which Crane was probably familiar.

II

In Garrettsville, also, the youth became acquainted with the Crane family's literary interests. Most were avid readers who exchanged books as gifts on special occasions.[14] Those gift books usually reflected the family's romantic tastes. R. W. B. Lewis is in agreement with numerous scholars in describing Hart Crane as an inheritor of the romantic tradition in literature, the "Romantic tradition in both its English and its American phases."[15] This is not surprising because the writers he identifies as contributing to Crane's romanticism include the family favorites: Shelley, Coleridge, Blake, Wordsworth, Keats, Poe, Bryant, Longfellow, Whitman, Emerson, and others.

While in Garrettsville, too, young Crane became familiar with the family's writing tradition. His great-uncle, Cassius Crane, was the editor of *The Garrettsville Journal*; various relatives, including his grandfather, uncles, aunts, and cousins wrote poetry with varying degrees of accomplishment. Two, Frederic (Uncle Fred) and Alice Crane, were both poets and musicians of special importance, not only because they demonstrate Crane's heritage of taste, temperament, and talent, but also because of the contributions they made to the poet's aesthetic development during his early and adolescent years.

A friend's description of Hart Crane as an "eloquent, swashbuck-

---

13. Carl Schmitt, in a telephone conversation of 23 February 1974.
14. Hart Crane followed the tradition. In 1916, his Christmas gift to his grandmother Crane was an inscribed copy of Henry Van Dyke's *The Blue Flower*, and to his father he gave The Pocket Book of Robert Louis Stevenson, also inscribed (BCM).
15. *The Poetry of Hart Crane: A Critical Study* (Princeton: Princeton University Press, 1967), p. 10.

ling intellectual" (*V*, p. 637), could aptly apply to his great uncle, Frederic Jason Crane, who, had he become a professional poet, might also have arrogantly proclaimed, "I believe I have it in me to become the greatest singer of our generation."[16] Frederic was appropriately named for the first poet in the family, his grandfather, Jason Streator, about whom was written, "The temptations of the city were too much for him. He became dissipated—made shipwreck of his brilliant talent—and soon was carried to his grave."[17] Fortunately this was not to be Frederic's fate. Ardently fond of music, he possessed a powerful voice, and as a youth had prepared himself for an operatic career. But when the time came for him to go to New York to enter his chosen profession, his mother, perhaps recalling the city's alleged malign influence upon her father, persuaded him to abandon his dream and enroll at nearby Hiram College. After several terms of teaching school and giving concerts in Illinois, followed by a lucrative two year barnstorming tour of the midwest as a singing lightning-rod salesman, Frederic returned to Garrettsville, purchased a partnership in Crane Brothers' Store, but never relinquished his love for music, drama, and poetry (ECM).

Heading the cast of any musical or dramatic production anywhere in the Portage County area was the name, "Frederic J. Crane." He also served as the literary and drama critic for the *Journal* with his witty eloquacious columns appearing over the signature "ENARC" —Crane reversed. In addition, Frederic was a prolific poet whose unpublished volume of more than three hundred poems circulated within the family. He did not seek national publication of his poetry but served for years as poet laureate of Garrettsville. Consequently, his poem, "Arlington Cemetery," was printed in Memorial Day issues of the *Journal*. It was he who was called upon to write commemorative verse for his alma mater, Hiram College, and the "in memoriams"— verses published as parts of the obituaries of the townspeople—a practice which he and his editor brother deplored but to which he resigned himself (FCL).

16. Horton, *Hart Crane*, p. 25.

17. *Semi-Centennial Celebration of the Settlement of Windham* (Ravenna, Ohio, 1861), p. 62.

Quite different from this occasional verse is the poetry Frederic usually wrote, which, like the work of John Greenleaf Whittier, is thoroughly romantic in its celebration of individualism, native legends, the simple life, the supernatural, the picturesque past, exotic places, and natural beauty. Unlike Whittier, however, Crane reveals through his poetry a generally cultured background with allusions drawn from art, world history, and music, as well as from literature. Because his poetry is derivative and sometimes frankly imitative, it suggests his literary preferences and therefore the writers to whom he most probably exposed his nephew. Throughout the poetry he reveals himself as a reader of Dante and Shakespeare, and later poets such as Burns, Poe, Bryant, Longfellow, Blake, and Emerson, all of whom he admired enough to appropriate their style and tone. He imitated the poetry of Burns, complete with Scottish dialect. The result is a series of "To . . ." poems, including, "To a Grasshopper," "To a Mosquito," and "To a Bedbug." Frederic's fondness for Poe is reflected in his lines from "Requiem":

> To my grave through life's December
> Come my dear one and remember
> That my love's a smoldering ember
> Struggling to leap forth to thee.

Crane lingered long over his complete works of Bryant, in whose style are such didactic nature poems as "To a Violet," which begins: "Posthumous child, first tribute on the bier/ Of guardian winter, dead in frosty age," and ends, "One has to look but once upon a flower,/ To wonder at the great Creator's power." Frederic considered Longfellow to be the proper reading level of a child, and having read to his daughter, Fredrica, from that poet's works for years, gave the complete poems to her on her eighth birthday. Of course, he wrote poems influenced by that writer—lengthy works about the Indians who had lived in the Portage County area. In one poem he wrote of the same local places his nephew did in "The Dance," the Indian village, streams, hills, and mill. Frederic's "Niagara" was no doubt influenced by Blake's "The Tyger," particularly the line, "Did he who made the rill make thee?" His affinity with and affection for Emerson and Shelley are shown in long philosophical poems about ancient relics and civilizations. Of the ruins along the Euphrates River he composed these lines:

> Deep graven frieze on lofty capitols
> That rose on fluted columns from their base
> Once firmly set, now prostrate, chronicle
> The fate that overwhelmed their time and race.
> Tuscan, Doric and Ionic art
> With Corinthian and Composite yield
> But shattered skeletons, fallen apart,
> Like unburied dead on battlefield.

And of Egypt's ruins he wrote, echoing the same masters:

> Prone on the desert's dusty crawling floor,
> The solemn visaged sphinx lies stretched at length,
> Like skin upon some mighty hunter's door,
> Stripped from ferocious beast by human strength,
> Each morning lighted by the wondering sun,
> Each night in shadow gloomed, his journey done.

Frederic had many other literary mentors, most of them romantics. So profoundly impressed was he by Whitman's poetry that he painstakingly copied much of it for Fredrica. Other favorites were Donne, Keats, Byron, Scott, and Coleridge (FCL).

Writers favored by Frederic were often those most appreciated by his nephew. Hart Crane wrote friends, "I *do* run joyfully towards Messrs. Poe, Whitman, Shakespeare, Keats, Shelley, Coleridge . . . [and] Dante" (*Letters*, p. 67), and "You know how much Blake has always interested me" (*Letters*, p. 100). Clearly, Frederic Crane's influence on Hart has been greatly underestimated. Fredrica, considerably younger than her cousin, says her earliest recollections of Hart and his family are vague; she admits that she recalls little of them until 1916 except that her father and the poet's mother used to play and sing together in area musicales. Hart's Aunt Bess, however, remembers young Hart's fascination with his Uncle Fred and his poetry, and she insists that some of the Burns burlesques were family affairs in which the youngster participated (much perhaps as in later years when he and his friends collaborated on parodies). Crane's appreciation of Burns obviously began early, as evidenced by his giving a copy of the Scotsman's verse to his Aunt Alice in 1914. More than likely he heard his uncle recite; this was almost unavoidable since Frederic often did so, even in his store, and as a result, nieces and nephews less interested than Hart in poetry avoided running errands to "Crane Brothers" and becoming a captive audience for his latest memorization (BCM). Hart also probably heard his uncle read poetry because his immediate family periodically visited Frederic's household where oral reading was a nightly affair (FCL). But if specific influences would be difficult, even impossible, to determine, the general one based on early association and artistic affinities becomes clearer.

III

The evidence of Alice Crane's influence on Hart's aesthetic development is more specific. A verse scrawled in adolescent script on the flyleaf of a collection of Burns's poetry reflects the love of music and verse which aunt and nephew shared:

> A song for happy feast days,
> A song for fortune's spurns,
> In merry and consoling lays—
> The cheery songs of Bobbie Burns.
>
> To Aunt Alice
> From Harold Crane

Christmas, 1914

With Alice, as with Hart, aesthetic interests furnished the focal point at which all the separate lines of her life converged. There seems to have been no area in her life—private or professional—in which those interests did not determine her choices. As a Hiram College student, her close friend was classmate Vachel Lindsey. It was equally fitting that of her two husbands, the first—William Wrigley—was a musician, and the second—Loring Williams—was a poet (ECM).

Alice was no mere dilettante who cultivated the arts superficially and sporadically. During her marriage to Williams, editor and publisher of *The American Weave*, she served as her husband's co-editor, publishing in this traditional poetry magazine such writers as Clement

Wood and Oscar Williams, and maintaining a salon where Cleveland artists, writers, and musicians frequently gathered. Also during this period she organized the Cleveland, Columbus, and New York City chapters of "Composers, Authors, and Artists of America," and served four years as national president of the organization.[18]

Although poetry was always secondary to her music, Alice wrote a great deal of verse, much of it published in the little magazines of the New York-New Jersey area when she maintained a piano studio at New York's Steinway Hall; occasionally it obtained national circulation (LW). Her poetry, like her music, reveals her romantic inclinations.

Alice spent much of her time composing music, and by the time of her death in 1964, had published more than thirty vocal and instrumental works. The piano pieces reflect her romanticism; they are filled with wide chord progressions, chromatic harmony, remote modulations, rippling runs and arpeggios. In composing vocal works, she frequently used existing poetry, and taught that poetry inspired music (LW). That which she selected for this treatment again reveals her romantic affections; among the works she used, whole or in part, were: Blake's "To Autumn," Wordsworth's "Lines Composed above Tintern Abbey," Whitman's "A Clear Midnight," Holmes's "The Chambered Nautilus," Walter De La Mare's "Music," Theodore Parker's "The Way, the Truth, and the Light," James Oppenheim's "Lilac-Magic," and Frederic Crane's "Night and Day." With her compositions she achieved a modicum of success, for some of them appeared in the repertoires of the Oberlin Women's Chorus and of such esteemed church organists as Emanuel Power Biggs of Boston and Richard Hobart of Cleveland.[19]

Nevertheless Alice Crane achieved no grand heights in either poetry or music. Possibly her greatest contribution was her influence upon Hart Crane during his adolescent years when she was his confidante and piano teacher. Loring Williams terms the influence "decided"

18. M. M. Girardeau, "In Memoriam: Alice Crane Williams," *Composers, Authors, and Artists of America*, 21 (Summer 1965), 15, and Loring Williams.

19. *Alice Crane Williams Catalogue* (New York: Paragon, 1959), pp. 2-3.

and "profound"; to commemorate the relationship he established the Hart Crane-Alice Crane Williams scholarships for musicians and writers at Hiram College. In an interview with Unterecker, Alice recalls those years:

> He was always talking about painting and writing in those days.
> . . . He'd sometimes come to my studio several times a week. I
> think it was there, in fact, that he decided he wanted to be a poet.
> I had a very fine library—standard collections of all of the good
> authors: Emerson, Whitman, Hugo, Browning. Once he stood
> there looking at all the books, "This is a wonderful collection,
> Aunt Alice," he said. . . . and then turned to me very seriously:
> "This is going to be my vocation," he said. "I'm going to be a
> poet" (*V*, p. 25).

IV

Alice is almost certainly the subject of Crane's early imagistic poem, "The Fernery," in which a woman's confusion is contrasted with her ordered surroundings. One identifying clue is the original title, "Portrait of Aunty Climax," suggesting a person as well as a state of being. Later, Crane sharpened his pun by reducing the title to "Auntie Climax," but in both an aunt-nephew relationship is implied. This is also suggested in the eighth line of the third version: "I have known myself a nephew to confusions."

Of Hart's aunts, only Alice and Elizabeth (Bess), his father's two sisters, were of the immediate family, and it is Alice whose life can better be seen as reaching an anti-climactic state. For although Bess studied music and art at Oberlin College and taught violin at Hiram Conservatory, she experienced neither Alice's expectation nor her disappointment. As a young woman Alice had shown great promise as a musician, but as a middle-aged one, that promise was woefully unfulfilled. To Crane, aspiring to a related career, his aunt's situation must have appeared sadly anti-climactic.

When Alice graduated from Hiram Conservatory in 1900, it was with much acclaim. As might be expected, The *Garrettsville Journal* (21 June 1900) applauded her highly. Several months later, New

York's respected *Musical Courier* was even more lavish with its praise, referring to her as "gifted and brilliant" (*GJ*, 25 October 1900). For the next three years Alice studied composition and piano technique, first in Berlin, then in Brussels. In Europe *The Berlin Times* hailed her as "one of the most gifted and ambitious artists the United States has sent to Germany" (*GJ*, 13 December 1900). Alice returned home "bringing with her the highest testimonials to her ability as a pianist" (*GJ*, 8 October 1903), prepared to fulfill her dream of composing great music and capturing audiences on the concert stage.

Her repertoire consisted of the music of romantic composers, from Schubert to Chopin, Beethoven to MacDowell; her reviews were unfailingly laudatory. Typical is one from *The Ohio State Journal* (30 October 1903) noting the "continued applause" and concluding with, "Her technical equipment is excellent, her method the Leschetisky [teacher of Paderewski], her youth promising much for her future." But despite critical acclaim, Alice discovered that to earn her living in music she would be compelled to teach, not only compose and concertize. She accepted teaching positions, first at Roanoke College in Virginia, then at Indiana Normal College in Pennsylvania. At the latter she married violinist William Wrigley, and together they performed in faculty ensembles during the school year and at Chautauqua during the summers. But by the time she had come to serve as Hart's music teacher, her career had reached its lowest point. Her husband was first violinist with the Cleveland Municipal Symphony (precursor of the Cleveland Orchestra), while she only maintained a studio in her home and occasionally taught at Notre Dame Academy. Her infrequent concerts were on the "garden-club circuit," and her grand future which had previously seemed assured was in doubt.[20]

Writing of biographical elements in other Crane poems, Unterecker says, "Awareness of such personal association should not, I think, influence us in judging any poem as a work of art; but it can help us comprehend part of the poet's creative process. We can see some of

20. Alice Crane's biographical notes are from family members and friends, various biographical dictionaries, recital programs, Cuyahoga County Court (divorce), *The Garrettsville Journal*, *The American Weave*, and archives of Indiana State College (then Indiana Normal), and Hiram College.

the ways personal material is worked and reworked until it is no longer personal" (*V*, p. 22). Alice's identity and Hart's process of reworking can be seen in the three extant versions of the poem, the first of which is dated by Weber as 1919:

PORTRAIT OF AUNTY CLIMAX

> The light that travels on her spectacles
> Will sometimes meet a mirror in her eyes.
> I've seen it so in lifting up a shade
> Beside her ancient fernery . . . And the dies
> In zig-zag motifs round her wide mouth
> No longer argumentative, show there
> Sleep many runes within the crimped and furled
> Grey wreathes of more-than-human faithful hair.
>   (Weber, *Hart Crane*, p. 78)

In addition to the title, identifying clues appear within the poem itself. The portrait matches Alice who wore glasses and occasionally wigs. In addition, it suggests not so much a woman who is immersed in momentary meditation as it does one who is rarely aware of the profuse life which surrounds her in her fernery, a physical fact and a metaphor for the world itself. Alice was such a woman. Describing her sister's self-absorption, Bess echoes others who commented on her introspection; she says, "Alice lived in a world apart; she was a mystery to us all." The dead or dormant imagination is suggested by the lines, "Sleep many runes within the crimped and furled/ Grey wreathes of more-than-human faithful hair," with "runes" suggesting unwritten poetry and particularly music—since notes resemble runic characters. The word also phonetically echoes "ruins," a relevant connotation, given Crane's penchant for punning (see "fast" in later version). "Primped and curled" hints at a concern for the external world; Crane conveys the subject's withdrawal more clearly with "crimped and furled," with "crimped" suggesting an obstructed imagination and "furled" a turning inward. "Wreathes" also suggests dead creativity.

Most of the original poem is retained in the second version, dated by Weber as 1920:

AUNTIE CLIMAX

The light that travels on her spectacles,
    Will seldom meet a mirror in her eyes.
I have watched when lifting up the shade
Beside her ancient fernery,—and there lies
A wreath of zigzags fast around her lips
Composed to darkness,—meshes that will wear—
Outlasting words that will flicker in the curled
    Grey crown she wears of perfect, borrowed hair.
              (Weber, *Hart Crane*, p. 78)

Here Crane sharpens the contrast between the woman and her world,
but the woman retains her identity as Alice. The wreath is transposed
to the woman's mouth, suggesting the death of her creative voice. Her
crown suggests suffering, not laurels; it is only of hair, both gray and
borrowed, suggesting Alice's tarnished and ephemeral reputation.

    Crane's finished version, undated, shows the most pronounced re-
visions:

THE FERNERY

The lights that travel on her spectacles
Seldom, now, meet a mirror in her eyes.
But turning, as you may chance to lift a shade
Beside her and her fernery, is to follow
The zigzags fast around dry lips composed
To darkness through a wreath of sudden pain.

—So, while fresh sunlight splinters humid green
I have known myself a nephew to confusions
That sometimes take up residence and reign
In crowns less grey—O merciless tidy hair.
              (*Complete Poems*, p. 14)

This version, although somewhat depersonalized by the second person viewpoint of the first stanza, contains more probable biographical
references to Alice. In 1916, Crane wrote of sending roses to Alice
who was "very ill" (*Letters*, p. 3), according to Bess, when she suffered an almost-fatal sickness. But the pain could have been emotional as well, because during the same period Alice was suffering the

anguish of choosing between her marriage and musical career (she divorced Wrigley, resuming her maiden name and profession). Crane's striking line, "so while fresh sunlight splinters humid green" perhaps recalls a childhood memory of a moment of beauty the poet shared with his aunt. Both Hart and Alice were passionately fond of flowers, surrounding themselves with them throughout their lives. As a small child visiting his grandfather's Garrettsville home, his first mission in the morning was to see what flowers had blossomed during the night. On one such morning a mist had lingered on the garden, refracting the sun's rays, reflecting them against the flowers and foliage. The dazzled child, overwhelmed with wonder, shot into the house shouting, "Aunt Alice! Aunt Alice! *Do* come see, there's a rainbow around every flower" (ECM). The line interpreted in this light provides a violent contrast between Alice and her world—the juxtaposition between "funerary" and "fernery." Crane empathizes with the subject, and in his admission that he had known confusions, Crane's "crowns less grey" is probably autobiographical; his own hair began to gray before he was twenty and was quite gray by the time he was thirty (HHH). The last words of the poem, "O merciless tidy hair," emphasize the contrast between the woman's placid exterior and her inner turbulence, and become an invective hurled against externally imposed order, order even Alice imposed on others when, during periods of emotional stress, she became compulsively neat, as if she were trying to restore order to the chaos of her life (ECM).

Alice Crane's presence in her nephew's poem confirms the indelible impression she made upon him; of all the family members, she probably shared more interests with him than did any of his other relatives. That she encouraged him is certain, but with Alice, as with Frederic, definitive contributions to Crane's development are difficult to assess, though the influence is evident in his work. Whereas Alice —the musician—celebrated her enthusiasm for Wagner's work by writing a poem "Lohengrin," Crane—the poet—used Wagner's music as a stimulus for his poems, possibly because Alice had taught him, as she did others in her lectures, that music inspired poetry.[21]

21. A thorough study of Crane's use of music should reveal the musical qual-

V

Certainly not all of Crane's taste, talent, and temperment derived from the Cranes. His mother, Grace, possessed a trained soprano voice and entertained hopes of becoming an actress (*V*, p. 534), and Hart's cousin, Helen Hart Hurlbert, publisher of *The Warren Tribune Chronicle*, is an accomplished organist in addition to being a writer and painter of marked ability. But she generously credits the Cranes for Hart's extraordinary talent and robust wit. However, Grace Crane, seeking recognition of the Harts's contribution to her son's genius wrote him:

> In signing your name to your contributions and later to your books, do you intend to ignore your mother's side of the house entirely? . . . It seems to me that Hart or at least H. should come in somewhere. I understand that the Cranes say you get your literary talent from them—Uncle Fred, for instance, being the example they point to. If you feel that way, leave "Hart" out— but if not, now is the time to fix it right. How would "Hart Crane" be? No partiality there. You see, I am already jealous, which is a sure sign I believe in your success (*V*, p. 74).

In fairness to Grace it must be said that she was aware her son was contemplating a name change. Earlier, his choice had been "Hal Crane," for he thought the name "memorable" and "masculine," and he admired Shakespeare's dashing prince, perhaps seeing himself as a similar romantic figure; equally important, it was reminiscent of Walt Whitman's abbreviated form. Before he had appended that name to any of his writings, however, Grace had dissuaded him from it by re-minding him that *Henry IV* was his father's favorite Shakespearean play (ECM). Although Crane obviously enjoyed the opportunities for punning that the name "Hart" provided, both in his poetry and private correspondence, it was his tragic need for his mother's ap-

---

ity of many of his lines, his conception of some of his poetry as "symphonic" (*Letters*, p. 232), his use of music as a metaphor for poetry, and his employ-ment of some musical terms—from antiphonal to tympanum—which he most likely learned from his music teacher, Alice Crane. Refer to *A Concor-dance to the Poems of Hart Crane*, comp. Hilton and Elaine Landry, Maurice Kramer, Robert DeMott (Metuchen, New Jersey: Scarecrow Press, 1973).

proval combined with his affection for her and his periodic animosity toward his father following his "curse of sundered parentage" that prompted him to call himself "Hart Crane."

The same circumstances led Crane sometimes to provide an erroneous view of his father's family, portraying them as culturally illiterate, thereby contributing to the oversight of the family's influence upon him. On January 23, 1927, a few months after the publication of his first book, *White Buildings* (1926), he wrote his mother, echoing her sentiments about the Cranes' literary obtuseness and taste: "Wait until they see it, and try to read it," he wrote; "I may be wrong, but I think they will eventually express considerable consternation; for the poetry I write, as you have noticed already, is farther from their grasp than the farthest planets." Elsewhere in the letter he added, "In a way it's a pity that none of the Crane family are readers of anything more important than such magazines as *The Saturday Evening Post* and *Success*" (*Letters*, p. 284). Yet the Cranes were readers of literature much more important than the publications Hart cited, indeed—the literature that had become a part of the poet himself.[22]

In discussing Crane's limited formal education, R. W. Butterfield writes:

> These factors considered, it may appear surprising that Crane became the kind of poet he did . . . he was (at his best) a superb conventional technician, a master of blank verse, a cherisher of archaisms, and a coiner whose neologisms often seem Elizabethan. . . . How shall we account for this highly literate verse, ringing with elusive echoes of earlier poetry?

Butterfield's answer is Crane's self-instruction.[23] However, his explanation supplies only a portion of the truth. The remainder lies in the

---

22. Within the same letter, however, edited also by Weber, are favorable comments about the Cranes; for example, "I've always thought that Bess was pretty good company, and so is Alice Crane." This and other similar omissions might have contributed to the oversight of Hart's family's influence since they minimize the Crane relationship. *Letters of Hart Crane and His Family*, ed. Thomas S. W. Lewis (New York: Columbia University, 1974), from which this passage is taken (p. 522), provides a more accurate view.

23. *The Broken Arc: A Study of Hart Crane* (Edinburg: Oliver & Boyd, 1969), pp. 6-7.

symbolic will written by the poet's grandfather, Arthur E. Crane, in which he bequeathed his interest in literature to his descendants. It represented a legacy propagated and perpetuated before and after its author, a legacy that initially provided a stimulating artistic milieu which Hart Crane—through his poetry—confirmed.

Gloria L. Young

"The Fountainhead of All Forms":
Poetry and the Unconscious
in Emerson and Howard Nemerov

For it is the inert effort of each thought . . . to solidify and hem in the life. . . . But the heart refuses to be imprisoned; in its first and narrowest pulses it already tends outward with a vast force and to immense and innumerable expansions.[1]

It is a commonplace of contemporary poetry, as Northrop Frye has pointed out, that "the natural metaphorical direction of the inside world is downward, into the profounder depths of consciousness"; this, he says, is a "Romantic inheritance."[2] It is not, however, commonplace to refer to Emerson as an important source of this inheritance. Emerson's marked influence on twentieth century poetry has been much discussed;[3] his aesthetic theory has been most clearly expounded

1. "Circles," *The Complete Works of Ralph Waldo Emerson,* ed. Edward Waldo Emerson (Boston: Houghton Mifflin, 1903-1904), II, 304. Subsequent references will be cited, volume and page, in the text.

2. "The Drunken Boat: The Revolutionary Element in Romanticism," *Romanticism Reconsidered,* ed. Northrop Frye (New York: Columbia University Press, 1963), pp. 7-8.

3. For instance, Harold Bloom has related Emerson to Walt Whitman and Wallace Stevens; to A. R. Ammons; and to E. A. Robinson, Hart Crane, and Alvin Feinman in *The Ringers in the Tower* (Chicago: University of Chicago

241

by Vivian C. Hopkins.[4] Yet, Emerson's intuition of the unconscious as a source of inspiration has not been thoroughly analyzed nor has his anticipation of contemporary theories of the unconscious in poetry been sufficiently recognized.

The purpose of this essay is to confirm that Emerson's ideas of the unconscious anticipate certain psychological, linguistic, and aesthetic theories of Carl Jung, depth psychologist, and Howard Nemerov, poet, critic, and theorist.[5] In each division of this essay—(1) description of the unconscious; (2) access to it; and (3) confrontation and interaction with it (process and product)—Emerson's ideas will be compared with those of Jung and Nemerov, with statements of other contemporary poets occasionally noted to suggest their awareness of the role of the unconscious in recent American poetry.

It is significant that Emerson sensed and described this "blind wisdom . . . seminal brain . . . which seems to sheathe a certain omniscience; and which, in the despair of language, is commonly called Instinct" (XII, 65), and in so doing he delineated concepts which would later be included in a larger circle, complete with psychological vo-

Press, 1971) pp. 217-234; 257-322. The most extensive treatment of Emerson as "spokesman and as catalyst" in American poetry is Hyatt Waggoner's *American Poets from the Puritans to the Present* (Boston: Houghton Mifflin, 1968).

4. *Spires of Form: A Study of Emerson's Aesthetic Theory* (Cambridge: Harvard University Press, 1951). Subsequent references will be cited in the text as *Spires*.

5. Howard Nemerov is a representative choice, having published (1947-1972) seven volumes of poetry, three novels, two collections of short stories, and two books of essays on poetry and fiction. He has edited and contributed to books on poetry. His bibliography of published works includes over 250 entries. He has taught at Hamilton, Bennington, and Brandeis colleges; he has been Visiting Professor at the University of Minnesota, Poet in Residence at Hollins, and Hurst Professor of English at Washington University, St. Louis. He has also served as Consultant in Poetry to the Library of of Congress. Nemerov states: "Poetry and criticism are as a double star, and . . . we shall do well to learn all we can of what poetry is, and try to see . . . how the art is constantly redefining itself. . . . And that includes doing not only criticism, but also theory" (*Poetry and Fiction* [New Brunswick: Rutgers University Press, 1963], pp. vii-viii). Subsequent references to *Poetry and Fiction* will be cited in text as *P.F.*

cabulary. Ralph Rusk has pointed out that for Emerson no truth was final, "a bigger circle would include the one just drawn." If this made Emerson's theories unstable, it was of little concern to Emerson, says Rusk, since he was always confident that "a little later on, if not now, they would be justified by a wise interpretation of experience."[6] Emerson probably would view contemporary theories of the unconscious as only another circle, since life "spawns and scorns system and system-makers" (X, 352).

Professor Hopkins, in her scholarly treatment of Emerson's aesthetic theory, discusses his concept of inspiration as beginning with the inflow from the Deity to a mind passively and receptively awaiting it. The difficulty is

> that the artist is prevented by reverence for the Deity from complaining when intuitions fail to flow into his mind. Aware of this problem, Emerson denotes the term *instinct* as the special source of power for the arts and literature. . . . The action of instinct, in Emerson's theory, is negative rather than positive; though not itself a light, it is the source of illumination for creative artists.
> (*Spires*, pp. 21-22)

Summarizing the "core of Emerson's theory of imagination," she defines it as the "power of the creative mind to refashion the objects of nature . . . into symbols of his own thought" (pp. 37-38), but she finds "the gap which exists between the intuition in the artist's mind and its transference to objective matter" is the "principal lack in Emerson's concept of form" (p. 137). It is the same "gap" that Carl Jung (as well as many contemporary poets) believes is bridged through language: the conscious mind submerges into the unconscious, brings up archetypal images (the raw material of the unconscious), and transforms them into symbols. Professor Hopkins admits that Emerson "has studied the sub-ego more carefully than any other contemporary critic, and that he has made definite use of it in relation to aesthetics," but "without in any real sense anticipating Freud's concept of the subconscious" (p. 183). Twenty years later, however, she sup-

---

6. Ralph L. Rusk, *The Life of Ralph Waldo Emerson* (New York: Scribner's, 1949), pp. 283, 237.

ports the view that Emerson's interpretation of dreams "anticipates some present-day psychological theories and methods."[7] It seems incredible that Emerson—operating in the dark, suspecting the presence of unconscious power, recognizing an unknown, non-self in his dreams, distrusting it as he distrusted anything unintelligible, struggling to name and describe this force—should have anticipated so much.

I

Constantly beset by the inability of language to describe his intuition of the unconscious, Emerson uses various and sometimes contradictory figures of speech, each suggesting some aspect of his "feeling" of the underlying psyche. Some personifications refer to the Over-Soul (real Being, Essence, God); others refer to a kind of Under-Soul (aboriginal Self, Earth Spirit, Primeval world); still others simply describe the qualities of the unconscious (aboriginal abyss, unknown country, alien energy, secret augury). The term "unconscious," used by Emerson, is the correct term, according to Jung, since it should not be designated as "*sub*conscious," being not merely "below consciousness but also above it."[8]

Emerson frequently used water to symbolize the unconscious:

> Earth Spirit, living a black river like that swarthy stream which rushes through the human body is thy nature, demoniacal, warm, fruitful, sad, nocturnal.[9]

7. "Emerson and the World of Dream," *Emerson's Relevance Today: A Symposium*, ed. Eric Carlson, and J. L. Dameron (Hartford: Transcendental Books, 1971), p. 66. Hopkins compares "Emerson's recognition of the sub- and ob-jective qualities of the phenomenon" to Freud's distinction between the *id* and the *ego*. She suggests, but does not develop, the idea that some of Emerson's dreams "illustrate Jung's theory of the 'collective unconscious' " (p. 64). See also Gay Wilson Allen, "Emerson and the Unconscious," *American Transcendental Quarterly*, 19 (Summer, 1973), 26-30.

8. C. G. Jung, *The Archetypes and the Collective Unconscious* (New York: Pantheon, 1959), p. 243. Subsequent references will be cited in the text as *A.C.U.*

9. Edward W. Emerson and Waldo E. Forbes, eds., *The Journals of Ralph*

Under all this running sea of circumstance, whose waters ebb and flow with perfect balance, lies the aboriginal abyss of real Being. Essence, or God, is not a relation or a part, but the whole.
(II, 120-121)

The waters of the great deep have ingress and egress to the soul. But if I speak, I define, I confine and am less. (II, 342)

Man is a stream whose source is hidden. Our being is descending into us from we know not whence. The most exact calculator has no prescience that somewhat incalculable may not balk the very next moment. . . . When I watch that flowing river, which, out of regions I see not, pours for a season its streams into me, I see that I am a pensioner; not a cause but a surprised spectator of this ethereal water; that I desire and look up and put myself in the attitude of reception, but from some alien energy the visions come. (II, 268)

Sensing the unconscious sometimes as a higher power, sometimes as a lower, Emerson acknowledges: "We see at once that we have no language subtle enough for distinctions in that inaccessible region." Realizing that there will be objections to representing "the Divine Being as an unconscious somewhat," Emerson answers that the "unconsciousness we spake of was merely relative to us. . . . We predicate nothing of its consciousness or unconsciousness in relation to itself" (*J.*, Apr. 27, 1840).

The term Emerson most frequently uses to name the unconscious "potential wit" is *Instinct*, described as a source of mental power

which pours all the others into its mould;—that unknown country in which all the rivers of our knowledge have their fountains, and which, by its qualities and structure, determines both the nature of the waters and the direction in which they flow.
(XII, 33-34)

Instinct is passive, potential, negative—"a shapeless giant in the cave, massive, without hands or fingers or articulating lips or teeth or

Waldo Emerson, (Boston: Houghton Mifflin, 1909-1914), VI, 347 (Feb. 7, 1843). Subsequent references will be cited in the text as *J*.

tongue; Behemoth, disdaining speech, disdaining particulars, lurking, surly, invincible, disdaining thoughts, always whole, never distributed, aboriginal, old as Nature." Beginning at this low point, "at the surface of the earth," it works first for the necessities of man and then "ascends stop by stop to suggestions which are when expressed the intellectual and moral laws." Instinct is "a taper, a spark in the great night. Yet a spark at which all the illuminations of human arts and sciences were kindled." And "inspiration," says Emerson, "is only this power excited, breaking its silence; the spark bursting into flame" (XII, 34-35). Inspiration, an "enlarged power," accomplishes what is "great and lasting" by leaning on the "secret augury" (VIII, 271), providing the source of genius (II, 64).

Carl Jung, also, used the metaphor of water to describe the unconscious:

> Therefore the way of the soul . . . leads to the water, to the dark mirror that reposes at its bottom. . . . This water is no figure of speech, but a living symbol of the psyche. . . . The dreamer descends into his own depths and the way leads him to the mysterious water. . . . But the breath of the spirit rushing over the dark water is uncanny, like everything whose cause we do not know— since it is not ourselves. It hints at an unseen presence, a numen to which neither human expectations nor the machinations of the will have given life. *It lives of itself.* . . . It is a spookish thing and primitive fear seizes the naive mind. (*A.C.U.*, p. 17)

In psychological terminology, Jung hypothesizes that

> In addition to our immediate consciousness, which is of a thoroughly personal nature and which we believe to be the only empirical psyche, there exists a second psychic system of a collective, universal, and impersonal nature which is identical in all individuals . . . is inherited . . . consists of preexistent forms, the archetypes, which can only become conscious secondarily and which give definite form to certain psychic contents. (*A.C.U.*, p. 43)

Jung differentiates between a "superficial layer of the unconscious," wholly personal, containing the "feeling-toned complexes" (Freud's concept), and a deeper "collective" layer, containing primordial archetypes that make up a "common psychic substrate of a suprapersonal nature." The archetypes, psychic contents not yet "submitted to conscious elaboration," are, therefore, an "immediate datum of psychic experience" (*A.C.U.*, pp. 3-4). Echoing Emerson's intuition of instinct's determining not only the nature of the waters but the direction in which they flow, Jung states that unconscious archetypes force man's "ways of perception and apprehension into specifically human patterns."[10] When man feels "menaced by alien powers" (*A.C.U.*, p. 105), he is not inventing but experiencing them.

Paralleling Emerson's and Jung's descriptions of the unconscious, Howard Nemerov uses images of water and light throughout his poetry. The dark and wrinkled sea symbolizes the ground of being, the unconscious, the alien, the Other, as well as the great mother whose salt water flows in man's veins and in his tears. Life, like raindrops or snowflakes, is always merging and flowing, from stream to river to sea. Light images (Emerson's flame) symbolize inspiration, imagination, and mind. It is the imagination that sees, listens, transforms, and reconciles the "pond as birthplace and deathplace, the liquid mother and mirror whence beautiful and terrible forms arise, and whereto they return."[11] Discussing his poem, "Painting a Mountain Stream," Nemerov describes an "unknowably large part of a material world whose independent existence might be likened to that of the human unconscious, a sleep of causes, a chaos of the possible-impossible, responsive only to the wakening touch of desire and fear—that is, to spirit; that is to the word."[12] "The image . . . most appropriate for this notion," he adds, is the image of a "stream, a river, a waterfall, a fountain, or else of a still and deep reflecting pool." One must bring to this world an attitude of "attentiveness and obedience," recognizing,

10. C. G. Jung, *The Structure and Dynamics of the Psyche* (New York: Pantheon, 1960), p. 133. Subsequent references will be cited in the text as *S.D.*

11. *Journal of the Fictive Life* (New Brunswick: Rutgers University Press, 1963), pp. 146-147. Subsequent references cited in the text as *J.F.L.*

12. "Attentiveness and Obedience," *Poets on Poetry*, ed. Howard Nemerov (New York: Basic Books, 1966), p. 241. Subsequent references cited in the text as *P.P.*

however, that it cannot be plumbed: "The visible way is always down / but there is no floor to the world" (*P.P.*, pp. 248-249).[13]

In "The Sanctuary,"[14] Nemerov envisions a trout sanctuary as the "pool of the skull" where images swim. On the floor of the pool, one sees "The numerous springs moving their mouths of sand," and the trout, "With a delicate bend and reflex / Of their tails . . . glide"

> From the shadowy side into the light, so clear,
> And back again into the shadows; slow
> And so definite, like thoughts emerging
> Into a clear place in the mind, then going back,
> Exchanging shape for shade.

The images appear in consciousness and then move back into unconsciousness, or hang "between the surface and the slate / For several minutes without moving, like / A silence in a dream." As the poet observes the phenomena, his life "Seems to have been suddenly moved a great / Distance away on every side," as though

> The quietest thought of all stood in the pale
> Watery light alone, and was no more
> My own than the speckled trout I stare upon
> All but unseeing. Even at such times
> The mind goes on transposing and revising
> The elements of its long allegory
> In which the anagoge is always death;

While the poet meditates, a trout "pokes through the fabric of the surface to / Snap up a fly. As if a man's own eyes"

13. Robert Bly believes the poet must bring forward another reality from "*inward* experience," "inward depth" (David Ossman, *The Sullen Art* [N.Y.: Citadel, 1963], p. 41). John Ciardi describes the "vital part of the poem" as being in the "unconscious mind" (*Mid-Century American Poets* [N.Y.: Twayne, 1950], p. xiv). John Wheellock calls the unconscious the "fourth Voice of Poetry," speaking out of "some older, wiser Self in which all selves are included" (*Poets of Today*, II [N.Y.: Scribners, 1955], p. 3). Robert Duncan notes the "swell and ebb" of primal waters, "amoebic intelligences," that "arouse in our awake minds a spell, so that we let our awareness go in the urgent wave of the verse." See *Poets on Poetry*, p. 135.

14. *The Salt Garden* (Boston: Little, Brown, 1955), pp. 44-45. Subsequent references cited in the text as *S.G.*

Raised welts upon the mirror whence they stared,
I find this world again in focus, and
This fish, a shadow dammed in artifice,
Swims to the furthest shadows out of sight
Though not, in time's ruining stream, out of mind.[15]

The archetypal images may be temporarily dammed through artifice, but being protected and holy, they revert back into unconscious content. Only the moment of flowing can be captured, not the essence; being imperishable, they are not "out of mind," though "out of sight" in "Time's ruining stream."[16]

In a long poem, "To Lu Chi," Nemerov describes the unconscious as a "pure and hidden reach,"

Some still, reed-hidden and reflective stream
Where the heron fishes in his own image.

The poem is a reflective debate between a modern poet and Lu Chi (A.D. 302). In the modern world, the poet tells Lu Chi, "They say, the arts, / And poetry first . . . must wither away." Even when "all civilisation / Quite visibly and audibly collapses," they still will not "consult those who consult the source." "What then? Nothing but this, old sir: *Continue*" Continue to

Look into the clear and mirroring stream
Where images remain although the water
Passes away.[17]

15. In "Monadnoc" Emerson sees the "constant mountain" as a sanctuary which "imagest the stable good / For which we all our lifetime grope, / In shifting form the formless mind, / And though the substance us elude, / We in thee the shadow find" (IX, 74).

16. Richard Eberhart's seals "that rise and peer from elemental water" resemble Nemerov's trout. In "Seals, Terns, Time," the poet is drawn by primordial forces from within and also by the mind, symbolized by the terns, whose "aspirations dip in mine." The poet is "pondering, and balanced on the sea, / A gauze and spindrift of the world." The unconscious is "hid," and the conscious is "thwarted." He is "pulled back in the mammal water, / Enticed to the release of the sky" (*15 Modern American Poets*, ed. George P. Elliott [N.Y.: Holt, Rinehart, Winston, 1965], p. 34).

17. *Mirrors and Windows* (Chicago: University of Chicago Press, 1958), pp. 90-94. Subsequent references cited in the text as *M.W.*

Similarly, for Emerson poetry is the constant attempt to "pass the brute body" and "to see that the object is always flowing away, whilst the spirit or necessity which causes it subsists" (VIII, 17).

II

The "unknown country in which all the rivers of our knowledge have their fountains" is there, but "How?" asks Emerson, is this source to be tapped? He answers that one must "invent means. . . . Power is the authentic mark of spirit" (XII, 73). One may sometimes reach it consciously, says Emerson: the "primeval world,—the Fore-World . . . I can dive to it in myself" (II, 23). The key is to release the will, "to forget ourselves, to be surprised out of our propriety" (II, 321-322). One must "subject to thought things seen without (voluntary) thought. . . . The feeling of all great poets has accorded with this. They found the verse, not made it" (VII, 49-50). New energy, "beyond the energy of his possessed and conscious intellect," is derived from "abandonment to the nature of things" (III, 26); "we sink to rise" (VIII, 42). The poet's effort is the "least part of his work of art" (VII, 43), his will "only the surrender of will" (I, 213). Thoughts enter and leave minds through "avenues . . . never voluntarily opened" (II, 286). Emerson mentions having written poems he does not remember composing nor correcting (*J.*, Jan. 1852), elsewhere noting that the artist is often "as much surprised at the effect" as others (VII, 46). Although one can occasionally dive into the unconscious through conscious effort, more frequently such states are "coy and capricious," not to be "too exactly" tasked and harnessed, having "a life of their own, independent of our wills" (XII, 77). At best, the experience is never consecutive—"A glimpse, a point of view . . . but no panorama" (VIII, 273).

Usually, access to the unconscious is gained through unconscious means: the dreams and fantasies of early childhood, mythology and fable, sleep, religious ecstasy, madness, the occult, and drugs. Emerson believes the dreams of childhood, myth and fable, and the dreams of sleep to be valid and genuine sources of inspiration, but he is suspicious of the others.

"A sleeping child" seems to Emerson "a traveller in a very far country" (*J*, Sept. 16, 1840). Mythology, stemming from the childhood of the race, "repeats itself in the experience of every child. He too is a demon or god thrown into a particular chaos, where he strives ever to lead things from disorder into order" (I, 206). Pan, an early and primitive intimation of the All, according to Emerson, is described by him in language echoing his description of Instinct: "refusing to speak, clinging to his behemoth way" (XII, 36). Fable, also, may have in it "somewhat divine" since it came "from thought above the will of the writer . . . that which flowed out of his constitution and not from his too active invention" (II, 108). If only, laments Emerson, "we could retain our early innocence, we might trust our feet uncommanded to take the right path. . . . But we have interfered too often" (XII, 37).

By acknowledging the powers of dreams, Emerson emphasizes the unconscious as a generative source of creativity: "In dreams we are true poets; we create the persons of the drama" and they "speak after their own characters, not ours" (VIII, 44-45). That in dreams he "must be the author of both parts of the dialogue . . . is ever wonderful" (*J.*, Oct. 24, 1866) to Emerson. It is only "by repairing to the fountainhead of all forms" that the artist can be illuminated, "for as soon as we let our will go and let the unconscious states ensue, see what cunning draughtsmen we are" (II, 337). Participation in dreams frees the poet of conscious fetters and transcends "all limit and privacy"; consequently, man becomes "the conductor of the whole river of electricity" (III, 40)—the water and the spark united. Dreams serve to unite the active and passive selves and cause the viewer to see himself as an object—as with a double consciousness. The following passage from "Demonology" is incredibly sound in terms of ideas prevalent today:

> Dreams have a poetic integrity and truth. . . . They seem to us to suggest an abundance and fluency of thought not familiar to the waking experience. They pique us by independence of us, yet we know ourselves in this mad crowd, and owe to dreams a kind of divination and wisdom. My dreams are not me; they are not Nature, or the Not-me: they are both. They have a double conscious-

ness, at once sub- and ob-jective. . . . Wise and sometimes terrible hints shall in them be thrown to the man out of a quite unknown intelligence. . . . Once or twice the conscious fetters shall seem to be unlocked, and a freer utterance attained. A prophetic character in all ages has haunted them. They are the maturation often of opinions not consciously carried out to statements, but whereof we already possessed the elements. (X, 7-8)

Through "miracles . . . enthusiasm . . . Animal Magnetism; prayer; eloquence; self-healing," reason may lose its "momentary grasp of the sceptre" and find the "power which exists not in time or space, but an instantaneous in-streaming causing power" (I, 73). Trances, visions, convulsions, and illumination, also, may be "varying forms of that shudder of awe and delight" when the individual soul mingles with the universal soul (II, 281-282). There are dangers, however, attending the "opening of the religious sense in men" since there is a "certain tendency to insanity" in such men, as if they had been "blasted with excess of light" (II, 281-282). The experience called by the ancients, "*ecstasy* or absence,—a getting out of their bodies to think," may come in "terror, and with shocks to the mind of the receiver" and may drive man mad (IV, 97). Genius, too, has its dangers. Emerson agrees with Aristotle that "no great genius was ever without some mixture of madness" and things grand and superior can be spoken only by the "agitated soul" (VIII, 279). Nevertheless, the result is worth the risk: "Men of large calibre, though with some eccentricity or madness . . . help us more than balanced mediocre minds" (IV, 98-99).

In addition, access to the unconscious may be gained through the occult: "omens, coincidences, luck, sortilege, magic and other experiences which shun rather than court inquiry." Although Emerson views the occult with suspicion, he agrees that it may give "hints" to man and "shed light on our structure" (X, 3). Animal magnetism, for instance, sometimes viewed by Emerson as a religious phenomenon and sometimes as a "black art," nevertheless, seems "to open again that door which was open to the imagination of childhood—of magicians and fairies" (X, 25). Denying the "impatience which cannot brook the supernatural . . . and the great presentiments which haunt us," he "willingly" says, "Hail! to the unknown awful powers which transcend the ken of the understanding" (X, 27). Still, such things are not to his liking. "I set down these things as I find them, but however poetic these twilights of thought, I like daylight" (X, 19).[18]

The poet, then, in reaching the unconscious, works to an "end above his will, and by means, too, which are out of his will" (XII, 71). The experiencing of the unconscious may bring "terror" and "shock" or "awe and delight." The "sublime" (II, 267) is felt when the emotion seems to come from above; but the "pain of an alien world," a world "not yet subdued by thought," is realized when it comes from below. Emerson asks if the *"dire"* may be the "act of the imagination when groping for its symbols in these parts or functions of nature which nature conceals because painful to the observer?"[19]

One "groping" explanation for man's occasional experience of an alien world may be that he is part of it at an unconscious, unremembered level. At the Jardin des Plantes, his feelings of "occult sympathies," as if "looking at our bone and flesh through coloring and distorting glasses," led him to speculate that men still have knowledge of the creatures they hunt (XII, 22). As early as *Nature*, Emerson felt an "occult relation between man and vegetable" (I, 10), and in "Powers and Laws of Thought," man seems to Emerson to be a "higher plant" (XII, 24). Man can know nature, having just come out of it, from the "chemic lump" to the plant to the quadruped to the man. "He is not only representative, but participant" (IV, 11). Yet, Emerson believed that what was ugly or beastlike would eventually disappear (I, 76), since in the "secular melioration of the planet" the

18. One means of access to the unconscious that Emerson finds invalid is drugs. He understands that "bards love wine, mead, narcotics, coffee, tea, opium, the fumes of sandalwood and tobacco" as means to add "extraordinary power to their normal powers," but, he says, "Nature will not be tricked, and inspiration owed to narcotics is 'counterfeit excitement'" (III, 27-28). See also "Circles" (II, 322), in which he adds to this list "wild passions, as in gaming and war, to ape in some manner these flames and generosities of the heart."

19. Hopkins, "Emerson and the World of Dreams," p. 66. Professor Hopkins gives the source of this quote as the Ms. Lecture, "Demonology," delivered February 21, 1839, at the Masonic Temple in Boston.

inharmonious in nature would "become unnecessary" and "die out" (VII, 276).

Like Emerson, Jung recognizes the power, energy, and danger which derives from the confrontation with the unconscious. The experience, Jung says, while "redeeming" and giving power, may also "unleash a dangerous enthusiasm" (*S.D.*, p. 315). Like Emerson again, Jung believes that one may enter the unconscious through certain conscious techniques employed by the "active imagination" (*A.C.U.*, p. 44):

> One concentrates one's attention on some dream image, or on visual impression, and observes the changes taking place in it. It brings a mass of unconscious material to light. . . . The experiences which result differ from dream only by reason of their better form, which comes from the fact that the contents were perceived not by a dreaming but by a waking consciousness.
> (*A.C.U.*, p. 190)

Art, intuition, telepathic phenomena are the result of such "creative fantasy" in which "primordial images are made visible" through conscious "perception via the unconscious" (*A.C.U.*, pp. 78, 282, 142).

The unconscious, containing "all the fantasy combinations" (*S.D.*, p. 69), reveals itself in the "psychic phenomena" of dreams, religion, trance states, visions, early childhood fantasies, primitive tribal lore, myth and fairy tale, magic, and insanity (*A.C.U.*, pp. 5, 7, 44). But the further away from immediate experience these archetypes of myth and religion become, the less meaningful they are to man. Emerson's sense of seeing one's self in a dream as an "object," a "pensioner," is described by Jung: "In the realm of consciousness we are our own masters; we seem to be the factors (makers) themselves. But if we step through the door of the shadow we discover with terror that we are the objects of unseen factors" (*A.C.U.*, p. 23). When dealing with the unconscious, Jung comments that "we are more possessed than possessing" (*A.C.U.*, p. 187).

Emerson's intuition of man's "occult relation" with the vegetable-animal world is paralleled by Jung who says that the unconscious contains "forgotten material" of the personal past plus inherited "behaviour traces" constituting the structure of the mind. The unconscious supplements the picture of the human personality with "living figures ranging from the animal to the divine, as the two extremes outside men, and rounds out the animal extreme, through the addition of vegetable" (*A.C.U.*, pp. 69, 188). For Jung, beast images and other negative archetypes belong to the "family of figures which describe the dark, nocturnal, lower chthonic element," sharing in the "daemonically superhuman" and the "bestially subhuman" (*A.C.U.*, pp. 234, 230), but they are not likely to disappear as Emerson optimistically predicted.

For Howard Nemerov, the unconscious is simply an unknown "other," which may, under certain conditions, enter consciousness. One cannot define it, since this requires a "talent for mystical experience" (*P.F.*, pp. 11-12), but one may gain access to it through "attentiveness and obedience." He is drawn to Keats' idea of negative capability, "when a man is capable of being in uncertainties, mysteries, doubts, without any irritable reaching after fact and reason": one looks, listens, and transforms (*P.P.*, pp. 248-249). In the process of combining the materials of the "world-in-language," Nemerov, like Emerson, finds that "once in a great while" the "poet surprises himself, or it surprises him, with thoughts beyond the reaches of his soul." The self may be "suddenly invaded by the Other, the Outside," offering the old dream of "divination and esoteric oracular utterance." Nemerov calls this the "heartbreaking dream of poetry itself, to persuade an indifferent and mighty Nature to respond to the human," a dream which cannot be accomplished by will alone.[20] The poet for Nemerov, as for Emerson, is oracular, vatic, "not speaking so much as spoken through by something other than himself," which may be thought of as "divinity, Muse, Goddess, Holy Spirit"; the poetic function of the Other is simply to be other, "hence to guarantee that the poet shall express not his silly little personal consciousness but the vast consciousness open to the Other" (*S.E.*, pp. 400-401).[21]

20. "Speculative Equations: Poems, Poets, Computers," *American Scholar*, 36 (Summer, 1967), 399. Subsequent references will be cited in the text as *S.E.*
21. Cf. Peter Viereck who discusses three stages of spiritual truth: the lowest, that of the external world, has "nothing abiding"; the second, spiritual but willed, is "mere surface"; the third, "true inspiration," cannot be kept by "im-

Nemerov chose "Runes" for *Poet's Choice*, calling it a drama, with progression from "statement through dispute to resolution."[22] The "statement" is in poem I: "This is about the stillness in moving things, / In running water. . . . That is my theme, of thought and the defeat / of thought before its object." Thought can only be caught in its flowing since "every tense / Is now." Nevertheless, "out of this head . . . Are basilisks who write our sentences" (poem IV). The descent into the waters of the unconscious is described:

> To go low, to be as nothing, to die,
> To sleep in the dark water . . .
> And through the tangle of the sleeping roots
> . . . and past the buried hulls of things
> To come, and humbly through the breathing dreams
> Of all small creatures sleeping in the earth;
> To fall with the weight of things down on the one
> Still ebbing stream, to go on to the end . . .
> Into the pit where zero's eye is closed. (poem VIII)

As water in the "soft green stalks and tubes" hardens into wood and as the seed is "compacted under pressures" into stone, so are the images soldified into language. The "truth," however, lies in the flowing quality of the symbol—in the memory of "how the water is streaming still" and of how the division of the seed "pours a stream, between / The raindrop and the sea, running in one / Direction, down, and gathering in its course / That bitter salt" (poem XII). Poem XIV describes the crossing of the threshold, "The water of the eye where the world walks," and poem XV, the resolution:

> To watch water, to watch running water
> Is to know a secret. . . .
> It is a secret. Or it is not to know
> The secret, but to have it in your keeping,

prisoning it or by mere daytime wisdom. It can be kept only by not trying to keep it, by not subjecting it to will" (*Poet's Choice*, ed. Paul Engle and Joseph Langland [New York: Dell, 1962], p. 156).

22. *Poet's Choice*, pp. 179-187. Subsequent references will be cited in the text as *P.C.*

> . . . it is not knowing, it is not keeping,
> But being the secret hidden from yourself.[23]

Nemerov describes the "voice of the eternally other" as a further voice of poetry, about which little can be said except that at certain times it is there, "the resonance that in our repetition of the poet's words seems to come from the outside, when the 'shadow of an external world draws near'" (*P.F.*, p. 92).[24] "Poetry," Nemerov adds, "is the art of contemplating this situation in the mirror of language" (Emerson calls the world the poet's "mirror and echo" [X, 191]). Through language, "the marvelous mirror of the human condition," Nemerov believes the poet can show "the relations between things." However, "the mirror is a limit, and as such, it is sorrowful; one wants to break it and look beyond." But outside the garden "where relations grow . . . is the wild abyss" (*P.F.*, pp. 11-13).

In "The Salt Garden," the persona of the poem has wrested a garden of relations from the ocean's floor with "much patience and some sweat." Sitting in his green garden, "in a decent order set," he watches the work that he has done "Bend in the salt wind." Becoming aware of "The ocean's wrinkled green," maneuvering in its sleep, he despises what he had planned—"For what can man keep?" In stanza

23. Emerson's Sphinx says to man: "Thou art the unanswered question" (IX, 24).

24. Like Nemerov, Theodore Roethke sees the unconscious as a source of power, the womb of nature in its creative essence: "I believe that to go forward as a spiritual man it is necessary first to go back. . . . Sometimes one gets the feeling that not even the animals have been there before; but the marsh, the mire, the Void, is always there, immediate and terrifying" (*Mid-Century American Poets*, pp. 69-71). Muriel Rukeyser says that the process of writing poetry has much "unconscious work in it. . . . My own experience is that the work on a poem 'surfaces' several times, with new submergence after each rising. . . . Another deep dive to its own depth of sleep and waiting and you may be ready to write" (*Waterlily Fire* [New York: Doubleday, 1963], p. 11). Sylvia Plath in "The Ghost's Leavetaking" speaks of the "chilly no-man's land" of early morning when she is half asleep and the "waking head rubbishes out the draggled lot / Of sulphurous dreamscapes and obscure lunar conundrums / Which seemed, when dreamed, to mean so profoundly much." The unconscious speaks "in sign language of a lost otherworld, / A world we lose by merely waking up" (*The Colossus* [New York: Knopf, 1962], pp. 39-40).

2, the gull, "like a high priest / Bird-masked, mantled in grey," "like a merchant prince / Come to some poor province," contemptuously surveys the garden. As it vanishes seaward, the gull utters a cry in a "strange tongue but the tone clear," which seems to tell the poet that the gull has come

> . . . brutal, mysterious,
> To teach the tenant gardener,
> Green fellow of this paradise
> Where his salt dream lies. (S. G., pp. 41-43)

The poet realizes he is only a tenant, a "pensioner," as Emerson says; the salt sea in his garden, his veins, and his tears, tells him he is "participant" only. The Other can invade man's rationally ordered world and menace his imagined unity. In Emerson's words, the "bitten world" ("the gnat grasping the world" [XII, 11]) may hold the "biter fast by his own teeth," and although man perishes, "unconquered nature lives on" (IV, 77); the "abysmal Forces, untameable and immense" may crop out in man's "planted gardens" (J., Oct. 27, 1845).[25]

Art mirrors through the "magic of language. . . . It is also the magic of impersonation, and not without its sinister aspect, the being possessed by spirits, or by the spirit" (P.F., p. 90). In "A Predecessor of Perseus," Nemerov reveals the need for art as shield against the chaos of the other. Perseus used the mirror of Athena's shield against the Gorgon, but the "predecessor" of Perseus had no mirror. "Stravaging through the Dark Wood," he rides forth on his quest, "and maybe he will keep on going / Until the grey unbearable she of the world / Shall raise her eyes, and recognize, and grin / At her eternal ama-

---

25. Theodore Holmes in "Idylls of Cape Ann" finds the exterior world as "what lies outside words." Our descriptions are "just the shores on which it laps. . . . It is the loneliness we know because we live at the edge of it" (An Upland Pasture [Nashville: Vanderbilt University Press, 1966], p. 12). Richard Eberhart, "The Horse Chestnut Tree," finds that in the desire to steal a "shining amulet," "we, outlaws on God's property, / Fling out imagination beyond the skies," the death will "drive us from the scene / With the great flowering world unbroken yet" (15 Modern American Poets, pp. 33-34).

teur's approach." The predecessor, "All guts no glass," will be "stricken in the likeness of himself."[26]

The limitation of the mirror of art is sorrowful. Like Emerson, who laments that "facts do not sit for their portrait . . . but lie in a web" (II, 334), Nemerov says, the "shapes" that "cannot be seen in a glass" are the ones "the heart breaks at" ("Holding the Mirror up to Nature," *M.W.*, p. 102):

> They will never become valentines
> or crucifixes, never. Night clouds
> go on insanely as themselves
> though metaphors would be prettier;
> and when I see them massed at the edge
> of the globe, neither weasel nor whale,
> as though this world were, after all,
> non-representational, I know
> a truth that cannot be told, although
> I try to tell you, "We are alone,
> we know nothing, nothing, we shall die
> frightened in our freedom."

The world goes on being itself, and the moon, known by poets "to be Artemis," sails away, beyond the serious poets with their "crazy ladies and cloudy histories."

"The idea of the Other" is for Nemerov, as for Emerson and Jung, "a somewhat dangerous as well as tempting idea, magical, religious, superstitious, according to your point of view" (*S.E.*, p. 401). In "The Scales of the Eyes," eighteen poems which constitute the "variations" of the "text," the quest to obtain the treasures of the unconscious becomes "a kind of spiritual exercise." Through poetry, one attempts "to pray one's humanity back into the universe; and conversely . . . to read, to derive anew one's humanity from nature."[27] The "text" is stated in the first poem of the series:

26. Nemerov, *The Next Room of the Dream* (Chicago: University of Chicago Press, 1962), p. 16. Subsequent references cited in the text as *N.R.D.*
27. *Poets in Progress*, ed. Edward Hungerford (Evanston, Ill.: Northwestern University Press, 1962), p. 125.

> To fleece the Fleece from golden sheep,
> Or prey, or get—is it not lewd
> That we be eaten by our food
> And slept by sleepers in our sleep?[28]

The poet preys on (prays to) the unconscious and is consumed by what he consumes (the unconscious determines him). The mind fleeces (steals from, preys) the Fleece (treasure, poem, reality) and reacts upon itself, so that the act of fleecing becomes synonymous with the result (Fleece). In poem VI, the poet finds that the world, "Already old when I began," is "not my oyster, nor / No slow socratic pearl grows here." Instead, like Emerson's boa constrictor, the world may close in on him: "The blind valves are closing / On only one grain of sand." Poem VIII brings recognition: "There is / No place I do not taste again / When I choke back the deeper sleep / Beneath the mined world I walk." The world of "mind" is dangerously "mined" with archetypes of the unconscious, which must be "mined" to obtain the "Fleece from golden sheep."

III

The act of "mining" the unconscious is part of the process of creative activity, resulting in the work of art, the product. Jung says:

> The creative process, so far as we are able to follow it at all, consists in the unconscious activation of an archetypal image, and in elaborating and shaping this image into the finished work. By giving it shape, the artist translates it into the language of the present, and so makes it possible for us to find our way back to the deepest springs of life.[29]

The process of the active imagination, acting on passive, unconscious material, brings to light symbols of transformation. The symbol is the middle way between conscious and unconscious perception, having

28. *New and Selected Poems* (Chicago: University of Chicago Press, 1960), pp. 117-131. Subsequent references cited in the text as *N.S.P.*
29. C. G. Jung, *The Spirit in Man, Art, and Literature* (New York: Pantheon, 1966), p. 82.

the quality of an image and being thus representable, but also pointing beyond itself to a "meaning that is darkly divined yet still beyond our grasp and [which] cannot be adequately expressed in the familiar words of our language. . . . It expresses not only a conception of the world . . . but also the way in which one views the world" (*S.D.*, pp. 331, 336). The symbol not only "conveys a visualization of the process" but also "brings a re-experiencing of it, of that twilight which we can learn to understand only through inoffensive empathy, but which too much clarity only dispels."[30] "Therefore," Jung states, "this is a psychic world, which allows us to make only indirect and hypothetical inferences about the real nature of matter"; "Between the unknown essences of spirit and matter stands the reality of the psychic—psychic reality, the only reality we can experience immediately" (*S.D.*, p. 384).

Similarly, Emerson frequently discusses the "inevitable dualism" which bisects nature (II, 97), saying that "only by taking a central position in the universe and living in its forms" (sinking to rise) can we know anything: "thoughts let us into realities" (VIII, 42, 272). Poets are the "standing transporters, whose employment consists of speaking to the Father and to matter" (VIII, 19); they are the "link" between "two craving parts of nature . . . the bridge over that yawning need, the mediator betwixt two else unmarriageable facts" (I, 207). The poet orders the world against chaos (X, 280); "the maker of a sentence . . . launches out into the infinite and builds a road into Chaos and old Night" (*J.*, Dec. 19, 1834). Although the marriage is always partial and sometimes contradictory, since "no sentence will hold the whole truth" (III, 245) and the world refuses "to be shut in a word" (*J.*, Oct., 1841); nevertheless, a certain bi-polar unity is possible, with "fact" as "fulcrum" of spirit (XII, 59). By naming objects of nature, the "veil which hid all things" becomes "transparent" (XII, 89); thus, language is a "demi-god," "material only on one side" (VII, 43).

Nemerov, too, notices a "growing consciousness of nature as responsive to language or, to put it the other way, of imagination as the

---

30. C. G. Jung, *Psychological Reflections*, ed. by Jolande Jacobi (Princeton, N.J.: Princeton University Press, 1970), p. 44.

agent of reality" (*P. P.*, p. 241). The dilemma of the relation of self with non-self, through which "infinity becomes finite, essence becomes existence," and spirit mingles with matter, is resolved by the "leap of likeness poetry shares with and derives from magic" (*P.F.*, 102, 160). In "De Anima" Nemerov discusses the spirit's "ransacking through the earth / After its image, its being, its begetting."

> These pure divisions hurt us in some realm
> Of parable beyond belief, beyond
> The temporal mind. Why is it sorrowful?
> Why do we want them together? (*N.R.D.*, p. 25)

The "link" that marries spirit and nature is vision culminating in language. The threshold (division, pain, limitation) of the eye is where the tapestry of art is woven:

> There is a threshold, that meniscus where
> The strider walks on drowning waters. . . .
>   Now that threshold,
> The water of the eye where the world walks
> Delicately, is as a needle threaded
> From the reel of a raveling stream, to stitch
> Dissolving figures in a watered cloth,
> A damask either-sided as the shroud
> Of the lord of Ithaca, labored at in light,
> Destroyed in darkness, while the spidery oars
> Carry his keel across deep mysteries. (*N.S.P.*, "Runes," p. 10)

Like Penelope, the poet weaves the fabric of art from the raveling stream of life. The damask's figures dissolve in a watered cloth, since, as Emerson has said, the "slippery Proteus is not so easily caught" (IV, 121). Meanwhile, the lord of Ithaca confronts the vast and brute sea with miniscule "spidery oars."

In "The Master at a Mediterranean Port," Nemerov calls the sea a "disputed field, it changes sides, / Is turbulent, is unreflecting, deep / And deep and deep." Man constructs his "arcs / And angles," but his curve remains fragmentary, for "yonder in white foam Poseidon rises." The mirror of art is valuable, however, and not "altogether false," but the "mastery" it establishes depends on "image," "stance," "way of seeing," or, as Emerson says, the "angle of vision" (XII, 10). The poem ends with a plea that the "doubleness of these laws" be respected.[31] Emerson, too, laments the "brute Fate" which may be "controlled by a law not adapted to man" (VIII, 407).

Both Emerson and Nemerov (like Jung) view poetry as uniting the me and the not-me through the psyche's participation in a creative process manifested by symbolic language. According to Emerson, the poet, "repairing to the fountain-head of all forms" (*J.*, 1867; also II, 337), brings forth the "gift to men of new images and symbols . . . poetry which tastes the world and reports of it, upbuilding the world again in thought" (VIII, 64). The power is in the image, since it is through the image that the "world realizes mind," and "better than images" is realized (VIII, 20). When the unconscious is tapped—"the whole art of man has been an art of excitation, to provoke, to extort speech from the drowsy genius" (XII, 69)—thought expands from a "barren thesis" and paints itself in symbols (XII, 71), symbols which are "fluxional . . . vehicular and transitive" (III, 34). The "incredible, inexplicable" poet, working to an "end above his will" by means which are "out of his will" (XII, 72), loses himself in his source (XII, 10). For Nemerov, symbolic language unites the me and the not-me in its mediation between thing and thought. He calls poetry a "species of *askesis*," a devotion to the "energy passing between self and the world" (*P.F.*, p. 131), and the energy is magically translated into language that can "act across distances and through an invisible medium."[32] The unconscious plays a large part in the process:

> My belief about poetry says that you write a poem not to say what you think, nor even to find out what you think—though that is closer—but to find out what *it* thinks. . . . And what is that *it* thinks? . . . The devil, the goddess, the unconscious, the language? . . . . Some such notion as this might account not only for the poetic belief in the other, the outside, but also for the well-

31. *The Image and the Law* (New York: Harper, 1947), p. 25. Subsequent references will be cited in the text as *I.L.*

32. Howard Nemerov, *Reflexions on Poetry & Poetics* (New Brunswick: Rutgers University Press, 1972), p. 40. Subsequent references will be cited in the text as *R.P.P.*

known recalcitrance of lyric poetry to paraphrase, its oracular
acceptance of ambiguity as the condition of life, and . . . the
sheer excess vitality and valency of the text over all its explica-
tions. (*R.P.P.*, pp. 160-161)

Emerson's metaphor of inspiration as a quick "flash of light" followed by darkness, "as if life were a thunder-storm wherein you can
see by a flash the horizon, and then cannot see your hand" (VIII, 272),
is echoed in Nemerov's poem "Winter Lightning," where "A sky torn
to the bone / Shattered the ghostly world with light":

> As if the storming sea
> Should sunder to its floor,
> And all things hidden there
> Gleam in the moment silently,
> So does the meadow at the door
> To split and sudden air
> > Show stone and tree. (*N.S.P.*, p. 22)

"So may the poem dispart / The mirror from the light / Where none
can see a seam."[33] Language as mirror may reveal the world so that it
seems seamless, but it is only a seeming; the world is an "as-if" world.
Yet, the poet may "in the lightning second's sight, / Illuminate this
dream / With a cold art" (*N.S.P.*, pp. 72-73). "Lightning second's
sight" suggests at least three qualities of the creative: instantaneous-
ness, illumination, and magic.

Nemerov views the "poet as magician"

> if we remember that magicians do not really solve the hero's
> problems, but only help him to confront these; as Merlin may be
> said to have helped Arthur, not so much by doing magic as by
> being for him a presence and a voice. . . . Our proper magic is the
> magic of language. (*P.F.*, p. 90)

Emerson's Merlin poems express his theory of the "mystic springs" of
inspiration, where angels will say, "pass in, pass in [and] . . . mount to
paradise / By the stairway of surprise!" But Merlin is a "master of

---

33. Emerson notes that usually the "world will be whole and refuses to be
disparted" (VII, 103).

the games," not a problem solver. Through ritual, the "mighty line" will "reconcile" the "two married sides" of every mortal (IX, 120-124). In Emerson's terminology, the living, creating word produces "artful thunder"; in Nemerov's, it produces truth "triply wound," the thing itself, the poet's perception, and language. In "The Book of Kells," he writes: "Out of the living word / Come flower, serpent and bird." "Kell," a dialectal term for "caul," the investing birth membrane, also means a net or web with which to capture or contain. Language is both creating word and capturing net. "In the river of the eye," however, "speech is three-ply / And the truth triply wound" (*S.G.*, pp. 81-83).

No thought can be conveyed but by symbols (*J.*, 1867), writes Emerson, and the truth of the symbol is in its flowing, since "nothing is secure but life, transition, the energizing spirit" (II, 320). Since being is always becoming, the imagination must flow and not freeze (III, 35). Echoing Emerson, Nemerov begins the poem, "Painting a Mountain Stream," with, "Running and standing still at once / is the whole truth," and he ends it with, "Paint this rhythm, not this thing" (*N.S.P.*, pp. 57-58). Emerson criticizes mystics who nail a "symbol to one sense" (III, 35), an idea repeated by Nemerov when he calls poetry and religion "the flowing and the static forms of the same substance" (*P.F.*, pp. 12-13). Only the flowing has vitality and the symbol cannot be fully explicated. As Emerson says, a poem is more than "a vehicle to carry a sentence as a jewel is carried in its case"; it is "inseparable from its contents" (VIII, 54). Nemerov's metaphor for the impenetrability of the symbol is that its interpretation is only "the next room of the dream." Ultimate, absolute truth is not measurable: Emerson states that "dream delivers us to dream, and there is no end to illusion" (III, 50), and Nemerov notes that the "connection" the poem makes may be merely a "solipsism from which we have no escape but by delusion into illusion" (*S.E.*, pp. 400-401).

Emerson's poet puts the world "under the mind for verb and noun" (III, 20), whereas Nemerov's concentrates on the verb. In "The Loon's Cry," the speaker of the poem, having fallen from "the symboled world, where I in earlier days / Found mysteries of meaning, form, and fate," envies past ages when the world was ordered by Christian symbols. He sees that having "traded all those mysteries in" for reality in things, that reality has "exhausted all their truth." As though answering his thought, a loon cries out, "Laughter of desolation on the river, / A savage cry," and the poet feels naked and cold in his isolation until he realizes that to be otherwise is to be "in ignorance and emptiness" like Adam before the fall.

> I thought I understood what that cry meant,
> That its contempt was for the forms of things,
> Their doctrines, which decayed—the nouns of stone
> And adjectives of glass—not for the verb
> Which surged in power properly eternal
> Against the seawall of the solid world,
> Battering and undermining what it built,
>
> And whose respeaking was the poet's act.

For Nemerov, nouns are stone (Emerson's "rigid names" compared to the "wild fertility of Nature" [VII, 138]), and only verbs denoting process provide the material of the poet. Even though they undermine what they have built, still, it is only through them the poet can define

> Both wretchedness and love. For signatures
> In all things are, which leave us not alone
> Even in the thought of death, and may by arts
> Contemplative be found and named again.
>   (*M.W.*, pp. 29-31)

Emerson's poet, "the symbolizer," "projects a scribe's hand and writes the adequate genesis" (VIII, 71), whereas Nemerov's recognizes that the universe is unique to the person viewing it: "The universe induces / a different tremor in every hand . . . ." "Miraculous. It is as though the world / were a great writing" ("Writing," *M.W.*, p. 96). "The eye altering alters all" (VIII, 319), says Emerson, and Nemerov entitles a poem "For the Eye Altered Alters All": "Number, said the skull Pythagoras, / Their transfixed eyes design the world." Mathematical conceptions, "Abstracts of night . . . would not know / God and Son and guarding Ghost / Out of the writings of cold saints" (*I.L.*, p. 24). The angle of vision determines the view.

Both poets refer to Plato's cave, Emerson, optimistically: "We are like persons who come out of a cave or cellar into the open air. This is the effect on us of . . . poetic forms" (III, 30). The "spirit," the absolute behind Nature, "is a great shadow pointing always to the sun behind us" (I, 61). More paradoxically, Nemerov phrases the dilemma in "Unscientific Postscript."

> There is the world, the dream, and the one law.
> The wish, the wisdom, and things as they are.
>
> Inside the cave the burning sunlight showed
> A shade and forms between the light and shade,

"Neither real nor false nor subject to belief," but as in life, "Reflexive, multiple." The resolution to the dilemma is "not to believe . . . but fully as orchestra to accept, / Making an answer, even if lament, / In measured dance, with the whole instrument" (*J.L.*, p. 69) a resolution accepted by Emerson as well.

From Nemerov's writings, one can postulate a contemporary theory of poetry: "The rational, conscious mind works on or through the irrational, unconscious mind to create a statement about the world. The world itself, independent of man, is knowable only through the imagination which conceives it in its moment of flowing and presents it in image, symbol, myth, magic, invocation. The experience, immediate, exalting, inspiring, and terrifying, cannot be translated into nonsymbolic language. The truth of the poem is paradoxical; the bridge of language is true but its co-respondent reality may not be." Emerson dotted many of these points on the fragmentary curve of his aesthetic theory. For all of his insistence upon his own poetic "hoarseness," he was, as Howard Vincent has said, the "Radiant Center. And I mean center for his own day, for our day, for modern man—even, going way out, for the Consciousness III dreamers."[34] The "early pulse" he contributed has expanded and radiated in spirals not only up and out but also in and down.

34. Letter from Howard Vincent to Gloria Young, Ogunquit, Maine (June 27, 1973).

Robert J Bertholf

Shelley, Stevens and Robert Duncan:
The Poetry of Approximations

I

In his discussion of the "plenitude of being" rising in the presence of the "Holy," which he calls the *Numen*, Rudolf Otto maintains that the precise description of this experience is impossible. "The consciousness of the 'wholly other' evades precise formulation in words, and we have to employ symbolic phrases which seem sometimes sheer paradox, that is *ir*rational, not merely nonrational, in import."[1] By indirection, symbolic formulas, and evocation, the presence of the *Numen* can be transferred into the visibility of language, and in this designation Otto focuses on one of the principal situations in the poetry of Shelley, Stevens and Robert Duncan. All three poets come into illuminated visions, which demand a profusion of approximate images and statements, and which push their poetry into an arena of action where the process of presentation qualifies as a significant portion of the poem's meaning. As Whitehead reminds us, the mind forever learns more about itself and its relationship with reality. No concept or formulation remains fixed as an absolute definition. "Process for its intelligibility involves the notion of a creative activity belonging to the very essence of each occasion. It is the process of eliciting into actual being factors in the universe which antecedently to that process exist only in the mode of unrealized potentialities. The process of self-creation is the transformation of the potential into the ac-

1. Rudolf Otto, *The Idea of the Holy*, trans. John W. Harvey, 2nd ed. (1950; rpt. New York: Oxford University Press, 1958), pp. 21, 59.

tual, and the fact of such transformation includes the immediacy of self-enjoyment."[2] In the transformations of potential energies, these poets evolve a mode of poetry which challenges the conventions of literary tradition and projects as an energized possibility a unique conception of form. Working out a poetry of approximate images that evokes the visionary experience of the holy, and which develops as a process of self-creation in the act of the mind realizing its attunement with a greater spiritual world, places Shelley, Stevens and Duncan at the very heart of the Romantic in literature.

Not only did Shelley engage himself in this process in such poems as "Mont Blanc," "Alastor," and "To a Skylark," but in his defense of the art of poetry, he writes, conscious of his limitations as a scribe of the infinite wonder:

> For the mind in creation is a fading coal, which some invisible influence, like an inconstant wind, awakens to transitory brightness: this power arises from within, like the colour of a flower which fades and changes as it is developed, and the conscious portions of our natures are unprophetic either of its approach or its departure. . . . when composition begins, inspiration is already on the decline, and the most glorious poetry that has ever been communicated to the world is probably a feeble shadow of the original conception of the Poet.[3]

The release from the domination of fixed doctrines of belief, which the Romantics claimed as their right, shifted attention away from the necessity of conforming to certain fixed laws, to the centrality of the perceiving and knowing self. This release, as R. A. Foakes has demonstrated,[4] allowed the poet to approach reality without preconceptions, and granted the free interpenetration of the world and the mind; as

2. Alfred North Whitehead, *Modes of Thought* (1938; rpt. New York: The Free Press, 1968), p. 151.

3. Roger Ingpen and W. E. Peck, eds., *The Complete Works of Percy Bysshe Shelley* (London: Ernest Benn, 1926-1930), VII, p. 135.

4. R. A. Foakes, *The Romantic Assertion: A Study in the Language of Nineteenth Century Poetry* (New Haven: Yale University Press, 1958), *passim*; see also Patricia M. Ball, *The Central Self: A Study in Romantic and Victorian Imagination* (London: The Athlone Press, 1968), pp. 5-21.

Wordsworth said, "an ennobling interchange / Of action from without and from within" (*The Prelude*, XIII, 374-375). It also obligated the individual poet to create, or continually re-create, himself by constantly redefining his private sense of involvement in the vaster world of spirit, which Shelley tells us visits "This various world with an inconstant wing." While alienation from reality brought depression, as Coleridge says in "Dejection: an Ode," and Wordsworth confirms in "Ode to Duty," the balancing affirmation in the dissolution of Blake's "Cloven Fiction" brought with it immersion in the primordial energies of creation that tested the fullest capacities of the poet for right expression. Shelley's discussion of the fading coal is just one of many examples of the interpenetration of the mind and the world in a spot of time, an instantaneous and fleeting glimpse of the wholeness of the ground of being itself, existing without morphology, that appears in this line of poetry I am sketching out.

In Shelley's case, the substance of each poem is not a description of a completely possessed vision. It is a projection of a possible means of moving from the selvages of the experience to the center of the wholeness that has vanished before its variations inform the substance of the poem. "How vain it is," he announces in his essay "On Life," "to think that words can penetrate the mystery of our being."[5] And in "To a Skylark," which takes the unseen bird as an emblem of the presence of wholeness, Shelley works through a series of analogies introduced by "like"—"Like a high-born maiden," "Like a glow-worm golden," "Like a rose embowered"—that demonstrates the frustrating leakages words contain. In this series, each analogy becomes an approximation, or a projection of a possible means of bringing into visible form the invisible source of musical harmony. The process of calling up fit approximations, then, underlies the progress of the poem, and in a tangible way, enters the poem as a proof of the impossibility to express what is known, but what is inexpressible. In its attempt to actualize the potential energies of the event, the poem is a fragmentary testament of a vision, and not the carefully tutored result of rational deliberation.

5. *Complete Works*, VI, p. 194.

M. H. Abrams' comments on the fragmentary or incomplete aspect of Romantic poetry link Shelley's formulations to those of Wallace Stevens and Robert Duncan:

> For example, organic growth is an open-ended process, nurturing a sense of the promise of the incomplete, and the glory of the imperfect. . . . And only in a 'mechanical' unity are the parts sharply defined and fixed; in organic unity, what we find is a complex inter-relation of living, indeterminate, and endlessly changing components.[6]

Stevens was always aware of the open process and spiritual vitality of reality.[7] In his early poems, he designed an antithesis between his mind (imagination) and the world (reality), which, as the revolving arguments of "The Man With the Blue Guitar" (1937) illustrate, battled one another, at times, into a synthesis. Stevens was never content with this synthetic vision.[8] He knew that the mind's versions of reality were not mechanically complete and could never be. "It is never the thing but the version of the thing" (*CP*, 332) he announced with the full recognition that it was his duty to release the open secret of the universe, which he knew existed, with all the majesty at his command. "There is always an analogy between nature and the imagination, and possibly poetry is merely the strange rhetoric of that parallel: a rhetoric in which the feeling of one man is communicated to another in words of the exquisite appositeness that takes away all their verbality" (*NA*, 118). In the later poetry, the synthetic vision disappears and in its place appear points of penetration into the "times of inherent excellence" (*CP*, 386), or "nebulous brilliancies" (*CP*,

6. M. H. Abrams, *The Mirror and the Lamp: Romantic Theory and the Critical Tradition* (1953; rpt. New York: W. W. Norton, 1958), p. 220.

7. References to the work of Wallace Stevens will be to the following texts and will appear in my essay with the indicated abbreviations: Wallace Stevens, *The Collected Poems* (New York: Alfred A. Knopf, 1954), as *CP*; Wallace Stevens, *Opus Posthumous*, ed. Samuel French Morse (New York: Alfred A. Knopf, 1957), as *OP*; Wallace Stevens, *The Necessary Angel: Essays on Reality and Imagination* (New York: Vintage Books, 1951), as *NA*.

8. On this aspect of Stevens' poetry see: Bernard Heringman, "The Poetry of Synthesis," *Perspective*, 7 (1954), 167-175.

317), in which the mind and the world uncover the common course of their infinite movements. Strings of analogies, often canceling one another, arise as projections to evoke the life of the mind so that the medium of expression dissolves in the "pure rhetoric of a language without words" (*CP*, 374).

As Helen Hennesey Vendler has shown, Stevens' poetry is riddled with qualified assertions, delivered with *may, might, could, perhaps* or *possibly*.[9] "As it is, in the intricate evasions of as," (*CP*, 486), Stevens was challenged to light his vision with the full force of a rhetoric which resisted the containment of the invisible wonder. In "Credences of Summer" (1947) and the following poems, he arrived at a sense of splendor in which the processes of the world and the processes of the mind revealed themselves as equal emanations of a common source, which he proclaimed his mythological center: "This is the barrenness / Of the fertile thing that can attain no more" (*CP*, 373). As in Shelley's awe at the power of Mont Blanc, Stevens' fertile vision of his attunement with genesis and growth spirited him to transfer his flicks of feeling of the "enormous life" (*NA*, 82) of the ideal into language:

> It must be visible or invisible,
> Invisible or visible or both:
> A seeing and unseeing in the eye. (*CP*, 385)

As the parables of "Esthétique du Mal" (1944) and the exquisite yet abstract speculations of "Notes Toward a Supreme Fiction" (1942) teach, he evolved a poetry based on the principles of change and variation—"It is only enough / To live incessantly in change" (*OP*, 50). Change and process vitalize imagination and reality, and the discovery of this motion led to the dissolution of the "Cloven Fiction." By projecting reality's cycle of death/rebirth as the imagination's own, Stevens was able to formulate a pattern of the imagination's life that was imitative of but disengaged from the cycle of reality. He cleansed his mind of predeterminations of thought and feeling by destroying existing images and "wormy metaphors" (*CP*, 162) and creating by

9. Helen Hennessy Vendler, *On Extended Wings: Wallace Stevens' Longer Poems* (Cambridge: Harvard University Press, 1969), pp. 13-37.

means of analogies a sense of the brilliance alive in the flowing of imaginative time. His poem, "An Ordinary Evening in New Haven" (1950), demonstrates the mind creating images as approaches to a mythological center. Hardly a unified system, the poem is a series of related speculations toward the central source, itself enacting the very process of the poem's substance. It is Stevens' grand poem of "the mind in the act of finding / What will suffice" (*CP*, 239).

Shelley's approximations and Stevens' incomplete analogies of the holy presence operate in the poetry of Robert Duncan.[10] For Duncan, the sounds of words, their vowels, become "notes of a scale, in which breaths move" (*T&L*, 67). The musical rhythms move him into the presence of primal creation itself:

> This creative life is a drive towards the reality of Creation, producing an inner world, an emotional and intellectual fiction, in answer to our awareness of the creative reality of the whole. If the world does not speak to us, we cannot speak with it. If we view the literal as a matter of mere fact, as the positivist does, it is mute. But once we apprehend the literal as a language, once things about us reveal depths and heights of meaning, we are involved in the sense of Creation ourselves, and in our human terms, this is Poetry, Making, the inner Fiction of Consciousness.[11]

Immersed in the "wholly other" of the first emergence of Eros, the incarnation of form (as in the Gnostic mysteries) at the initiation of all forms, Duncan announces the grandeur of the central energies. His work is a poetry of beginnings, in which he recreates the mysteries of his own birth, an act he conceives as coincident with universal creation and motion.

---

10. References to the work of Robert Duncan will be to the following texts and will appear in my essay with the indicated abbreviations: Robert Duncan, *The Truth and Life of Myth: An Essay in Essential Autobiography* (1968; rpt. Freemont, Michigan: The Sumac Press, 1972), as *T&L*; Robert Duncan, *Bending the Bow* (New York: New Directions, 1968), as *BB*; Robert Duncan, *The Opening of the Field* (New York: New Directions, 1960), as *OF*; Robert Duncan, *Tribunals* (Los Angeles: Black Sparrow Press, 1970), as *T*.

11. Robert Duncan, *The Sweetness and Greatness of Dante's Divine Comedy* (San Francisco: Open Space, 1965), n.p.

The art of the poem, like the mechanism of the dream or the intent of the tribal myth and dromena, is a cathexis: to keep present and immediate a variety of times and places, persons and events. In the melody we make, the possibility of eternal life is hidden, and experience we thought lost returns to us.[12]

In an attempt to formulate and express the presence of first energies, "in the lateness of the world / primordial bellowings / from which the youngest world might spring" (*OF*, 50), he includes in his Chrestomathy the approximate fictions of Dante, Whitman, Shelley, Blake and Pound. As his poetry is a fiction of genesis, so he thinks of the great poems of the world as alternate fictions that come into his consciousness as he enters the aura of genesis itself. "It is not that poetry imitates but that poetry enacts in its order the order of first things," he explains as a means of declaring that the holiness of life reveals itself in the form of the poem as fictions which approximate a larger generative order. In this consciousness, he continues, "the poet desires to penetrate the seeming of style and subject matter to that most real where there is no form that is not content, no content that is not form."[13] As the intricate movements of sound and meaning in "The Venice Poem" (1949) reveal (and in their elegant variations of melody), Duncan thinks of his poetry as a developing process, which, in its approximations, catches the moment of clarity at the peak of its wholeness.

> Poems come up from a ground so
> to illustrate the ground, approximate
> a lingering of eternal image, a need
> known only in its being found ready.
> (*OF*, 60)

In a discussion in his "Passages Poems," which I will comment on later, he says: "I number the first to come *one*, but they belong to a series that extends in an area larger than my work in them. I enter the poem as I entered my life, moving between an initiation and a terminus I cannot name" (*BB*, V). Each of the poems in this series is an

12. Robert Duncan, "Rites of Participation," *Caterpillar*, No. 1 (1967), 21.
13. Robert Duncan, "Towards an Open Universe," in *Poets on Poetry*, ed. Howard Nemerov (New York: Basic Books, 1966), p. 138.

approximation of the whole poem, a projected version, incorporating previous fictions, put out as Duncan's attempt to recreate himself by illustrating the dance of the phonemes in the cadences and processes of language as it engages itself in the music of genesis. The poems, not complete in themselves, are fragments of the full vision, and they enact in their incompletion the process of the mind releasing itself in the influx of first energies. The form of the poem is the process of its meaning realizing itself. In Duncan's world, the arrival of the movement of the poem is greeted with humility and grace, as well as fear and awe, because he has been allowed entrance into the sacred presence of the creating processes themselves.[14]

While the presence of the *Numen* and the activities of approximations are common to these poets, another feature at the heart of the Romantic ties these poets together. Denying the comfortable sanctions of social, philosophical or religious doctrine, they join the procedure of creating for themselves a fictive habitation for the self to occupy. They are all mythopoetic poets. Shelley, for example, was aware, as Duncan is, that his poetry moves in a much larger poem, of which Ovid's *Metamorphosis*, Dante's *Divine Comedy* and Milton's *Paradise Lost* are also participants. He writes:

> And let us not circumscribe the effects of the bucolic and erotic poetry within the limits of the sensibility of those to whom it was addressed. They may have perceived the beauty of those immortal compositions, simply as fragments and isolated portions: those who are more finely organized, or born in a happier age, may recognize them as episodes to that great poem, which all poets, like the co-operating thoughts of one great mind, have built up since the beginning of the world.[15]

Yet, in adding to the great poem, Shelley was also aware that he was creating for himself an imaginary landscape, formed with the morphology of the parts of the poem he was able to wrest from the invisible realm. In another way, the process of searching out approximate versions of the one poem in the terms and images of reality made

14. See Rudolf Otto, pp. 12-24.
15. *Complete Works*, VII, p. 124.

it possible to fix his perceiving self in the flow of the vision, and to create a version of himself in the habitation of the whole physical poem. As in "Ode to the West Wind" and "Hymn to Intellectual Beauty," he was aware of the existence of the cyclic process of spiritual reality and offered prayers of supplication to join that reality. When the joining occurs through the ritual of invocation, the self of the poems is born as a distinct possibility in the area of the whole poem.

> Emerson too was aware of the primordial genesis of all poetry. For poetry was all written before time was, and whenever we are so finely organized that we can penetrate into that region where the air is music, we hear those primal warblings, and attempt to write them down, but we lose ever and anon a word, or a verse, and substitute something of our own, and thus miswrite the poem. The men of more delicate ear write down these cadences more faithfully, and these transcripts, though imperfect, become the songs of the nations.[16]

Again the idea is clear that the poem exists before the poet arrives to transcribe the parts of its message into language. The written poem is an imperfect rendering; through it the poet participates in the forces of the great poem and gains a definition, however partial, of himself in terms of primal warblings. And Whitman, in whom Duncan finds a base as a poet, writes in a similar vein:[17]

> All apparent contradictions in the statement of the Deific nature by different ages, nations, churches, points of view, are but fractional and imperfect expressions of one essential unity, from which they all proceed—crude endeavors or distorted parts, to be regarded both as distinct and united.[18]

16. "The Poet," in *Selections from Ralph Waldo Emerson*, ed. Stephen Whicher (Cambridge: Riverside Press, 1957), pp. 224-225.

17. See Robert Duncan, "Changing Perspectives in Reading Whitman," in *The Artistic Legacy of Walt Whitman: A Tribute to Gay Wilson Allen*, ed. Edwin Haviland Miller (New York: New York University Press, 1970), pp. 73-102.

18. From "Carlyle from American Points of View," in Walt Whitman, *Prose Works 1892*, Vol. 1 *Specimen Days*, ed. Floyd Stovall (New York: New York University Press, 1963), p. 260.

In his poetry Whitman creates a fictive "I" that assimilates to itself as many of the imperfect expressions as possible and then projects outward as much of the total vision of the "cosma-float" possible as the passional and democratic location of that "I." He had the sense that the poet is only the passing servant of a process that has no beginning and no end; but a process, as Shelley says, that brings to light parts of the whole which are modified in the imagination of the actual into realized forms of the self, alive, in a world created in the terms and energies of first forms. In the reiteration and repetitions of the parts of the whole, the individual poet adds to the revealed poem, and thus generates himself in the *Numen* of the whole poem.[19]

Stevens enters the line here too. After he reduced the abstractions of "Notes" to the human, everyday world in "Esthétique du Mal," and then discovered in "Credences" that there was a holy credence table he could go to for spiritual rebirth, he joined the company of these visionary poets of the great poem. In his essay, "Effects of Analogy," he discusses among others a type of the imagination which dominates the intricate structures of the late poems, especially "An Ordinary Evening":

> One relates to the imagination as a power within him not so much to destroy reality at will as to put it to his own uses. He comes to feel that his imagination is not wholly his own but that it may be part of a much larger, much more potent imagination, which it is his affair to try to get at. (*NA*, 115)

The "rock" or the "centre" became Stevens' fictive images for the potent imagination which he tried to possess and be possessed by. At the same time that the course and form of the poems altered to include more of the possibilities of the potency, Stevens returned to the Connecticut landscape as a subject. In doing so he attempted to define a geography of the imagination which reflected its region.

> The image must be of the nature of its creator.
> It is the nature of its creator increased,

19. See Philip Wheelwright, "Notes on Mythopoeia," in *Myth and Literature: Contemporary Theory and Practice*, ed. John B. Vickery (Lincoln: University of Nebraska Press, 1966), pp. 59-66.

Heightened. It is he, anew, in a freshened youth
And it is he in the substance of his region,
Wood of his forests and stone out of his fields
Or from under his mountains. (*OP*, 118)

This geography, together with the creation of the imagination's time scheme, pushes the poems into the realm of the mythopoetic, where the infinite repetitions of daily affairs wedded to visionary concerns specify the emergence of a fictive self dwelling in the central poem.

And Robert Duncan joins Shelley, Whitman and Stevens in these matters:

Love, desire, and beauty, in the poet's Theogony, precede mankind. They were once forces that came to be forms. We experience something, the meaning of things seems to change when we fall in love, as if life were a language we had begun to understand. It is the virtue of words that what were forces become meanings and seek form. Cosmic powers appear as presences and even as persons of inner being to the imagination.[20]

Unlike Stevens' actual landscape, Duncan's geography is completely fictive. "Often I am permitted to return to a meadow," he writes

as if it were a scene made-up by the mind,
that is not mine, but is a made place,

that is mine, it is so near to the heart,
an eternal pasture folded in all thought
so that there is a hall therein

that is a made place, created by light
wherefrom the shadows that are forms fall. (*OF*, 7)

He calls this "a place of first permission, / everlasting omen of what is." Duncan's field of poetic action is alive with the original impulses to creation, and when he enters it, in a vision of the whole, he participates in creation itself. Like the other poets mentioned here, with the rehearsals of approximation, he moves through the rites of participa-

20. Robert Duncan, "Two Chapters from H.D.," *Triquarterly*, no. 12 (1968), 70.

tion into the full membership of the visionary company of mythopoetic
creators. "He," George Whalley tells us in a discussion of visionary
poets, "has adjusted himself to a state of translucence, of medium-like
conduction: he has co-operated in a minute moment of the universal
and eternal process of coming-to-birth, the self-bodying of reality."[21]
In the poems of this company, the parts come together in interdependent relationships, and are not joined closely by the dictates of rational
structures. This open-ended world, where additional glimpses of the
great poem are always welcome, permits the continuing growth of the
revealed forms of the invisible world.

There is no

good a man has in his own things except

it be in the community of every thing;

no nature he has

but in his nature hidden in the heart of the living

in the great household. (*BB*, 79)

II

In his Preface to "Alastor," Shelley writes the youthful poet "images to himself the Being whom he loves," and: "The intellectual
faculties, the imagination, the functions of sense, have their respective requisitions on the sympathy of corresponding powers in other
human beings. The Poet is represented as uniting these requisitions,
and attaching them to a single image."[22] The vision of the "veiléd
maid" (l. 151), the single image of love and desire, is contained and

21. George Whalley, *Poetic Process* (Cleveland: The World Publishing Company, 1967), p. xxx.
22. All references to Shelley's poetry will be to: *Shelley's Poetical Works*, ed.
Thomas Hutchinson (London: Oxford University Press, 1967), p. 14, and
will be indicated by either page or line numbers in the text.

complete for the journey of the best portions of an exhausting quest. In this formulation, the goal of the quest is teleological. The object of desire is known before the quest begins, and when the poet fails to touch the "dissolving arms" (1. 187) of his imagined lover, he must enter the world of the dead, which the poem postulates as equivalent to the world of dreams, where the original vision arose. Through "the Poet's blood, / That ever beat in mystic sympathy / With nature's ebb and flow" (ll. 651-653), the singularity of his search and his over-reaching ["He overlaps the bounds" (1. 207)], the poet binds himself to "Nature's vast frame, the web of human things" (1. 719). His obsessive preoccupations force him into a straight, linear decline out of the realm of dreams, out of the world of the living.

In "Hymn to Intellectual Beauty," an incantation to the transient but pervasive power of the universal imagination, Shelley shifted away from the linear, teleological quest, and approached a definition of numenous experience in line with his facilities as a poet of process. For in this poem, which runs through applications of approximations of the "inconstant glance" (1. 6) of the mysterious beauty and terror of the vision, Shelley advanced out of his depressive separation from reality and moved into a participation with its flow. Otto's "wholly other" possessed him; and his fealty at meeting this messenger of the holy was to summon up, with versions of reality, the unseen and unseeable force of the universe:

> Like hues and harmonies of evening,—
>   Like clouds in starlight widely spread,—
>   Like memory of music fled,—
>   Like aught that for its grace may be
> Dear, and yet dearer for its mystery. (ll. 8-12)

By shifting away from the teleological quest to the evocation of a vision, Shelley arrived at a procedure of poetry in which accumulated similes, appositions and images illustrate the essay of the mind coming to terms with a poetic duty, which he knows will always remain unfinished, but a duty he has no choice of rejecting. The incomplete expression evolving out of the forms of poetry stands as an unfinished and unfinishable account of a vision that defies completion. Shelley

attempts to move into the area of the presiding spirit with his procedures, but failing to be welcomed, and thus reborn, he imposes a rational order on the poem. At the same time that he allows the organic
accumulation of the parts within the poem, the Aristotelian bearing of
a beginning, middle and end offers the appearance of a completed
definition.

"But a voice / is wanting," Shelley tells us in *Prometheus Unbound*,
"the deep truth is imageless" (II. iv. 115-116), and in "Mont Blanc"
his mode of expression initiates a process of approximate images that
intimates the powerful truth of silence and the sublime without cate-
gorically defining it. As in "The Clouds" and "Arethusa"—a poem
Duncan set to a new measure[23]—Shelley projects the water cycle's
open-ended continuance as the underlying principle of change in reality that best embodies the presentations of the holy to the imagination's life. In a real sense, the poem's message is fully delivered after
the initial declaration, "The everlasting universe of things / Flows
through the mind and rolls its rapid waves" (ll. 1-2) with various
avatars through the physical universe. The vision emerges almost as
a direct tautologous statement; but the interchange of energies flowing in and out of his consciousness pushes the rest of the poem into
a complex series of images, grammatical appositions and approximations which provoke from their easy movement the sense of a mind
creating itself, immersed in, yet not fully approaching, the dynamic
centrality of visionary brilliance. As Jerome J. McGann assures us, "the
imagination rises to upbuild itself into ever new forms, and only by
describing this endlessly generative process itself does it approximate
the ideal source of all generation and life."[24]

In the "unremitting interchange / With the clear universe" (ll. 39-
40) of the cyclic process, figured in the flow of the glacier and the
run of the Arve—and the ravine as the channel of the poet's receiving

23. Robert Duncan, *Roots and Branches* (1964: rpt. New York: New Directions 1969), pp. 78-81.
24. Jerome J. McGann, "Shelley's Veils: A Thousand Images of Loveliness,"
in *Romantic and Victorian: Studies in Memory of William H. Marshall*, ed.
W. Paul Elledge and Richard L. Hoffman (Crabbury, New Jersey: Associated
University Presses, Inc., 1971), p. 216.

mind—Shelley associates the massive setting of Mont Blanc he described in a letter with the emergence of a vast, universal power.[25]

> Thus thou, Ravine of Arve—dark, deep Ravine—
> Thou many-coloured, many voicèd vale,
> Over whose pines, and crags, and caverns sail
> Fast cloud-shadows and sunbeams: awful scene,
> Where Power in likeness of the Arve comes down
> From the ice-gulfs that gird his secret throne,
> Bursting through these dark mountains like the flame
> Of lightning through the tempest. (ll. 12-19)

The mountain itself assumes the religious regalia of "a secret throne" (l. 17), robed in "solemn harmony" (l. 24), and the pines, in their "mighty swinging" (l. 23) from the "devotion" (l. 21) of the wind, are transformed into a huge ceremonial censor. These pines, as "Children of elder time" (l. 21), or present appearances of antique mysteries, contribute to the evocation of the sense of the primordial sources shrouded in the flickering lights and lightning of cosmic involvement. Not only with the process of grammatical approximation, then, but with connotative associations which expand the physical scene into the arena of the living imagination, Shelley spreads out the fictive map of his full immersion in the visionary world. In the ceaseless motion of piling up attributes of the physical scene alive in the poet's mind, the mountain still remains the habitation of "some unsculptured image" (l. 27), that final statement that would make clear the crude compoundings of approximations, and gathering connotations of holiness that could reform the faulted religious "voices of the des-

25. Shelley wrote: "On all sides precipitous mountains the abodes of unrelenting frost surround this vale. Their sides are banked up with ice & snow broken & heaped up & exhibiting terrific chasms. . . . They pierce the clouds like things not belonging to this earth. The vale itself is filled with a mass of undulating ice. . . . It exhibits an appearance as if frost had suddenly bound up the waves & whirl[l]pools of a mighty torrent . . .: the waves are elevated about 12 or 15 feet from the surface of the mass which is intersected with long gaps of unfathomable depth, the ice of whose sides is more beautifully azure than the sky" (*The Letters of Percy Bysshe Shelley*, ed. Frederick L. Jones [Oxford: Clarendon Press, 1964], I, p. 500).

ert" (l. 28). Yet, the realization of the impossibility of possessing
the one image, though possessed by its power in the miracle of rebirth, lapses, as all visions do, and the final lines turn to a direct discussion of penetration into the unknown world that has motivated
the first part of the section:

> I seem as in a trance sublime and strange
> To muse on my own separate fantasy,
> My own, my human mind, which passively
> Now renders and receives fast influencings,
> Holding an unremitting interchange
> With the clear universe of things around. (ll. 35-40)

The discussion of searching for "some faint image" (l. 47) leads back
to the center of the section, where the process itself was enacted with
the creative brilliance of a mind reaching into the excitement and music of primal life.

Section two contains the heart of the vision and the major series
of approximating images. The main concern of the third section is
Shelley's astonishment that Mont Blanc "still, snowy, and serene" (l.
61) remains a physical structure after it stood out from itself as his
mythological center. This shock comes after further speculations about
the nature of the vision, the possibility of the vision as a dream, and
the important lines, "I look on high; / Has some unknown omnipotence unfurled / The veil of life and death?" (ll. 52-54).[26] Moments
before the mountain shimmered in beauty and terror as the generative power of the mind and the world, but now, after the vision has
faded, the image has lost its holy glow in the mundane. In another
sense, the mountain has been veiled—that is, concealed by the approximate images that Shelley hoped would reveal it. And he is left to
speculate at the end of the section about the barrenness and wildness
of the geography, and to attribute, almost as an afterthought, pro-
prieties of morality:

26. See E. B. Murray, "Mont Blanc's Unfurled Veil," *KSJ*, 19 (1969), 39-
48, especially his comments on Harold Bloom's unconscionable alteration of
"unfurled" to "upfurled."

> The wilderness has a mysterious tongue
> Which teaches awful doubt, or faith so mild,
> So solemn, so serene, that man may be,
> But for such faith, with nature reconciled;
> Thou has a voice, great Mountain, to repeal
> Large codes of fraud and woe; not understood
> By all, but which the wise, and great, and good
> Interpret, or make felt, or deeply feel. (ll. 76-83)

Sections four and five end the poem but do not provide it with a tight unity. The central proposition of section four comes in the lines:

> All things that move and breathe with toil and sound
> Are born and die; revolve, subside and swell.
> Power dwells apart in its tranquillity,
> Remote, serene, and inaccessible: (ll. 94-97)

Shelley recognizes that the cyclic processes of the invisible world can only appear in the morphology of the physical universe. In the same way that the power of the numenous vision energizes the variety of rhetoric and images in his poem, the power realizes itself in the flux and impermanence of reality. Unchanging itself, it causes change alike in the mind and the world. This assurance leads to the deliberate statement of the progress of the glacier and its destructive passage down the mountain, forming the "majestic River" (l. 123), which in turn evaporates to make the moisture for the snow that falls in silence on the mountain again. The final lines lead to Duncan's notion of literal reality containing the language of creation itself:

> And what were thou, and earth, and stars, and sea,
> If to the human mind's imaginings
> Silence and solitude were vacancy? (ll. 145-146)

Shelley seals his poem with the simplest of notions: if a man recognizes in the process of the mind and nature a vast and overwhelming sameness, then nature, as Bryant tells us in "Thanatopsis," "speaks/ A various language." The demonstration of the cyclic visitation of the visionary *Numen* has been enforced by a further example of the cyclic process of nature; and these processes, though uniquely felt, are part

of a vaster one that has been in motion since primordial time. At the
end, the poem refers to its own spoken message but leaves the conclusion of the speculations of approximation open. Unlike the structure
of "Hymn to Intellectual Beauty," "Mont Blanc" does not conclude;
the message of the poem, as it extends itself outward in the form of
the poem, embodies a cyclic process of holy visitation that is as endlessly repetitive as winter leading to the blooming of spring.

By allowing the action of his poetry to course in phase with the
processes of reality, Shelley, for a time, released himself into the clear
fluency of visionary rebirth. In such a coursing each statement of the
Numen opened other possibilities for a closer approach to that sought-
for apocalypse of being, which finally arrived in "The Triumph of
Life." In Stevens' world, also, the announcement of one penetration
into the seemings of reality released multiple changing analogies of
the central energies. As a "patron of origins" (*CP*, 443), Stevens was
certain that a more comprehensive poem existed, that glimpses of it
arrived unexpectedly, and that, perhaps, he could render a closer semblance from the imagination's reservoir of images. "One poem proves
another and the whole" (*CP*, 441), he says, assuring himself that
the appearance of a single poem invites the belief that the universal
poem might yet appear in its wholeness.

In "Credences of Summer," Stevens welcomed a sparkling accord
with reality, in which the long-fought battles between reality and
imagination resolved themselves into the peaceful occasion of con-
traries (in the Blakean sense), recognizing that both were emanations
from a common source, but appearing in different morphologies. In
this apocalyptic vision of the holy, Stevens reached out through the
imagery of the sacred mountain, as Shelley had done:

> It is the rock of summer, the extreme,
> A mountain luminous half way in bloom
> And then half way in the extremest light
> Of sapphires flashing from the central sky,
> As if twelve princes sat before a king.
> (*CP*, 375)

Yet, he was not able to approach the luminous mountain without the
evasions of metaphors and analogies. He knew that the "puissant

flick" (*CP*, 517) arrived and departed in desperate swiftness, and saw that this procedure matched the procedure of reality, just as Shelley claimed for the water cycle. But in "The Auroras of Autumn" and "The Rock," Stevens attempted to specify the inviolable necessity of the imagination's life he discovered in "Credences" and to assert a process of poetry which assumed to itself the revelation of the mystery of Being. "From the imaginative period of Notes," Stevens wrote in a letter to Bernard Heringman:

> I turned to the ideas of Credences of Summer. At the moment I am at work on a thing called An Ordinary Evening in New Haven. This is confidential and I don't want the thing to be spoken of. But here my interest is to try to get as close to the ordinary, the commonplace and the ugly as it is possible for a poet to get. It is not a question of grim reality but of plain reality. The object is of course to purge oneself of anything false. . . . This is not in any sense a turning away from the ideas of Credences of Summer: it is a development of those ideas. That sort of thing might ultimately lead to another phase of what you call a seasonal sequence but certainly it would have nothing to do with the weather: it would have to do with the drift of one's ideas.[27]

As he approached reality closely, Stevens designated the numenous experience in the analogy of a magical river, and called it Being:

> It is certain that the River
>
> Is not Swatara. The swarthy water
> That flows round the earth and through the skies,
> Twisting among the universal spaces.
>
> It is not Swatara. It is being.
> (*CP*, 444)

In "An Ordinary Evening," the season has changed from summer to autumn, and the metaphors of the fertile times of August are no longer appropriate for the physical decline of October. The project

---

27. *Letters of Wallace Stevens*, ed. Holly Stevens (New York: Alfred A. Knopf, 1966), pp. 636-637.

of this "endlessly elaborating poem" (*CP*, 486) is to uncover the
central rock of autumn's being, and display the outpouring of its beneficent energies in the process of the poem while it demonstrates the
mythic rebirth of the self in pristine youth, clothed in the leaves of the
new season.

> The mobile and the immobile flickering
> In the area between is and was are leaves,
> Leaves burnished in autumnal burnished trees
>
> And leaves in whirlings in the gutters, whirlings
> Around and away, resembling the presence of thought,
> Resembling the presences of thoughts, as if,
>
> In the end, in the whole psychology, the self,
> The town, the weather, in a casual litter,
> Together, said words of the world are the life of the world.
>   (*CP*, 474)

It is off the point to condemn the poem's "lack of forward motion"
as Helen Hennesey Vendler does, or to announce, stiffly, that it is not
"successful as a total poem," as Joseph Riddel does.[28] Instead, it is
more fruitful to approach the dynamics of the poems from the lines:

>   The hibernal dark that hung
>   In primavera, the shadow of bare rock,
>
> Becomes the rock of autumn, glittering,
> Ponderable source of each imponderable,
> The weight we lift with the finger of a dream,
>
> The heaviness we lighten by light will,
> By the hand of desire, faint, sensitive, the soft
> Touch and trouble of the touch of the actual hand.
>   (*CP*, 476)

In a real sense, poetry is the subject of all of Stevens' poetry. And at
the core of the subject is the necessity to avoid as much as possible

28. Helen Hennessy Vendler, p. 309; Joseph N. Riddel, *The Clairvoyant Eye:
The Poetry and Poetics of Wallace Stevens* (Baton Rouge: Louisiana State University Press, 1965), p. 263.

the repetitions of images and analogies that have been used by other poets, and himself; and to arrive in the freshness of perception at the freshness of expression, which, in the quickness of delivery, dissolves, leaving the sense of the occasion—here the rock of autumn—without the interference of language lodged in specified definition. In his release from the bonds of tradition, and his claim that it was the poet's duty to create a mode of belief in an age of disbelief, Stevens championed the projection of fictions as a means of satisfying the fundamental longing for the "wholly other." "The final belief is to believe in a fiction, which you know to be a fiction, there being nothing else. The exquisite truth is to know that it is a fiction and that you believe in it willingly!" (*OP*, 163). Stevens also knew that poetry itself was equally a fiction, structured sounds standing for a presence that is without structure and without form.

"An Ordinary Evening," then, is not a unified poem, tightly organized with a beginning, middle and end; it is a poem which starts, and stops, and between the starting and stopping appear thirty-one fictive versions about the relations of imagination and reality. It is part of a ceaseless meditation that begins before the poem does and goes on after it. In the strictest sense, the poem is a fragment, a partial statement of one season's workings and reworkings to clear a blessed clairvoyance from the particulars of daily activities. In another sense, it is a poem of "open form," a massive proposition in a field of action —namely the imaginative geography of Connecticut—which fractures literary conventions. In its entertainment of the invisible flux of original genesis which resides in "a permanence composed of impermanence" (*CP*, 472), as the presiding genesis of form, "The poem is the cry of its occasion, / Part of the res itself and not about it" (*CP*, 473). The poem participates in this changing permanence of the imagination's life in such a way that "the style of a poem and poem itself are one" (*OP*, 209), or, in such a way that the poem gathers its parts and projects them outward to enact the process of the arrival of the parts as coincident with the meaning of the parts themselves.

In the varied speculations about the composition of the houses of the mind, the architecture of poetic statement, the poem runs through numerous parables, versions, and demonstrations about the fellowship or battles of imagination and reality. The desire for the "celestial ease in the heart" (*CP*, 467), the propounding of the "brilliancy at the central of the earth" (*CP*, 473), the "Being part of everything come together as one" (*CP*, 482), are examples of possible statements of the rock of autumn; but these few do not stand as absolute definitions in a poem riding out the nonteleological waves of linguistic variations in the process of the mind. "Professor Eucalyptus" (*CP*, 481) is simply an example of the endless search for the whole, as the "ephebe" (*CP*, 474) and the "Romanza" (*CP*, 480) of Orpheus are further examples. The main point of these rehearsals of approximation is that in the process of presenting them, without the luxury of logical and structural connectives, Stevens demonstrates the path of the mind approaching the numenous experience:

> The glass of the air becomes an element—
> It was something imagined that has been washed away.
> A clearness has returned. It stands restored.
>
> It is not an empty clearness, a bottomless sight.
> It is a visibility of thought,
> In which hundreds of eyes, in one mind, see at once.
>   (CP, 488)

Once the clearness shows forth, he realizes words can not contain the vision completely, though he reaches here for the complementary imagery of "Mont Blanc." He is left with the happy condition of generating from the center as many fictions as the proprietry of his ingenuity allows. "These," Stevens says, "are the edgings and inchings of final form" (*CP*, 488) which will never be welded into a solid, dogmatic statement. The poem remains, in its incompletion, a demonstration of the complete freedom of a mind approaching through the rituals of rhetoric a center of wholeness, then writing out of that wholeness a picture of the process of mythic rebirth in the flow of creation itself.

Stevens' imperative to free his mind of precessions of thought and feeling challenged him to conjure a poetry of process in which the destruction of old ideas and the creation of new ones substantiated the repetition of that freedom. Because of the very thorough purging of these predeterminations, which he understood as fictions anyway, he was forced into the estranged position of the necessity to deal only with the ingenuity of his own mind; with the ability of his separate mind to generate again and again, without modifications, versions of the central energies. While a good in itself, this procedure flirted with the hostile potential of arriving at a stasis—a condition he guarded against by postulating and working out the attunement of the imagination's life with the turning of the seasons. Each new season demanded a refreshed definition, or a fictive version of the mind's engagement with the vitality of its processes. Especially in his later poetry, Stevens became an a-historical poet who refused to enter the household of the universal imagination's fictions, which Robert Duncan announces as the imperative to the communal ground of all poets past and present:

> The poem that moves me when I write is an active presence in which I work. I am not concerned with whether it is a good or a bad likeness to some convention men hold; for the Word is for me living Flesh, and the body of my own thought and feeling, my own presence, becomes the vehicle for the process of genetic information. (*T&L*, 23)

Duncan's "Passages Poems" grow up out of the active presence of the accumulated information of all poets of the imagination's life; of poets who deliver in their visions of appearances of the original genetic arrangements of life's beginning. And unlike Stevens, who arrived at the point of a poem without a beginning and an end, but a poem nonetheless obligated, internally, to the most impeccable principles of man-made conventions, Duncan arrives at the point in which the poem is completely released from convention, and presents its form as the morphology of the musical and mystic energy which excites it.

> The morphology of forms, in evolving, does not destroy their historicity but reveals that each event has its origin in the origin of all events; yes, but in turn, we are but the more aware that the first version is revised in our very turning to it, seeing it with new eyes. (*T&L*, 50-51)

In his projection of an emotional and intellectual fiction, Duncan gives the sense of reaching a readiness of tensions in which cosmic

powers reveal themselves simultaneously with the re-visions of previous fictions of the one great poem. They both ride through to him
on the melody of his vision. And when the vision fails, he must wait,
as Shelley and Stevens did, for its next visitation—it is delivered, not
manufactured. His "Passages Poems," as the second to appear, "At the
Loom," suggests, can be considered a vast and intricate tapestry in
which, at the moment of vision in the community of the universal
imagination, he weaves versions of mythic genesis. In a discussion
of the lines of development of modern poetry Duncan writes:

> But just as when we weave a complex of lines a cloud or atmo-
> sphere appears, a texture or cloth, something more than the
> threads told, and out of that texture appear, not only the figures
> we were translating into our design, but other figures of the
> ground itself; so a "life" appears in the work itself. . . . In the me-
> dium, our work and this thing become mixed, changed then. A
> ground appears as a new condition of what we are doing.[29]

At his loom in these poems, Duncan weaves together threads from
many sources and many different areas of information, but in the delicate arrangement he creates a new ground of being, as the habitation
for the projection of a fictive self, that had not existed before. In this
sense he creates an "area of selfcreation" (BB, 15); he enters the
flow of the mythopoetic process in which the evolving design of the
poems activates a new version of the old myths in the consciousness
of the present.

The evolving design of the poems can also be thought of as a collage. "The great art of our time," he writes, "is the collagist's art, to
bring all things into new complexes of meaning."[30] And in the spacious
project of these poems to bring together the historical fictions and the
violence and strife of our time, the collagist's techniques are clearly
visible. With diagrams, prose and mythological references woven together by the fluidity of his imagination in "The Collage: Passages

29. Robert Duncan, "Nights and Days: Chapter One," *Sumac*, No. 1 (1968),
133.
30. Robert Duncan, "Beginnings: Chapter I of the H.D. Book, Part I," *Coy-
ote's Journal*, Nos. 5/6 (1966), p. 21.

6," he enacts a collage, and then announces, giving an indication of the scope of the whole series of poems:

> [I mean to force up emblems again into these passages of a poetry, passages made conglomerate, the pyramid that dense, a mountain, immovable; cut ways in it then and trick the walls with images establishing space and time for more than the maker knows he acknowledges, in it.] (*BB*, 19)

Neither obscure nor esoteric, the poems assume to themselves political, social and poetic events of today which have correspondences in the past—because those events were driven into form by the same primal energies—and present them in a massive tapestry, a "*grand collage*" (*BB*, vii), as evidence of the continuance of the generative center's presence.

> In terms of my own Darwinian persuasion—for I see Creation as a process of evolution of forms, and these forms in turn as arising and surviving in a ground of individual variations and mutations where the multiplicity is not superfluous but the necessary condition of potential functions.[31]

In his individual variations and mutations, Duncan moves away from Stevens' position that the mind must free itself from all previous fictions, to the position that the mind *must* take them into itself; and then, in the magic of creation, project them as a polysemous version of the whole. And in doing this he extends the incipient notion of open form in "An Ordinary Evening" to the full discharge of a poem realizing its unique configuration from the energies within, without the imposition of conventions, to the idea of what he calls "poems without closure." Duncan's grand poem of the mind then becomes an open ended series which evolves in seeking incompletion out of the poet's passages into the immediate mysteries of primal life itself.

Whitehead reminds us that "Language is expression of one's past into one's present. . . . In this way, an articulated memory is the gift of language."[32] As Duncan explains with great care in "Spelling: Pas-

31. Robert Duncan, "Man's Fulfillment in Order and Strife," *Caterpillar*, Nos. 8/9 (1969), 233.
32. Alfred North Whitehead, 33.

sages 15," "the history of words" (*BB*, 49) and their accurate definitions are primary to his work as a poet. And in a discussion of the
music of words, a music which offers him a past order of meaning
older than himself he says:

> But now the poet works with a sense of parts fitting in relation to
> a design that is larger than the poem. The commune of Poetry
> becomes so real that he sounds each particle in relation to parts
> of a great story that he knows will never be completed. (*BB*, vi)

The story Duncan attempts to tell, in all its glorious incompletion, is
of his own involvement in the flow of cosmic forces, which he takes
to be as immediate as the daily events in his kitchen. He did not know
his own birth and will not know his own death, but between the beginning and end of consciousness, he knows of his attunement in the
great poem that all poets have contributed to. At the beginning he returns to "Tribal Memories: Passages 1" and there uncovers the articulate, universal memory, from whom all images flow:

> Mnemosyne, they named her, the
>   Mother with the whispering
>   feathered wings. Memory,
> the great speckled bird who broods over the
>   nest of souls, and her egg,
>   the dream in which all things are living,
> I return to, leaving my self.
>   (*BB*, 10)

She appears later in "Before the Judgment: Passages 35" as "She
whose breast is in language   the Over-Whelming" (*T*, 19), and
as "Nature, our Mother" who "hides us, even from ourselves" (*BB*,
46). Yet she is only one of many examples of the myths of genesis
that are woven into the fabric of these poems. "Pegasos/that great
horse Poetry,   Rider/ we ride, who make up/the truth of What Is"
(*BB*, 122), also comes in, as does Eros and his various names as "Pro-
togonos, Erikepaios, Dionysos" (*BB*, 46), as alternate sources for the
sounds of poetry and words. And in a centering passage, Duncan announces his allegiances:

> Grand Mother of Images,   matrix
> genetrix,   quickening in rays
>   from the first days of the cosmos,
>
>   turning my poet's mind in tides of
>   solitude, seductive reveries, fears, resolves, outrage
>   yet
>   having this certain specific agent I am.
>   (*BB*, 75)

Duncan's repetitive recoursing to the varied sources of his language represents a new beginning in each instance, and a moving out to collect in the pattern of the poems as much of the full engagement of himself with the cosmos as possible. As each poem is incomplete, so the whole series of poems remains an approximation of a larger poem. With the setting out of the details of these stories, as well as with the great influx of information from Plato, Hesiod, Rimbaud (especially the list of directives in "The Architecture: Passages 9"), Duncan attempts to define an area, or field, with imaginary boundaries, that will be his habitation as a poet, and that will stand as the fictive meadow for his mythic rebirth. The retellings of the intricate myths of creation and the statement of the doctrines of the ancient mysteries enter the poems—sometimes as direct quotations as in the citing of Boehme's *The Aurora* ("Passages 31: The Concert"), because Duncan conceives of Boehme, and many others, as participating in the same essential poem that he is writing. Each has a direct place in his poem, because, as the scribe of the numenous world, he becomes the sounding medium for what has been articulated from the universal memory. While he seeks comprehensiveness, he knows that all such definitions are, and must remain, incomprehensive:

> nor poet
> nor writer of words
>
>   can contrive to do justice to the beauty of that
>   design he designs from
>
>   we pretend to speak   the language is not ours
>   and we move upward beyond our own powers into
>   words again   beyond us   unsure measures

the poetry of the cosmos $(T, 11)$

A poem for Duncan is not the record of cognitive deliberations, but a process of dancing with a moving vision and discovering in the course of writing the path the poem takes. "Each poet seeks to commune with creation, with the divine world: that is to say, he seeks the most *real* form in language. But this most real is something we apprehend; the poem, the creation of the poem, is itself our primary experience of it."[33] Each of these poems begins with the excitement of the numenous presence and emerges as the configuration of the energy caught in the music of language. "The Golden ones," Duncan tells us, "move in invisible realms,/wrapt round in our thought as in a mist" $(T, 19)$. The internal tensions of the poems move between the necessity to respond to the presence of the golden ones, the first forms, and the human limitation of being unable, even in the cadences of song, to bring into the visible line the shadows of the invisible. In unique notation of dependent interrelationships, each poem works out the turning movement of the stars in the movement of the mind; each is a testament to a process revealing forms of the most real.

> Incidents of me   the eye sees
>
> a leaf among many leaves   turning upon the stream, the screen,
>
> the words upon the page   flow away into   no hold I have
>
> What did it say?

>   (A PASSAGE)   Kraftgänge
>
> . . . for the stars have their kingdom in the veins of
> the body which are cunning passages (and the sun
> has designd the arteries)   where they drive forth
> the form, shape and condition of man
>
> $(BB, 66)$

33. Robert Duncan, "Towards an Open Universe," pp. 135-136.

With all reverence, Duncan honors his station as a poet of the sacred who recognizes in Christ's passion the essential experience of the poetic act. Yet, he also recognizes that the contrary of creation is destruction, and in our time, war, as well as the perils of Satan in political life come into the imaginary boundaries of the evolving field of action. "I thought," he tells us,

> to come into an open room
> where in the south light of afternoon
> one I was improvised
> passages of changing dark and light
> a music dream and passion would have playd
> to illustrate concords of order in order,
> a contrapuntal communion of all things.
>   (*BB*, 78)

Yet his masters in poetry and music are dead. And as "The Multiversity: Passages 21" and "Up Rising: Passages 25" illustrate, corrupt politics the tyranny of government in its denial of individual freedom, and the scourge of war dominate our days to such an extent that good —the household of the holy imagination—is denied its beneficent appearance. The poems, with their arena of action fully described in terms of generative brilliance, turn bitterly to a condemnation of satanic subversion. In this grim reality, however, Satan is redeemable, and out of the darkest conditions when the nation is over-run with "faces of Princes, Popes, Prime Usurers, Presidents,/ Gang Leaders of whatever Clubs, Nations, Legions" who meet "to conspire, to coerce, to cut down" (*BB*, 44), he can still prophesy the emergence of a new America, redeemed, in tune with Whitman's notions of democracy,

> And from the dying body of America I see,
> or from my dying body,

>   emerge

> children of a deed long before this deed,
> seed of Poseidon, depth in which the blue above
> is reflected
>   released.
>   (*BB*, 132)

In his study of myth Claude Lévi-Strauss assures us: "There is no single 'true' version of which the others are but copies or distortions. Every version belongs to the myth."[34] There was a myth, a central act of genesis which revolved in the stars and in the mind of man before the versions of tradition arrived to add corrobating evidence of the essential reality of the invisible forces. Shelley, Stevens and Duncan all participate in their own versions of this most real invisibility of the numenous life, and in their poetic approximations of this presence generate it again in developing forms of expression. For the unbounded energy of generation cannot be contained in the prisons of convention, and the luxury of dogmatic conclusions. Its essence is freedom, and it resists almost completely release into the medium of words. As it is an evolving process, so the poetry must engage itself in the process of the mind, and enact in its open movement the movement it seeks to release into clarity. These three poets have tried to write out in parables of approximations their own sense of this numenous experience; and in doing this they engage themselves in a divine act of the mind that brings with it the possibility of redeeming the process itself, and the men who engage in it. Far from the wicked act of attempting to kill the presence of power as Ahab does, Shelley, Stevens and Duncan seek out community with the forces of reality's creation and attempt to evoke the power with the majesty of language dissolving at times to remove its own interference to the *Numen*. The poetry of approximation turns to supplications of wonder and the statement of the real possibility of mankind's holy redemption:
Children of Kronos, of the Dream beyond death,

> secret of a Life beyond our lives,
>   having their perfection as we have
>
>   their bodies a like grace, a music,   their minds   a
>   joy, abundant
>
>   foliate, fanciful in its flowering

34. Claude Lévi-Strauss, "The Structural Study of Myth," in *Structural Anthropology*, trans. Claire Jacobson and Brooke Grundfest Schoeph (1963; rpt. New York: Doubleday & Company, Inc., 1967), p. 215.

come into these orders as they have ever come,   stand

   as ever, where they are acknowledged,
   against the works of unworthy men, unfeeling
     judgments and cruel deeds.

(*T*, 24)

Part Six

"Seventy Years Later":
A Checklist

How sweet the silent backward tracings!
The wanderings as in dreams—the meditation of old times
resumed—their lives, joys, persons, voyages.

Whitman, "Memories," *Sands at Seventy*

Dean W. Keller

A Checklist of the Writings of
Howard P. Vincent

1932-1937

"The Date of Wycherley's Birth." *Times Literary Supplement.* 3 March 1932. p. 155.

"The Death of William Wycherley." *Harvard Studies and Notes in Philology and Literature.* 15 (1933), 219-242.

"A Pope Problem." *Times Literary Supplement.* 14 February 1935, p. 92.

"Two Letters of Colley Cibber." *Notes & Queries.* 168 (January 5, 1935), 3-4.

"George Colman the Younger: 'Adopted Son.'" *Philological Quarterly*, 15 (1936), 219-220.

"Two Unpublished Letters of Vanbrugh." *Notes & Queries*, 173 (August 21, 1937), 128-129.

"William Wycherley's *Miscellaneous Poems*." *Philological Quarterly*, 16 (1937), 145-148.

1939-1944

"Some *Dunciad* Litigation." *Philological Quarterly*, 18 (1939), 285-289.

"Three Unpublished Letters of Abraham Cowley." *Modern Language Notes*, 54 (1939), 454-458.

"Warton's Last Words on the Rowley Papers." *Modern Language Review*, 34 (1939), 572-575.

"The Childhood of Henry Fielding." *Review of English Studies*, 16 (1940), 438-444.

"Tobias Smollett's Assault on Gordon and Groom." *Review of English Studies* 16, (1940), 183-188.

"Henry Fielding in Prison." *Modern Language Review*, 36 (1941), 499-500.

"A Sarah Helen Whitman Letter about Edgar Allan Poe." *American Literature*, 13 (1941), 162-167.

"Christopher George Colman, 'Lunatick.' " *Review of English Studies*, 18 (1942), 38-48.

"Early Poems by Henry Fielding." *Notes & Queries*, 184 (March 13, 1943), 159-160.

[Review] *Study Out the Land*. By T. K. Whipple. Berkeley: University of California Press, 1943. *Accent*, 3 (1943), 191-192.

"William Wycherley's 'Posthumous Works.' " *Notes & Queries*, 185 (July 3, 1943), 12-13.

Letters of Dora Wordsworth. Chicago: Packard and Company, 1944. Edited, with an introduction by Howard P. Vincent.

1947-1952

"An Attempted Piracy of *The Duenna*." *Modern Language Notes*, 62 (1947), 268-270.

Collected Poems of Herman Melville. Chicago: Packard and Company (Hendricks House), 1947. Edited, with an Introduction and Notes by Howard P. Vincent.

Complete Works of Herman Melville. Chicago: Packard and Company (Hendricks House), 1947—. General Editor, Howard P. Vincent.

[Review] *Journal of a Visit to London and the Continent by Herman Melville, 1849-1850*. Edited by Eleanor Melville Metcalf. Cambridge: Harvard University Press, 1948; and *Melville's Billy Budd*. Edited by F. Barron Freeman. Cambridge: Harvard University Press, 1948. *Accent*, 10 (1949), 58-60.

The Trying-Out of Moby-Dick. Boston: Houghton Mifflin, 1949.

"White-Jacket: An Essay in Interpretation," *New England Quarterly*,

22 (1949), 304-315. Reprinted in Rountree, Thomas J., editor, *Critics on Melville; Readings in Literary Criticism*. Coral Gables, Florida: University of Miami Press, 1972, pp. 72-75.

[Review] *Melville's Use of the Bible*. By Nathalia Wright. Durham, North Carolina, Duke University Press, 1949; and *Herman Melville, A Critical Study*. By Richard Chase. New York, Macmillan Company, 1949. *New England Quarterly*, 23 (1950), 109-112.

[Review] *Herman Melville*. By Newton Arvin. New York: William Sloane, 1950. *Saturday Review of Literature*, 29 April 1950, pp. 21. 36.

Moby-Dick, or, The Whale. By Herman Melville. New York: Hendricks House, 1952. Edited, with an Introduction and Notes, by Luther Mansfield and Howard P. Vincent.

1954-1959

Reader and Writer. Boston: Houghton Mifflin, 1954. Edited by Harrison Hayford and Howard P. Vincent.

[Review] *Moby-Dick Centennial Essays*. Edited for the Melville Society by Tyrus Hillway and Luther S. Mansfield. Dallas, Texas: Southern Methodist University Press, 1953. *American Literature*, 26 (1954), 444-445.

Reader and Writer. 2nd ed. Boston: Houghton Mifflin, 1959. Edited by Harrison Hayford and Howard P. Vincent.

[Review] *The Fine Hammered Steel of Herman Melville*. By Milton Stern. Urbana: University of Illinois Press, 1957. *American Literature*, 31 (1959), 85-86.

1961-1966

[Review] *The Long Encounter: Self and Experience in the Writings of Herman Melville*. By Merlin Bowen. Chicago: University of Chicago Press, 1960. *American Literature*, 33 (1961), 84-85.

Kent Studies in English, Kent, Ohio: Kent State University Press, 1964. Howard P. Vincent, General Editor.

The Trying-out of Moby-Dick. Paperback ed. Carbondale: Southern Illinois University Press, 1965.

Bartleby the Scrivener: A Symposium. Kent, Ohio: Kent State University Press, 1966. Also issued in paperback edition, 1966. (Melville Annual, 1965) Edited by Howard P. Vincent.

1968-1973

Daumier and His World. Evanston, Ill.: Northwestern University Press, 1968.

Melville & Hawthorne in the Berkshires: A Symposium. Kent, Ohio: Kent State University Press, 1968. (Melville Annual, 1966). Edited by Howard P. Vincent. Contains Vincent's essay on Melville's *White-Jacket*, " 'And Still They Fall From the Masthead'." pp. 144-155.

[Review] *The Recognition of Herman Melville: Selected Criticism Since 1846*. Edited by Hershel Parker. Ann Arbor: University of Michigan Press, 1967. *New England Quarterly*, 41 (1968), 307-308.

"Ishmael, Writer and Art Critic." *Themes and Directions in American Literature: Essays in Honor of Leon Howard*. Edited by Ray B. Browne and Donald Pizer. Lafayette, Indiana: Purdue University Press, 1969, pp. 69-79.

The Merrill Checklist of Herman Melville. Columbus, Ohio: Charles E. Merrill Publishing Company, 1969. Compiled by Howard P. Vincent.

The Merrill Studies in Moby-Dick. Columbus, Ohio: C. E. Merrill Publishing Company, 1969. Edited by Howard P. Vincent.

A Guide To Herman Melville, Columbus, Ohio: Charles E. Merrill Publishing Company, 1969.

Reader and Writer. 3rd ed. Boston: Houghton Mifflin, 1969. Edited by Harrison Hayford and Howard P. Vincent.

[Review] *A Formula of His Own: Henry Adams's Literary Experiment* By John J. Conder. Chicago: University of Chicago Press, 1970. *New England Quarterly*, 43 (1970), 669-672.

The Tailoring of Melville's White-Jacket. Evanston, Ill.: Northwestern University Press, 1970.

[Review] *White-Jacket: or The World in a Man-of-War*. By Herman

Melville. Edited by Harrison Hayford, and G. Thomas Tanselle, with a historical note by Willard Thorp. Evanston and Chicago: Northwestern University Press and the Newberry Library, 1970. *American Literature*, 43 (1971), 292.

Twentieth Century Interpretations of Billy Budd; A Collection of Critical Essays. Englewood Cliffs, N.J.: Prentice-Hall, 1971. Edited by Howard P. Vincent.

[Review] *The Poetry of Melville's Late Years: Time, History, Myth, and Religion*. By William Bysshe Stein. Albany: State University of New York Press, 1970. *American Literature*, 44 (1972), 325-327.

The Spirit Above the Dust; A Study of Herman Melville. By Ronald Mason. Second edition. New Foreword by Howard P. Vincent. Mamaroneck, N.Y.: Paul P. Appel Publisher, 1972. pp. 11-12.

[Review] *Melville Dissertations: An Annotated Directory*. By Joel Myerson and Arthur H. Miller, Jr. Philadelphia: The Melville Society of America, 1972. *American Reference Books Annual, 1973*. Littleton, Colorado: Libraries Unlimited, Inc., 1973. pp. 497-498.

Contributors

Robert Bertholf is Assistant Professor of English at Kent State University. He is a graduate of Bowdoin College and the University of Oregon (Ph.D., 1968). He has published on Wallace Stevens, Charles Olson, Robert Duncan, and contemporary poetry in *ELH, Bucknell Review, Boundry 2, Caterpillar* and elsewhere. He is editor of *Credences*, a poetry journal, and is completing a full length study of Wallace Stevens and the Romantic tradition.

Thomas M. Davis received his Ph.D. from the University of Missouri in 1968. During 1965-1969, he taught at Southern Illinois University where he served as Director of General Studies. He has edited several text books, including *14 by Emily Dickinson*, and he has published in *American Literature* and *Early American Literature*. Currently he is Professor of English at Kent State University, and he is working on the manuscripts of Edward Taylor.

Robert J. DeMott, born in 1943 in Connecticut, is a graduate of Assumption College, John Carroll University and Kent State University (Ph.D., 1969). He has published on Thoreau, Ezra Pound, Robinson Jeffers, Hart Crane and John Steinbeck. He is an editor of the *Steinbeck Quarterly* and of *The Back Door*, a poetry journal. He teaches courses in American literature at Ohio University where he is Associate Professor.

Marjorie Dew is a graduate of the College of Wooster, and Kent State University where she received her Ph.D. in 1966. Her dissertation on Melville and Existentialism was directed by Howard Vincent. She has published on Melville, Owen Wister and others, and is Professor of English at Ashland College.

Alex Gildzen, Assistant Curator of Special Collections at the Kent State University Libraries, is the author of several small press volumes of poetry, including *Into the Sea* (1969) and *The Origin of Oregano* (1971). He reviews for *American Reference Books Annual* and has had articles in magazines varying from *American Cinematographer* to *Papers of the Bibliographical Society of America*.

Harrison Hayford, a graduate of Tufts College and Yale (Ph.D., 1945), is Professor of English at Northwestern University, where he has taught since 1942. He is general editor of the Northwestern University-Newberry Library edition of Herman Melville's works, and he is an editor of the *Journals and Miscellaneous Notebooks of Ralph Waldo Emerson*, being published by Harvard. With Hershel Parker he has edited *Moby-Dick as Doubloon*, Melville's *Billy Budd*, and *Moby-Dick*.

Wilson Heflin was born in Alabama in 1913 and was educated at Birmingham-Southern College and Vanderbilt (Ph.D., 1952). He taught at the University of Alabama and since 1946 has been at the U.S. Naval Academy where he is now Professor of English. He has published on Herman Melville and was President of the Melville Society in 1958.

David G. Hoch received his Ph.D. from Kent State University in 1969 where his dissertation was directed by Howard Vincent. He is presently Associate Professor of English at the University of Toledo, and he has published on Thoreau, as well as facets of popular culture.

Dean H. Keller is Curator of Special Collections and Professor of Library Administration at Kent State University. His M.A. in Library Science is from Kent State (1968), and he attended Indiana University on Lilly Fellowship in Rare Books during 1966-1967. He is the author of five books and numerous articles and is editor of the *Serif Series* of bibliographies and checklists.

Sydney J. Krause, Professor of English at Kent State University, has published widely on American literature in *PMLA*, *American Literature*, *Bulletin of the New York Public Library* and elsewhere. He edited *Essays on Determinism*, and his *Mark Twain as Critic* was published by Johns Hopkins. He was a Fulbright lecturer in Denmark in 1968-1969, and is now Director of Kent's Bibliography and Textual Center, which is publishing an edition of Charles Brockden Brown.

Sanford E. Marovitz is an Associate Professor of English at Kent State University. A graduate of Lake Forest College, he received his Ph.D. from Duke

University (1968) where he held a Woodrow Wilson Fellowship. He taught at Temple University and at The University of Athens, Greece, under the Fulbright program. He has published on American literature in *American Quarterly*, *Philological Quarterly*, *Modern Fiction Studies* and *American Literary Realism*. He is writing a book on the influence of Shakespeare and Hawthorne on Melville.

Paul Metcalf, born in 1917, the second son of Henry Knight and Eleanor Melville Metcalf, was raised and educated in New England and briefly attended Harvard. As a member of the Hedgerow Theatre, he worked under Jasper Deeter, and later studied writing informally with Charles Olson and Conrad Aiken. His principal publications include *Will West* (1956; reissued 1973 by the Book Store Press), *Genoa* (1965) and *Patagoni* (1971). New works include *Apalache*, a long poem, and *The Middle Passage* (Jargon Society). Issue #12 of *Lillabulero* is devoted to him.

Eric Mottram lectures on American literature at King's College, University of London. He has been a Visiting Professor at Kent State University and at SUNY, Buffalo. He has published widely on American literature, especially on contemporary writers. He edits *Poetry Review* and has published two books of poetry, *Gardiner's Island and Points of Honour* and *The Expression*, as well as a book on William Burroughs.

Henry A. Murray was born in 1893 and educated at Harvard (A.B.), Columbia (M.D., M.A.), Presbyterian Hospital, Rockefeller Institute, and Trinity College, Cambridge (Ph.D., biochemistry). A former Director of the Harvard Psychological Clinic, he is now Professor Emeritus of social relations at Harvard. His publications include *Explorations in Personality* (1938), *Assessment of Men* (1948), *Myth and Mythmaking* (1960), and approximately one hundred papers on various topics—biochemical, embryological, and psychological —three of them on aspects of the life and work of Herman Melville, for fifty years his principal avocation.

Vivian Pemberton was a graduate student at Kent State University where she pursued Crane, Faulkner and Patchen research under Howard Vincent. She is currently Assistant Professor of English at the Trumbull Regional Campus of Kent State in Warren, Ohio. Her works in progress include a consideration of Crane's early poetry, and expansion of her M.A. thesis, "Some Family Figures Behind Hart Crane."

Edward Stone, born in New Jersey in 1913, was educated at the University of Texas and Duke University (Ph.D., 1950). He has taught at Newcomb College, Georgia Tech, Duke University, University of Virginia, and, since 1956, at Ohio University where he is Distinguished Professor of English. His books include *What Was Naturalism?*, *The Battle and the Books: Some Aspects of Henry James*, *Voices of Despair*, and *A Certain Morbidness*. He has been a Fulbright lecturer to Mexico and Argentina. He is presently completing a study of Herman Melville and popular culture.

Nathalia Wright is Professor of English at the University of Tennessee. She was born in Athens, Georgia, received her B.A. from Maryville College and her M.A. and Ph.D. from Yale University. She has held fellowships from the Guggenheim Foundation and American Association of University Women. She is the author of *Melville's Use of the Bible*, *Horatio Greenough: the First American Sculptor*, *American Novelists in Italy*, and numerous scholarly articles; she is also editor of *Washington Irving's Journals and Notebooks 1803-1806*, and *Letters of Horatio Greenough*.

Donald J. Yannella is a Professor of English at Glassboro State College (N.J.), where he has taught since 1964. He earned his Ph.D. at Fordham in 1970. He has edited several volumes of Cornelius Mathews' writings and has published in *American Quarterly*, *New England Quarterly*, and other professional journals. His book on Emerson is soon to be published by Twayne, and he is currently editing the diaries and journals of Evert Duyckinck.

Gloria Young was educated at the University of Virginia, Akron University, and Kent State University (Ph.D., 1971). Her dissertation on Melville and Conrad was directed by Howard P. Vincent. She teaches at the Geauga County Regional Campus of Kent State University and she has published on Conrad and e.e. cummings.